Austin Presbyterian Theological Seminary

COMPLETING A CENTURY OF SERVICE

James S. Currie

EAKIN PRESS   Austin, Texas

FIRST EDITION
Copyright © 2002
By James S. Currie
Published in the United States of America
By Eakin Press
A Division of Sunbelt Media, Inc.
P.O. Drawer 90159 ◁❒ Austin, Texas 78709-0159
email: sales@eakinpress.com
💻 website: www.eakinpress.com 💻
ALL RIGHTS RESERVED.
1 2 3 4 5 6 7 8 9
1-57168-727-0

Library of Congress Cataloging-in-Publication Data

Currie, James S.
    Austin Presbyterian Theological Seminary : completing a century of
service / James S. Currie.– 1st ed.
        p.   cm.
    Includes bibliographical references and index.
    ISBN 1-57168-727-0 (alk. paper)
    1. Austin Presbyterian Theological Seminary. 2.   I. Title
BV4070.A93 C87 2002
230'.07'35176431–dc21   2002011440

Dedicated to
Thomas W. Currie, Jr.
whose own life of
faithfulness and devotion to Jesus Christ
through pastoral ministry, scholarship, and service
has been an inspiration to many and
a reflection of Austin Seminary's primary purpose of
preparing men and women for the pastoral ministry

CONTENTS

Acknowledgments   vii
Foreword   xi
Preface: The Community   xiii

  1. The Maxwell Years   1
  2. An Extraordinary Gift: The Jean Brown Bequest 25
  3. Regrouping and Reunion   31
  4. The Stotts Years   42
  5. The Shelton Years   75
  6. Lectures   95
  7. The Seminary Beyond the Seminary   104
  8. From the Students   127
  9. Unsung Heroes   150
10. Toward the Second Century   164

Appendix A   173
Appendix B   185
Endnotes   193
Index   207

ACKNOWLEDGMENTS

In 1978 *Austin Presbyterian Theological Seminary: A Seventy-fifth Anniversary History* was published by Trinity University Press. Written by Dr. Thomas W. Currie, Jr., son of the seminary's third president, this volume concludes with the advent of the sixth president of Austin Seminary, Dr. Jack Martin Maxwell. I am deeply indebted to my father for many things, not the least of which is a love for and an appreciation of those who have gone before us in the faith. In the acknowledgments of his volume, he admits to his own love for Austin Seminary and how that bias might obscure its flaws or leave them unreported. And yet, the story that is told is comprehensive and thorough. In light of that, it is with both humility and trepidation that I have undertaken the assignment of writing the story of the seminary from 1977 to the present.

The humility arises in knowing that what appears here might be compared to the seventy-fifth anniversary history of the seminary. The trepidation comes with knowing that it is always dangerous to write history while many, if not most, of the principals are still alive. Not only can one's account be challenged, let alone written differently, by participants in the story itself, but the luxury of historical perspective which the distance of time would afford the writer of another generation is not available.

I wish also to thank President Robert M. Shelton for inviting me to undertake this task. However, if risking comparison to the author of the predecessor volume were not enough to prove one's foolishness, then trying to cover a period of time through which Dr. Shelton has served as faculty member, academic dean, and president should dissuade one from the job altogether. He has been at the seminary since 1971 and probably knows more about the years covered in this volume than anyone else, alive or dead. While the duties of president are exceedingly demanding, he has made himself available to me for many hours of questions and conversation. In addition, Dr. Shelton has provided full access to documents, as well as to faculty and staff for interviews. For his openness and cooperation I am most grateful.

The executive assistant to the president, Linda Cunningham, proved to be especially helpful not only in providing official documents, but also in verifying details and in locating and contacting certain persons for the purposes of this history. Kris Toma, archivist for the seminary, and Randal Whittington and David Gambrell, both in the office of public relations, assisted in collecting pictures for this volume. My thanks to each of them.

I would be remiss if I did not thank all those who agreed to be interviewed for this project, as well as those who responded in writing to my request for information and reflections on their experience at Austin Seminary. To faculty, staff, administrators, students, former students, trustees, former trustees, and former employees of the seminary, thank you.

To those who read drafts of chapters and offered suggestions and critiques, I am most indebted. Their close reading of the manuscript saved me many embarrassing errors. Rev. Jerry Tompkins was especially helpful in this regard, reading each chapter and providing suggestions which improved the text immensely. Dr. Prescott H. Williams, the fifth president of Austin Seminary and professor of Old Testament languages and archaeology, graciously agreed to update the appendix having to do with faculty members. Kris Toma updated the appendix having to do with the Board of Trustees.

This work has been underwritten by the generosity of Thomas F. and Mary Ruth Williams of Houston, Texas. They have been faithful disciples of Jesus Christ and have, over the years, supported the work of his church in a variety of ways. I am profoundly grateful for this expression of their support of this project and of Austin Seminary. As of this writing, both are active members of Westminster Presbyterian Church, Houston.

Thanks must also go to the Session and congregation of Westminster Presbyterian Church, Houston, for their patience and encouragement as I have undertaken this project. It is a joy to serve as pastor of that fine church.

Finally, I wish to acknowledge my debt of gratitude to my wife, JoAnn, whose companionship, friendship, love, and grace contribute toward making life a delightful and joyful adventure. Her faith, support, and encouragement in this endeavor have been invaluable. She has also offered specific suggestions which have improved this work. She has enriched my life beyond measure.

This volume is dedicated to my father, the Rev. Dr. Thomas White Currie, Jr., who by his own love for Austin Seminary and example of Christian discipleship has taught me the high calling and the unparalleled joy it is to be a servant of the Master.

James S. Currie
Houston, Texas
Lent 2002

FOREWORD

As Austin Presbyterian Theological Seminary began making plans for the celebration for its Centennial year, one of the highest priorities was to engage a church historian to write the history of the seminary for the concluding twenty-five years of its existence. In 1977 a volume had been published by Dr. Thomas White Currie, Jr., which chronicled the prior seventy-five years of the institution's life, entitled *Austin Presbyterian Theological Seminary: A Seventy-fifth Anniversary History.* The new envisaged work would bring the seminary's story up-to-date.

The seminary was most fortunate to enlist one of its alumni, Dr. James Stuart Currie, to do the needed research and to write the proposed volume. His careful research and creative linking of facts and events are fine examples of responsible scholarship and recording of history. The seminary is indebted to him for his labor and for this completed volume. It will serve effectively as an important part of the institutional memory of this fine school.

Austin Seminary is also profoundly grateful to Thomas and Mary Ruth Williams of Houston, Texas, for generously funding this valuable project. Their extraordinary financial support made a variety of research methods possible for the author, and ensured the publication of this volume.

While this volume will be of greatest interest to many who have been and are presently a part of Austin Seminary, it also should prove to be of value to anyone interested in theological education and the important task of the education and formation of pastors of congregations and other leaders of the church. This history, like all responsible history, is more than the recording of facts and figures;

it is also an account of one theological school's attempt to be faithful to its mission.

I am delighted to commend this volume to present and future readers.

Robert M. Shelton, President
Austin Presbyterian Theological Seminary

PREFACE: THE COMMUNITY

The word *community* is often used to describe a body of people, regardless of size. This word, however, is seldom defined. One can talk about "the Houston community" or "the Dallas community." But one can also talk about "the neighborhood community" or "the church community." Is the same thing meant when alluding to a metropolitan area as to a congregation?

In describing Austin Seminary, many refer to "the seminary community." What does that mean? Does it refer to the relationships that emerge in the classroom between student and professor and between student and student? Does it refer to the collegiality among faculty members? Does it refer to the community of single students living in the dormitory? Does it refer to the spouses and families of students? Does it refer to the seminary administration, at all levels—president, dean, vice presidents, registrar, administrative assistants, public relations workers, library staff, office managers and secretaries, janitorial staff, cafeteria staff—in short, all those who help make the seminary operate in an effective way? And does it make sense to talk about an institution in terms of a community?

In 1986 Craig Dykstra delivered the Robert F. Jones Lectures as part of the Mid-Winter Lectures at Austin Seminary. In one chapter of his book *Growing in the Life of Faith: Education and Christian Practices,* which resulted, in part, from those lectures, Dykstra argues:

> The single most important thing about theological education in the future of the church and culture is that these schools actually *be* communities-of-faith-and-learning, guided by a theological vi-

sion in which faith and learning are bound inextricably together in something like the essential intimacy of love's knowledge.[1]

In that statement and in that chapter, Dykstra maintains that seminaries are communities, and that they are more than communities of learning. They are communities of "faith and learning," a phrase that is taken from the standards established by the Association of Theological Schools (ATS). According to Dykstra, while there are many different kinds of communities, seminaries form a peculiar kind, in that they combine the faith of the church with the scholarship of the academy.

The notion of community has been associated with Austin Seminary for a long time, perhaps from the very beginning, when its survival was by no means certain. One Austin Seminary graduate who became a leader in the church at the national level recalls a sense of community as being very important during his seminary years. The Rev. James E. Andrews, Class of 1956 and stated clerk of the General Assembly of the Presbyterian Church, U.S., for ten years (1973–83) and of the Presbyterian Church (U.S.A.) for twelve years (1984–96), writes that it was during his student years that he began to learn the meaning of community. Referring to the influence James Millard, field education director at the seminary and later stated clerk of the General Assembly of the PCUS, had on him, Andrews recalls:

> Along with the rest of the small seminary teaching staff, he taught me what it means to be in community. Seventeen years later he hired me to assist him in the Office of the General Assembly where he was stated clerk, and three years after that he recommended me to succeed him upon his retirement. For 25 years the development of community was a primary goal for the office staff working with me, not only for our work in the office, but also for our work with the committees and other groups for which we had responsibility. It was evident to many of us over those years that the renewal of sense of community was very important for the future of the Presbyterian Church.[2]

In the predecessor volume to this one, Professor John Jansen submitted the following:

When some years ago an accrediting team from A.T.S. was here, we we were asked to describe the seminary. As we all reached for short descriptive phrases, Stuart Currie said it best—for us all. He described the seminary as a "community of the Word." And I've always remembered those words because they say it for me. I suppose at every seminary—and almost every year, whether during opening retreats or during times when students hit the "slough of despond"—the question is asked whether indeed we are truly a community. But whenever some particular illness or sadness or crisis faces us, I've found that we all discover anew what community means. And what kind of community? What binds the academic and the personal concerns together is the Word. I've been through several curriculum changes here, but always it is the Word that is seen as central. This is far more than a "departmental" conviction but one that binds us all together—as much in the teaching of homiletics, etc. as in the biblical field per se. I'm persuaded that this has made for the quality of faculty comradeship in our common effort as well as for the quality of our whole life together as a seminary. Of course "community" is never a finished achievement—but it is a gracious reality.[3]

Stuart Currie's description certainly brings focus and purpose to one's understanding of the seminary, but in understanding the community itself to include all who are related to the seminary in one way or another, be they near or far, we find the applicability of "a community of the Word" even more appropriate. It is a community that acknowledges Christ's claim on it, in all its parts, and its desire to carry out its life together bound to him.

An awareness of a sense of community persists into the years covered by this volume. Rev. Steve Plunkett, who earned his M.Div. from Austin Seminary in 1980, writes the following regarding his years there:

As I reflect on my years at Austin Seminary in the late '70s, I think not so much of a place but of a community. As an institution, the seminary was undergoing a difficult time with issues of leadership but, as I look back on it, it is not those institutional issues which come to mind, but a community of scholars helping us, by God's grace, to become ordained servants of Jesus Christ.

The faculty had a number of people on it who understood that, in addition to being teachers, they were servants of the church, and this made all the difference.[4]

The Austin Seminary community has been one that, in the words of the apostle Paul, has "rejoiced with those who rejoice and has wept with those who weep" (cf. Romans 12:15). It has known the joy as well as the pain that go with a closely knit community. That it is a community of the Word makes it no less immune to deaths of faculty members, spouses, students. But the Word which is at the center draws the community even closer together and serves as a compass that guides us.

But, in fact, the seminary community is made up of several smaller communities: the community of faculty members, the community of students, the community of staff and office workers, the community of spouses, the community of families. And even within these groups, there may be smaller communities, communities based on ethnicity, age, or some special interest.

This broader view of the seminary community is one that goes beyond the campus. The issues that accompany it were vividly depicted in the May 1993 issue of *Windows,* a seminary publication which appears four times a year and provides articles and news of the seminary. That issue focused on "Learning from and Ministering to Crisis." Spearheaded by Kay Lewis, a master of arts student and widow of Professor Alan Lewis, who died of cancer in 1994, this issue included articles by professors, a secretary, and several students, all of which dealt with crises they had experienced (divorce, abortion, disease, and death). The point is that the seminary community goes beyond its immediate *raison d'être.* The issues confronting society also confront the seminary community at large.

Far from being purely an academic community, this community of the Word resembles that larger community of the Word, the church. Indeed, it is part of it and has contributed to it in significant ways, providing denominational leaders, seminary presidents, strong scholars, and committed pastors. Former General Assembly stated clerk Jim Andrews recalls discovering the connection of community between the seminary and the larger church during his student years:

As we learned more about the ministries ahead of us, we learned to feel ourselves a part of that community called the Presbyterian Church. We knew even as students what some of the needs of the seminary were, even before new projects were announced. ... Balancing needs and resources can be best accomplished when the people trying to plan have a sense of community with their partners. It was good training for those times when we would work with congregations and sessions in meeting the needs of church programs. The balance between Austin Seminary and the Church has impressed me as the most important aspect of the community spirit which is characteristic of both. Over the past four decades either the Church or the seminary has found it necessary to catch up to its vision of the other. At such times, it was the basic values of our theological education plus a focus on the congregation that kept the relationship working.[5]

This community lives and labors in the world. Even though there is a sense in which no seminary can prepare its students for everything they will encounter in their ministry, there is another very real sense in which the seminary experience prepares its students for ministry in the church both academically and experientially. Jesus Christ is at the center of seminary life and at the center of the life of the church. He is the Word that gives identity and purpose to the community. Even as the Austin Seminary community grows and increasingly reflects the ethnic and cultural diversity of society, and even as a variety of communities emerge within the seminary community, it remains a part of the larger community of faith in the world.

Andrews graduated from Austin Seminary in 1956. Forty-two years later, in 1998, Barbara M. Farwell, a member of the Class of 1992, wrote:

There used to be a lot of complaints and discussion about whether we were really a "community" at APTS. I always thought we were imperfect, as all communities, but nonetheless a place where we could find encouragement and nurture from each other. We had our squabbles; we argued about inclusive language in chapel and classes; we couldn't figure out what to do about the homeless who panhandled us and the woman (named Carol) who camped on campus for weeks during my senior year. We disagreed about theology and how to do ministry. We weren't always nice to each other. But we were a community, bound together by God's grace.[6]

This volume will concentrate on the customary understanding of the seminary community, that is, administration, faculty, staff, students, alumni/ae, and Board of Trustees members. But in doing so, I hope that the broad sense of the "community" will be kept in mind, including not only spouses and family members, but all the churches that are affected by Austin Seminary. The larger church, with all its parts, is the community of the Word. Austin Presbyterian Theological Seminary is part of that community.

CHAPTER ONE

The Maxwell Years
(1976–83)

On February 20, 1976, the Board of Trustees of Austin Presbyterian Theological Seminary elected Jack Martin Maxwell as the sixth president of Austin Seminary, effective April 1. He succeeded Prescott H. Williams, Jr., and was the first president to have no prior association with the school, although he had earned his bachelor's degree across the street at the University of Texas. Having earned his master of divinity and his Ph.D. at Princeton Theological Seminary, Maxwell went to the Presbyterian church in Sewickley, Pennsylvania, where he served as pastor for seven years (1969–76). It was from that pastorate that he came to Austin.

In the seven years of the Maxwell presidency, many changes and improvements took place that would have lasting significance for the seminary, but these years also proved to be difficult ones.

The service of inauguration for the new president took place Tuesday, September 28, 1976, in the sanctuary of First Presbyterian Church in Dallas. With the participation in this service of such denominational leaders as Dr. James E. Andrews, stated clerk of the Presbyterian Church in the United States, Dr. Lois Stair, moderator of the 183rd General Assembly of the United Presbyterian Church in the United States of America, Dr. James I. McCord, president of

Princeton Theological Seminary and former professor and dean of
Austin Seminary, and Dr. David L. Stitt and Dr. Prescott Williams,
former presidents of Austin Seminary, there was a sense of drama
and expectation in the eye of the casual observer. Not yet thirty-
seven years old when he was elected to the presidency, Maxwell represented a new generation.

Maxwell's inauguration took place at a time when America had
gone through tumultuous events. It had been two years since
Richard Nixon resigned as president of the United States, a result
of his participation into a coverup of illegal activity by his subordi-
nates in breaking into the Democratic National Headquarters in the
Watergate Hotel in Washington, D.C., in 1972. Several public officials in the Nixon administration either resigned or were convicted
of crimes, or both.

The last Americans had been taken by helicopter from the
United States embassy in Saigon, Vietnam, on April 30, 1975, when
that city fell to the communists, concluding an ordeal that lasted
more than eight very turbulent years. Public unrest and protests
during those years reflected a growing dissatisfaction with American involvement in that war. Gerald Ford succeeded Nixon as president, but his pardon of Nixon contributed to his defeat and the
election of a former governor of Georgia from Plains, Georgia, by
the name of Jimmy Carter, in November 1976.

Those events, combined with assassinations and racial unrest in
the 1960s, led to a spirit of cynicism and general distrust of institutions of any stripe among many, particularly young people. While
professor and dean at Union Seminary in New York in the 1960s,
Austin Seminary alumnus and former Austin Seminary professor
Ellis Nelson not only witnessed much of the unrest among students, but was called on to negotiate with students at Union Seminary who had occupied the president's office to protest American
involvement in Vietnam. While that had taken place several years
before, it does give an indication of how traditional institutional authorities were being challenged in ways they had not been before.
Jack Maxwell became president of Austin Presbyterian Theological
Seminary at a time when the national spirit was something less than
robust.

During the first four years of Maxwell's tenure as president, the
national spirit would continue to experience demoralization. A

stagnant economy meant double-digit unemployment and interest-rate figures. And in spite of international peace accords between Egypt and Israel, in November 1979, Iranian Muslim fundamentalists seized Americans in the American embassy in Tehran and held fifty-two of them captive for 444 days, releasing them on the day of the inauguration of Carter's successor, Ronald Reagan.

It must be said that, ecclesiastically, there were more hopeful signs. For some time, efforts had been made toward reconciliation and reunion between the two principal Presbyterian denominations, separated since the American Civil War. Although Austin Seminary had on its faculty ministers who had come from other branches of the Presbyterian church (for example, John Jansen from the northern stream and Robert Shelton from the Cumberland stream), the calling of a minister member of the United Presbyterian Church (northern) to a seminary which was part of the Presbyterian Church, U.S. (southern), whose presidents all had heretofore belonged to that denomination, was a sign of movement in the direction many presbyteries had already gone in the form of union presbyteries. The presence at Maxwell's inauguration of the moderator of one denomination (Lois Stair) and the stated clerk of the other (James Andrews), as well as the president and former president of seminaries each representing sister denominations (James I. McCord of Princeton and David Stitt of Austin), was visible evidence of the hope for eventual reunion.

In his inaugural address, entitled "So That the World May Believe," Maxwell pointed to the centrality of worship in the life of the church, asserting that the congregation is where the integration of worship, theology, and ethics takes place.

> I am persuaded that the parish is not only the most exciting place to be, but that the local congregation is indeed "God's colony" with a mission and a message upon which the redemption of the world turns. Whether it gathers in tent or in tabernacle, and whether it scatters wearing the blue collar or the white collar vestment of secular society, the local congregation is the footprint of incarnation.[1]

This emphasis on the local congregation was consistent with Austin Seminary's historic commitment to training persons for the parish ministry. Indeed, Maxwell explicitly affirmed that commitment in his closing statement: "However you may define your agenda, I can testify to this: Austin Presbyterian Theological Seminary is committed in all its parts to train men and women for the parish ministry—'so that the world may believe' that Jesus Christ is Lord."[2]

Improvements to the Physical Plant

One of Maxwell's early priorities was to address some of the needs of the physical plant of the seminary. One pressing need was providing for an expanding library. Constructed in 1949–50 at a cost of $190,602, the library needed more space if it was going to be able to accommodate the needs of students and faculty alike. At its fall meeting in 1976, the Board of Trustees authorized a change in the seminary by-laws which would permit a loan for the purpose of expanding the Stitt Library. The loan was not to exceed $300,000.[3] The project would add 10,000 square feet of additional space to the Stitt Library. With more than 103,000 volumes in 1976, and with an average annual increase of about 2,300 volumes per year, the library clearly needed more space.[4] The Library Expansion Committee consisted of the board members Robert Trull (chairman), Joe Culver, and Bill Murray, and librarian Calvin Klemt and business manager Herman Harren. Scheduled date of completion was February 1978. While the expansion project was underway, one section of the McMillan Building was used as "the library," which was, in essence, an expanded reading room. Student assistants served as "runners" to retrieve books requested by students, faculty, and other patrons. Eventually, the addition to the Stitt Library would cost $600,000.

Further changes to the seminary's physical plant were approved at the board meeting the following spring. A former faculty home on campus was remodeled and dedicated as the Smoot Center for Continuing Education, named after Richmond Kelley Smoot, who served not only as pastor of First Southern Presbyterian Church, but simultaneously was professor of church history of Austin Seminary's predecessor institution, the Austin School of Theology (1884–95), professor of church history and polity at Austin Seminary (1902–5), and on the Board of Trustees (1899–1904).[5]

The oldest building on campus was Lubbock Hall. It and Sampson Hall (razed in 1962–63) were built in 1908, the first buildings constructed on the current site, which had been purchased the year before. At its spring meeting in 1977, the board authorized borrowing up to $300,000 to renovate Lubbock Hall, which served as the refectory. The estimated cost of this project was $186,000.

However, the bids on the renovation of Lubbock Hall turned out to be excessive. At a meeting of the Executive Committee of the board in April 1978, Dr. Maxwell announced that "the Seminary will serve as its own general contractor with Jack Hodges, superintendent of buildings and grounds, being the construction superintendent."[6] Work was to begin in May. The renovation was completed in late 1978 and cost around $200,000.

Another part of the physical plant that required attention was married student housing. The minutes of the Board of Trustees' fall 1977 meeting indicate that there was a new need: "Within little more than a generation, the statistics have changed from almost 100% single students to 80% married students."[7] In 1951–52, apartments for married students had been constructed on University Avenue, south of Thirtieth Street. In 1957–58, more married student housing was built, in the 2900 block of University, just north of those that were built in 1952, and on Thirtieth Street. Homes on West Twenty-ninth Street and East Thirtieth Street were purchased by the seminary in the 1950s and used by married students.

The combination of an increase in the number of married students and the deterioration of the homes on Twenty-ninth and Thirtieth streets led the board to authorize the razing of existing houses and the construction of new brick homes. In May 1980 the board authorized the administration to proceed with this project. It was completed in 1982.

In May 1983 the board acted on two more recommendations having to do with the seminary's physical plant. One was the expansion of the Trull Building, which housed most of the administration offices. This affected the business office primarily. The southeastern portion of the building was expanded toward Twenty-seventh Street. The cost for this expansion was estimated to be $112,000. The board granted its approval.

At the same meeting, permission was granted to purchase a new pipe organ for the Chapel at a cost of $150,000. Having been constructed in 1941–42, the Chapel also required attention in other areas. Repairs to the inside walls and the outside tower had become necessary.[8]

According to Herman Harren, vice president for business affairs, no one was sure where the money for this project would be found, but when the need was announced, the money was there. Harren, who had been business manager of the seminary since 1971 and had become vice president for business affairs under Maxwell, recalled that he had bought some old Austin brick in the mid-1970s without knowing how it might be used. It turned out that the brick, taken from the old F. W. Woolworth building, perfectly matched the brick needed for the outside repairs of the Chapel and the addition to the Trull Building. Some of the bricks were also used for the new married student housing.[9]

Faculty Development

In addition to these improvements during the presidency of Jack Maxwell, there were other needs that were perceived and addressed. One had to do with strengthening the faculty. One of Maxwell's early goals, it is agreed, was to raise faculty salaries.[10] Rev. Tom Schmid, who served on the Board of Trustees from 1974 to 1983 and again from 1984 to 1993, has the following recollections of this priority for the new president:

> Jack worked very hard to bring Austin Seminary faculty salaries into a competitive range with other seminaries, and particularly the other three of the PCUS. We used to go to board meetings and he would hand out graphs showing what faculties were paid at Columbia, Louisville, and Union, and Austin was always the lowest. He got the board to institute a five-year plan to bring Austin Seminary's faculty salaries more in line with the other three, and faculty members had some major raises in a very short period of years. As well, there were tables developed and distributed that showed what faculty members would be making at the level of Professor, Associate Professor, Assistant Professor, and with the number of years of service.[11]

But, as important as that issue was, perhaps more important was the issue of change and continuity within the faculty community. Austin Seminary was in a period of transition that had begun a few years earlier. Walter Johnson, homiletics professor, died of cancer in 1970. Robert Shelton was called the following year to fill that position. After twenty-six years as president, David Stitt resigned in 1971. Rachel Henderlite, professor of Christian education, retired in 1971. David Ng filled that position in 1975. Stuart Currie, professor of New Testament language and exegesis, died of a massive heart attack in April 1975. John Alsup began the following fall as visiting professor of New Testament and, after a year, joined the faculty as assistant professor of New Testament. Jim Wharton, who had taught Old Testament since 1956, left in 1975 to become pastor of Memorial Drive Presbyterian Church in Houston. Merwyn Johnson arrived in 1974 to teach theology.

In the midst of these changes, there were faculty members who continued to give strength and stability to the seminary. Prescott Williams, who had taught Old Testament at the seminary since 1959 and had served as academic dean since 1966, succeeded Stitt in the president's office in 1972, retaining the responsibilities of academic dean. Others who provided continuity during this time included John Jansen, who had come in 1958 to teach New Testament, George Heyer, who began teaching the history of doctrine in 1964, Gene March, who had taught Old Testament since 1964, Ross Dunn, who had taught ethics since 1967, Dick Junkin, who had come to Austin to teach church history in 1970, and Calvin (Cal) Klemt, who had served as librarian since 1966.

Maxwell represented a new generation for Austin Seminary and would have the opportunity to influence the shape of the faculty for the foreseeable future.

At the same called meeting of the board in 1976 in which Jack Maxwell was elected president, Dick Junkin, who had taught at the seminary since 1970, was elected professor of church history and academic dean. He had served as acting dean since the resignation of Prescott Williams as president and dean in 1975.

With Junkin's move into the dean's office, clearly there was need for a faculty member in the field of church history. On the basis of faculty action and Maxwell's recommendation, at its May 1977 meeting the Board of Trustees elected Robert S. Paul as professor of ecclesiastical history and Christian thought. Maxwell and

Paul had known each other in Pittsburgh, where Paul had taught at Pittsburgh Theological Seminary. Paul accepted the call and began his teaching duties in Austin the following autumn.

Paul had already achieved distinction in his field of church history and as a churchman. Born in Surrey, England, Paul served as a pastor in England for nine years (1945–54) before accepting a call to the Ecumenical Institute of the World Council of Churches in Geneva. At the same time, he was on the staff of the Graduate School of Ecumenical Studies, which was part of the University of Geneva. He was in Geneva from 1954 to 1958. In 1958 he moved to Hartford, Connecticut, where he was Waldo Professor of Church History at the Hartford Seminary Foundation. In 1967 he moved to Pittsburgh Theological Seminary, where he served as professor of modern church history until 1977, when he accepted the call issued by Austin Seminary.

Paul's experience as pastor, churchman, and scholar contributed to the seminary's positive reputation, both in the church and in academic circles. His interest in ecumenical work at the international level brought a renewed interest in that area to the campus. Prior to his work in Geneva, Paul had attended the founding assembly of the World Council of Churches in Amsterdam in 1948. He had also participated in the International Congregational Council and in Presbyterian-Reformed/Roman Catholic and Presbyterian-Reformed/Lutheran conversations.

Paul's prodigious list of publications was a very attractive feature of his resume. Although faculty members were afforded the opportunity to publish articles and accounts of their current interests and research through the faculty edition of the Austin Seminary *Bulletin,* and although many of them published articles in other journals, it became clear that President Maxwell believed that a higher priority ought to be given to faculty publications. Over the years, Austin Seminary had produced an unusually high number of leaders in the church, but its appeal was largely a regional one. One way to gain greater exposure for the seminary would be by having a faculty that had published widely. While this goal was not to be at the expense of excellence in the classroom, Robert Paul's arrival in Austin represented a fresh emphasis in this area.

Among his publications prior to coming to Austin were *The Lord Protector: Religion and Politics in the Life of Oliver Cromwell*

(1955), *The Atonement and the Sacraments* (1960), *An Apologeticall Narration: Editor of a Facsimile Edition of 1643* (1963), *Ministry* (1965), *The Church in Search of Its Self* (1972), and *Kingdom Come!* (1974).[12] While at Austin, Paul completed a massive history of the divines that gathered at Westminster in 1643 and met through 1647. The book, *Assembly of the Lord: Politics and Religion in the Westminster Assembly and the 'Grand Debate,'* covered the developments of the ecclesiastical and theological debates within the assembly while the troops of Oliver Cromwell were doing battle with those of King Charles I outside Westminster's walls. Paul's book was published in 1985 by T. & T. Clark.

In addition to contributing articles to faculty editions of the Austin Seminary *Bulletin,* Paul would also serve as chairman of the faculty committee that produced that publication. With his own impressive list of publications, it was appropriate that he serve in this capacity.

There were other significant faculty appointments during Maxwell's tenure as president. Former board member Tom Schmid recalls:

> We had some stellar teachers, but the pattern seemed to be that most of them were graduates of Austin Seminary who had returned to teach after they got their doctorates. We began to see newer faculty members who came from out of the region. I say this without casting aspersions on the treasured faculty of the earlier era, but I believe that it was the broadening of the faculty that helped Austin Seminary begin to move out of being a small regional seminary into one which is nowadays much more geographically broadly based and far reaching. It was Jack Maxwell who seriously engaged in a new kind of faculty recruitment for the seminary, and I think it was related to some larger issues, such as the reunited Presbyterian Church (U.S.A.) and the fact that by that time distances within the nation were not perceived to be as great as they were even fifteen or twenty years earlier.[13]

With the departure of Merwyn S. Johnson in 1980 for Erskine Theological Seminary in Due West, South Carolina, there arose a need for someone in the field of theology. George Stroup, with degrees from Rice University, Yale Divinity School, and Vanderbilt

University, had taught at Princeton Seminary for six years (1974–80) when he received and accepted a call to teach at Austin Seminary. Stroup stayed at Austin Seminary until December 1985, when he moved to Decatur, Georgia, to join the faculty of Columbia Seminary. It was while he was at Austin that he wrote *The Promise of Narrative Theology* (1981), as well as *Jesus Christ for Today* (1982), one volume in the "Library of Living Faith" series.

In 1980 Dr. Maxwell, with the concurrence of the faculty, invited John R. "Pete" Hendrick to become professor of mission and evangelism at Austin Seminary. In addition, Hendrick was to direct the Continuing Education and the Doctor of Ministry programs, duties that came under the title "Director of Professional Development." Hendrick, a 1952 graduate of Austin Seminary with a Ph.D. from New York University, had served as "Instructor of Bible at the seminary from 1956 to 1959 and had served as pastor of three small churches in Arkansas, a suburban church in San Antonio, and the downtown church in Beaumont, Texas."[14] He came to Austin from Houston, having served as executive presbyter of Brazos Presbytery in southeast Texas for seven years (1973–80). His appointment at the seminary came on the heels of two developments: first, a clear decline in membership in the Presbyterian church; and second, an urging by the Evangelism Office of the Program Agency of the United Presbyterian Church that theological institutions address the matter of evangelism in theological education.[15]

Hendrick's *Opening the Door of Faith: The Why, When and Where of Evangelism,* the basis of which was the Settles Lectures on Mission and Evangelism which Hendrick delivered at Austin Seminary in 1972, was published by John Knox Press in 1977.

Throughout the 1980s, courses offered in the fields of mission and evangelism, doctor of ministry projects dealing with evangelism, and visiting lecturers, particularly those invited to give the Settles Lectures, kept evangelism in the forefront as a topic of interest and discussion. In 1985 a course in evangelism and mission became a requirement for seminary graduation. The April 1985 faculty issue of the Austin Seminary *Bulletin* was devoted to "Presbyterians and Evangelism." Eventually, thanks to financial contributions from members of First Presbyterian Church, Houston, Hendrick's position became an endowed chair honoring the former pastor of that congregation and his wife, John William and Helen Lancaster. Dr.

Lancaster had served on the board for twelve years (1959–65; 1967–73) and had served as chairman for ten years (1962–72).

Maxwell's establishment of a faculty position in the field of evangelism and mission in 1980 reflected insight into, and appreciation for, a need in the Presbyterian church not found in all Presbyterian seminaries at that time. It anticipated the interest in evangelism and spirituality that would grow in the next two decades.

Another contribution by Maxwell that would have a significant impact on the future of Austin Seminary was the appointment of women to the faculty. Until this time, the only woman to have served on the faculty was Rachel Henderlite, the first woman ordained to the ministry in the Presbyterian Church, U.S. Henderlite was ordained in 1965 and came to Austin that same year to teach in the field of Christian education. She remained until her retirement in 1971.

Cynthia Campbell joined the faculty in September 1981, having completed her Ph.D. at Southern Methodist University. Without forming a search committee, according to Tom Schmid, Maxwell announced to the board Campbell's appointment to the faculty.[16] Campbell not only taught in the areas of theology and ministry, but in 1984 was also appointed director of the Doctor of Ministry program, which had begun in 1974.

Although women students had been an integral part of the seminary community for several years, Campbell's presence on the faculty signaled a fresh recognition and affirmation of women in ministry in the Presbyterian church. While she came to the seminary in an unorthodox way, Maxwell's evaluation of her as a gifted servant of the church was confirmed by the positive way in which she was received into the seminary community and by her contributions to it. Furthermore, in 1988 Campbell accepted a call to serve as pastor of First Presbyterian Church in Salina, Kansas, a fact that received attention throughout the church as a step in the direction of increased acceptance of women in leadership positions within the church. In January 1995 Campbell left Salina to become president of McCormick Theological Seminary in Chicago.

In 1979 Laura Brookings Lewis graduated from the seminary and accepted a call to be the associate pastor of Hope Presbyterian Church in Austin. Lewis had earned a master's degree in Christian education at the Presbyterian School of Christian Education in

Richmond, Virginia, in 1971. After serving as a D.C.E. at First Presbyterian Church in Salisbury, North Carolina, Laura and her husband, Robert, decided to move back to Austin. Because she had already taken courses at the seminary when she was an undergraduate at the University of Texas, and because of her work at PSCE in Richmond, Lewis finished her M.Div. work in December 1978 and graduated the following May.[17]

In 1982 Lewis accepted a call from the seminary to become assistant professor of Christian education. The three-year appointment began in September of that year. She succeeded David Ng, who had moved to New York to work in the national offices of the United Presbyterian Church, and she thus became the second woman on the seminary faculty during Maxwell's presidency. Former board member Tom Schmid recalls that Maxwell "referred to this as the 'growing your own' method of faculty recruitment inasmuch as the call to Laura included the stipulation that she would pursue a Ph.D., which she did at the University of Texas."[18] The degree was granted in 1991.

In addition to her teaching duties, Lewis would later (from 1996 to 1998) serve on the nine-member denominational committee that would draw up a new catechism for the denomination. That catechism would be presented to and approved by the General Assembly in 1998. Actually, the committee drew up two catechisms, one for children and youth, and one for adults. Lewis's leadership reflected the growing role of women in the church and broadened the exposure of Austin Seminary.

In 1981 W. Eugene March announced that he would not return to the seminary after the 1981–82 academic year. At the time of the announcement, March had no call to another work. Eventually, he was called to be the A. B. Rhodes Professor of Old Testament at Louisville Theological Seminary, where he has served with distinction both as professor and as academic dean. To replace March, the board elected and called John Andrew Dearman to begin his teaching duties in the fall of 1982. Having earned his M.Div. from Princeton Theological Seminary and his Ph.D. from Emory University, Dearman came to Austin after a teaching stint at Louisiana State University in Baton Rouge.

There were two further faculty appointments of note during Maxwell's tenure as president. The academic year 1982–83 was John

Jansen's last year to teach before retirement. Having come in 1958, Jansen had endeared himself to faculty and students alike. His late-night hours at his typewriter in his campus office contributed to the admiration and respect he enjoyed among students. A prolific writer and a devoted churchman, Jansen found himself the recipient of a "Festschrift" (a collection of essays in his honor) in the June 1983 issue of the faculty edition of the Austin Seminary *Bulletin.* The edition bore the title "Doctor Ecclesiae" and included four essays by Austin Seminary colleagues as well as three by scholars at other institutions (including one by Gene March, who had moved on to Louisville Seminary).

In his introductory remarks, Jack Maxwell offered the following observations:

> I first met John Jansen through his writing: *Let Us Worship God: An Interpretation for Families,* published in the Covenant Life Curriculum. It remains the clearest and most effective book I have ever used with laypeople. Then more than seven years ago I met the man and quickly learned why he can write so convincingly and persuasively on worship: In both its corporate and devotional forms worship is at the center of his life. We are so envious of his command of the hymns and devotional literature of the Church that we kid him about it sometimes. One colleague is fond of saying, "When John knows that his argument is in trouble, he quotes a hymn." He often does, and it is always an apt hymn that never fails to take an argument beyond the capacity of prose and seal it in poetry.
>
> For more than this we give thanks for his faithful scholarship, his still boundless energy, his diligent attention to the tedium of committee work, his lofty preaching and his great capacity to be our counselor and friend. ...
>
> John Frederick Jansen is a giant among us, his colleagues believe, and in him we know that we have encountered one who has learned to live by the Spirit and walk by the Spirit, and that to the honor and glory of God.[19]

In retirement Jansen continued to work in his campus office and teach a course or two each year. A year in advance of the effective date of Jansen's retirement, at its May 1982 meeting the Board of

Trustees showed its affection for this New Testament scholar and friend by electing him professor emeritus of New Testament interpretation, effective July 1, 1983.

To fill the position vacated by Jansen's retirement, the seminary called Lewis Donelson to be assistant professor of New Testament, beginning no later than September 1, 1983. Having grown up as a Presbyterian in Memphis, Tennessee, Donelson had received degrees from Duke University and Louisville Theological Seminary, and a Ph.D. from the University of Chicago. He served as a pastor for two and a half years in Holly Grove, Arkansas, before beginning his doctoral work in Chicago. Austin Seminary was his first teaching appointment and, so far, has been his only teaching appointment. Although he has been contacted about positions elsewhere, Donelson says he remains at Austin because the personal relationships and the academic stimulation available there are more difficult to cultivate, he believes, at other, larger seminaries.[20]

The final faculty appointment during Maxwell's tenure at Austin Seminary proved to be providential. C. Ellis Nelson, a graduate of the seminary and former professor of Christian education at Austin, retired as president of Louisville Theological Seminary on July 1, 1981. Upon his retirement, Nelson went to San Francisco Theological Seminary to serve as professor of Christian education. While in San Francisco, Nelson was contacted several times by Maxwell to consider coming to Austin to teach when he retired from SFTS. Maxwell, Dean Shelton, and Nelson "worked out a plan for me to teach about half time for three years while Laura Lewis was working on her Ph.D. degree."[21] At its May 1983 meeting, the Board of Trustees appointed Nelson "Visiting Professor of Christian Education" for January 1 through December 31, 1984.

Nelson and his wife, Nancy, moved to Austin in December of 1983. Jack Maxwell resigned as president of Austin Seminary on November 10, 1983, a matter that will be discussed later in this chapter. The board asked Nelson to serve as interim president, effective January 1, 1984. Nelson's familiarity with the seminary and its history, his experience as a seminary president, and his humility and grace as a devoted churchman made it seem to some that his appointment by the board the preceding May was a blessing beyond expectations. Maxwell's resignation came as a surprise to many, including Nelson, but the appointment of the interim president brought a sense of relief and confidence to all who cared about Austin Seminary.

Although not an academic appointment, one innovation relating to the life of the community initiated by Maxwell deserves mention. According to former board member Tom Schmid, it "was Jack's idea that the seminary have a campus pastor, although I think the subject had been talked about for several years, and it was at his behest that the board called C. D.Weaver to that position."[22]

Having served as pastor of the Grace Presbyterian Church in Gainesville, Florida, for twenty years, Weaver moved to Austin in January 1983. His official title was "Minister-in-Residence." He describes his role as one of supporting students beyond the classroom. In addition to providing access to counseling services when needed, Weaver sought to organize small groups that might lead to friendships and networks that would last beyond their student life at seminary. He saw his role as helping to lay the groundwork for a life in ministry that meant knowing how to take care of oneself in ministry.[23]

At its November 1987 meeting, the Board of Trustees concurred with a recommendation of President Jack Stotts that Weaver's position bear a new title—dean of students and campus minister. Although his basic duties as campus minister remained the same, Weaver's administrative responsibilities did increase. For example, he assumed greater responsibility for the needs of international students on campus, developing a network of referral services.

Weaver served as the first and only person in that position until his retirement in the summer of 1999.

Development Office

In 1973 President Prescott Williams invited Jerry Tompkins to come to Austin Seminary to serve as the seminary's first vice president. Tompkins, a graduate of the Class of 1955, had been serving as pastor of Trinity Presbyterian Church in Midland, Texas. There were seven areas of responsibility which Tompkins was assigned: publications and publicity; alumni relations and organization; constituency relations; working with the Synod of Red River in providing educational resources to the synod; continuing education;

foundation contacts for the purpose of securing funds for buildings and programs; and working with the Development Committee of the Board of Trustees.[24]

Until Tompkins arrived on November 1, 1973, the responsibility for raising funds for the seminary had been lodged solely in the president's office. From the seminary's very beginnings, the seminary's financial survival and stability virtually depended on the president's ability to tap the resources of the school's constituents, making the case for the need for theological training of pastors for the church. That Austin Seminary not only survived but thrived is testimony to the persuasive abilities and the tireless efforts of Sampson, Vinson, Currie, Stitt, and Williams.

For a variety of reasons, however, it became clear that institutional development would require an office of its own which would be devoted to cultivating relationships with alumni and constituents. In addition, this office would develop associations with philanthropical foundations from which grants might be procured, and discover ways in which the seminary could publicize its needs as well as its offerings. "Marketing" and "target audience" were to become two of the watchwords that were to characterize American society, and one ignored their potential at one's own peril.

In working with alumni and constituents within the synod in the early 1970s, Tompkins was at the very beginning of Austin Seminary's gradual move toward the specialization that required an office of development. With the arrival of Jack Maxwell, that move became a conscious and deliberate one. His initiative in establishing a separate development office was an important and, it would soon be seen, necessary one. Other institutions had established such offices and had recognized the benefit.

In 1975 Joe Culver was elected to the Board of Trustees. A member of First Southern Presbyterian Church (now Central Presbyterian) in Austin, Culver had worked at the University of Texas since 1955. From 1969 to 1973 he had been the director of human resources, and from 1973 to 1977 he had served as the assistant vice president for development. Maxwell approached Culver to consider leaving the university to come to the seminary as vice president for development. Sensing a call to serve the church in a more involved way, Culver resigned as a member of the board, effective June 30, 1977, and began work at the seminary on July 1, 1977.

During Maxwell's first year, in addition to Tompkins' other responsibilities, he helped Maxwell become acquainted with the synod—attending presbytery meetings, soliciting invitations to preach, and speaking at various gatherings of ministers. After Culver's arrival at the seminary in the Development Office, he built on Tompkins' work in constituent relations. Tompkins was then free to turn his attention to assisting senior students in finding calls and in developing and administering a more ambitious Continuing Education program.

The combination of sound business acumen, a love for the church, and a gracious and humble spirit formed in Joe Culver a devoted and effective development officer for the seminary. The good relationships Culver, Maxwell, and Tompkins developed with individual pastors and churches went a long way toward the successful renovation of Lubbock Hall, the expansion of the Stitt Library, and the renovation of the West Lounge in the McMillan Building. The Smoot Center for Continuing Education was upgraded.

In addition, Culver saw to it that an IBM System 6 computer system was installed, thus introducing modern technology to the seminary and enabling the school to keep efficient and quickly accessible records in virtually every area. The good working relationship between Culver and Tompkins was reflected in the fact that alumni giving increased 2,000 percent in 1977–78.[25]

The calling of Joe Culver to Austin Seminary was, in the words of former board member Tom Schmid, "a master stroke" by Maxwell. Schmid goes on to recall:

> It was when Joe came to work for Austin Seminary that we began to have phonathons, alumni solicitations, systematized mailings, much more deliberate contacts with major and lesser donors and potential donors. I don't think Austin Seminary was behind most American seminaries in the 1970s in this respect. In fact, if a survey were made of all the Presbyterian seminaries at the time, I'd guess that there were only Princeton and a couple of others who had more sophisticated development programs. But the fact is that Jack recognized where seminaries needed to go in regard to development efforts, and where Austin Seminary in particular needed to go, and he made it happen with Joe Culver.[26]

Trustee chairman Clarence Frierson recalls that when Maxwell came to Austin, the financial situation was critical:

> As I looked at the numbers I could see that the seminary was going "broke." The operating budget was very small and yet was consuming all the income plus all increases in value of the endowment. Our faculty salaries were well below most comparable institutions. In face of all this Jack recommended that faculty salaries be increased and the board approved his recommendation without a clue as to how it was to be funded. To meet this financial crisis Jack recommended that we hire a full-time development officer (Joe Culver) and start an annual giving plan. We had neither.[27]

While matters related to the seminary endowment will be examined in the next chapter, it should be noted here that between 1976 and 1980 the seminary's annual operating budget grew from $770,500 to $1,409,250. In 1976 the seminary's endowment was $7,815,000. In 1980 the investment portfolio was $11,213,291.[28] Clearly, the establishment of an Office of Development by Jack Maxwell and the work of Jerry Tompkins and Joe Culver went a long way toward strengthening Austin Seminary's financial base, both for the present and the future.

Both Jerry Tompkins and Joe Culver left the seminary in 1980. Tompkins' resignation was effective June 30. He left the seminary to accept a call to be the president of the Presbyterian Children's Homes of Texas, the headquarters of which are today in Austin. Joe Culver left shortly thereafter to return to the Business School at the University of Texas. Maxwell had approached Dr. William K. Hedrick, pastor of Trinity Presbyterian Church in Midland and graduate of Austin Seminary, to consider working in the seminary's development office. Hedrick recalls:

> One day at Mo-Ranch, Maxwell called and wanted to know if I would be interested in working on the development staff at the seminary. First, I didn't know it had such a staff. I thought Jerry Tompkins was still trying to put together fund-raising dinners. Second, I said I was a pastor, not an administrator. Maxwell was very persuasive. He said he was not looking for someone who was trying to flee

the pastorate, but someone who loved the pastorate enough to make
it possible for others to be prepared for the calling.[29]

According to Hedrick, one of the reasons he thought Maxwell
wanted a seminary alumnus in the development office was to cultivate support from other Austin Seminary graduates. "Besides,"
Hedrick continued, "Joe Culver was an experienced development
officer and I would get to work under him and get trained by the
Lilly Endowment."[30] With some hesitation, but out of love for the
seminary, Hedrick agreed to accept the call.

Between the time Hedrick accepted the call and the time he
moved to Austin, Culver announced his resignation. The minutes
of the Executive Committee of the Board of Trustees indicate that
Hedrick's title was "Director of Development, effective August 1,
1980."[31] In May 1982, the Executive Committee changed Hedrick's
title to "Vice-President for Development."[32] Hedrick remained at
Austin Seminary in that capacity until November 1991, when he accepted a call to become pastor of Second Presbyterian Church in St.
Louis, Missouri.

Hispanic Ministry

According to the "Seventy-fifth Anniversary History" of
Austin Seminary, a serious interest in cultivating a relationship with
the Hispanic community and offering courses in Spanish had been
evident since 1921.[33] Over the years, professors in charge of the
"Spanish-speaking Department" included Robert F. Gribble and
R. D. Campbell. In the 1960s, the Office of the Hispanic American
Institute was established. Jorge Lara-Braud, an Austin Seminary
graduate, was its first director. Ruben P. Armendariz was its second.
The institute eventually closed.

While there have been many outstanding Hispanic graduates of
Austin Seminary who have carried out significant and effective ministries in the Presbyterian church, the Presbyterian seminary closest
to the Mexican border and in a state with a large Spanish-speaking
population has found it difficult to claim the allegiance of the Hispanic community in a widespread way. Nevertheless, Jack Maxwell
saw it as an important relationship to attempt to cultivate and one

that should be addressed. There may, no doubt, be several reasons that can explain this frustrating predicament.

In December 1982, Maxwell appointed Dan Garza to the position of assistant to the president for Hispanic ministries. Garza graduated from Trinity University in 1961. After a two-year stint in the U.S. Army, he entered Austin Seminary in 1964 and graduated in 1968. His first pastorate was Bethel Presbyterian Church in San Antonio. Following that pastorate, Garza served First Presbyterian Church in Edinburg, Texas, as associate pastor of Gethsemane Presbyterian Church, Fort Worth. In 1979 he worked for the synod's Mexican-American Coordinating Council. According to Tom Schmid, Maxwell saw Austin Seminary as being peculiarly positioned to strengthen the synod's work among Hispanics: "I do remember that it was Jack Maxwell who made a particular motion at a Synod of Red River meeting at First Church in Fort Worth, about 1980 or 1981, that synod's Hispanic ministry 'should not fail for lack of funds.'"[34]

When asked about the relatively small number of Hispanic students attending Austin Seminary over the years, Garza mentions several contributing factors. One is that the pool of qualified candidates has always been relatively small. Perhaps a more important factor is the synod's dissolution, in 1955, of the old Tex-Mex Presbytery, which was made up mostly of Hispanic congregations. The thought behind this action, apparently, was that assimilation of Hispanic congregations into already existing presbyteries made up primarily of Anglo congregations would be healthy for everyone. There was also the hope, it seems, that this action would lead to compensation for Hispanic ministers that was equal to that given to Anglo ministers. According to Garza, at one time there were eighty-five preaching points in the Tex-Mex Presbytery. The synod's dissolution of that body "took the wind out of the sails of the Hispanic church."[35]

Garza's presence and his recruitment efforts, no doubt, have played an important role in keeping the seminary's relationship with the Hispanic community viable and positive. And, in spite of the constant need for greater efforts in this area, at the very least, Jack Maxwell discerned the opportunity that lay before Austin Seminary and sought to address it.

What Went Wrong?

Considerable accomplishments and progress took place at the seminary during Jack Maxwell's tenure as president. The investment portfolio had virtually doubled, and buildings were being expanded, renovated, or constructed. But morale among students and faculty was at a low point during the latter years of his presidency. Two tenured faculty members, both of whom were graduates of Austin Seminary and highly admired and respected, Gene March and Dick Junkin, felt compelled to resign their positions at the seminary. The Synod Covenant Review Committee received letters urging it to recommend that the Board of Trustees ask Maxwell to resign. And the Board of Trustees, in fact, eventually asked for, and received, a letter of resignation from Jack Maxwell on November 8, 1983. How could a president who was so intelligent and full of such promise lose the support of virtually everybody necessary for the running of a seminary?

The answers are difficult, if not impossible, to compile. Nevertheless, some observations may be in order.

First, most agree that Jack Maxwell brought much talent to the office of president of Austin Seminary. Second, Maxwell demonstrated a pastoral side which few had the opportunity to experience. For example, he served as a supportive pastor and colleague to Bob Shelton, professor of homiletics and liturgics, when Shelton's wife, Barbara, was dying of cancer in 1980. He showed equally sympathetic pastoral care to student Thamar Aguirre when she also was diagnosed with cancer and died while enrolled at Austin Seminary.

In reflecting on the hospitality of several seminary faculty members during his student days, Walker Westerlage, a 1981 graduate and pastor of Trinity Presbyterian Church in Mansfield, Texas, writes of a side to Maxwell that very few persons saw: "I recall dinner with Jack and Sandy Maxwell, listening to Jack play the piano and tell of his encounter with Elvis."[36]

However, often what was experienced instead was an abruptness and rudeness with students, faculty, and constituents in the church which, not surprisingly, led to a loss of support for Maxwell and the seminary.

Dick Junkin, academic dean throughout most of Maxwell's presidency, offered the view that, for all the good things that may have happened, part of Maxwell's difficulties as president can be traced to his failure to demonstrate, consistently, respect for those inside the institution as well as for those outside it. This inconsistency led to confusion. But Junkin also suggests that the Board of Trustees as well as the faculty and staff bear some responsibility for allowing matters to reach the point that they did.[37]

The frustration of the faculty and staff can be seen in the departure of several faculty and staff members during the Maxwell years. David Ng left for the denominational headquarters of the United Presbyterian Church in New York City. Gene March announced his resignation before having a call, but accepted an endowed faculty chair of Old Testament at Louisville Theological Seminary. Six months before Maxwell resigned, Dick Junkin accepted a call to be a peace associate for Central America in the Division of International Mission of the PC(USA). He moved to San Jose, Costa Rica, where he stayed for five years. Jerry Tompkins left to become president of the Texas Children's Homes. Joe Culver had chosen to leave the seminary and return to the university, across the street.

Some seminary graduates tried to share their concern for the seminary with Maxwell. Others who loved the school spoke to faculty and board members. Some expressed their concern to the Synod Covenant Review Committee. While many acknowledged that the seminary was having problems, it seemed that most wanted to believe that the problems could be weathered.

Rev. Ted Foote, Class of 1979, writes the following of that time:

> That the seminary presidency of Dr. Jack Maxwell was, finally, among the seminary and synod constituencies, a most troubled period is incontestable. That Dr. Maxwell, on the one hand, and many church leaders and faculty, on the other, ended up alienated is also incontestable.
>
> That chapter of the seminary's story may unfortunately illustrate how seminaries like Austin Presbyterian need presidents who possess, with whatever other consummate skills they might have, at least convincing "people skills" and an abiding inclination to practice tactfulness no matter how much, situationally, brusqueness might be preferred.[38]

Robert Shelton, successor to Dick Junkin as academic dean, suggests that there are four constituencies to which a seminary president is responsible and whose support the president must have in order to be effective: the Board of Trustees, the faculty, the student body, and the larger church.[39] By November 1983, it seems, Maxwell had lost the support of all four bodies and, thus, tendered his resignation when representatives of the Executive Committee of the board met with him. The letter is dated November 8, 1983, and the resignation was effective December 31, 1983.

Clarence N. Frierson, chairman of the board, issued an announcement to the seminary community and a press release to the general public. A generous severance package for Maxwell was agreed upon.[40] In 1985 Maxwell accepted a call to become pastor of the Newtown Square Presbyterian Church in Newtown Square, Pennsylvania.

What Went Right?

In spite of much that had gone right and in spite of a sense of uncertainty regarding the future, there was a sense of relief with Maxwell's departure. A time for reflection and healing could begin. Dick Junkin, who had left the seminary six months before Maxwell resigned, points to several reasons for the seminary faculty and staff to look back with pride and satisfaction. First, the faculty kept at its work of educating men and women for the gospel ministry. "The atmosphere was depressed, but we nevertheless educated students, worked at our relationships with the wider church, put out our publications, and so forth. I am proud that we kept at it!"[41]

Cynthia Weeks Logan, 1979 graduate and former member of the Board of Trustees, echoes Junkin's sentiment. During the difficult years, she writes:

> never did we lack for anything which might nurture our experience of the seminary as a community. Those beloved professors saw to it that we never "got the short end of the stick" in quality of education, or in the overall positive seminary experience. They nurtured community in and for us. ... They never took out on us any

frustrations they might have been feeling. We did not suffer, although we can only imagine how they were suffering themselves![42]

Second, many of Austin Seminary's constituents were able to separate the current problems from their love for and commitment to the institution. Few of those constituents were permanently alienated. Affection for the institution, its mission, and all that it represented were larger than the adversities it had undergone. There was hope that the ship could be set right.

Third, Junkin continues, "we by and large hung together. We did not let the institutional stresses divide us into competing factions. We had no open, nasty fight among ourselves."[43] The high regard and respect which the constituents held for the seminary was, apparently, shared by the faculty. The work of the seminary was too important to let the immediate conflict cause them to lose sight of that work.

Upon Maxwell's resignation, leadership duties of the president were distributed among the triumvirate of Bob Shelton (academic dean), Bill Hedrick (vice president for development), and Herman Harren (vice president for business affairs). A search for both an interim president and a president was authorized by the Board of Trustees.[44] Having accepted the seminary's invitation to be visiting professor in the field of Christian education, Ellis Nelson was to move to Austin in December. In Nelson, Austin Seminary not only had an alumnus, a former professor, and someone who was devoted to the school, but also someone who had experience as a seminary president (Louisville Theological Seminary). He became the board's choice to serve as interim president at this particularly painful time in the seminary's life. Nelson's experience, love for the seminary, and calming presence provided the school with an opportunity to catch its breath and reset its sights on the future.

CHAPTER TWO

An Extraordinary Gift:
The Jean Brown Bequest

Over the years, countless persons have contributed in a variety of ways, often sacrificially, to Austin Seminary. Certainly, one measure of health of an institution, as well as of the support it may enjoy, is its financial condition.

When the first Board of Trustees of Austin Seminary elected T. R. Sampson to serve as the school's first president and "financial agent of said Seminary," the only tangible asset credited to the seminary was the property of the old Stuart Seminary at the corner of Ninth and Navasota streets. Furthermore, Sampson was to be paid $2,500, but he had to raise that money himself. He was also charged with seeking "money for an operating budget and a $100,000 endowment, professors to teach, and as the goal of all, candidates anxious to be better prepared to pursue their calling to the ministry." After more than $53,000 had been raised, the Synod of Texas gave permission for classes to begin in 1902 "if $100,000 in endowment funds had by then been received."[1]

One of the primary reasons the seminary was able to open its doors in October 1902 was the gift of $75,000 by Mrs. Sarah C. Ball of Galveston. This endowment gift was to provide funding for a professor to teach systematic theology and Old Testament languages and exegesis.[2]

Over the years, of course, many people, churches, and foundations have made significant financial contributions to Austin Seminary which have enabled it both to survive and to thrive. And while each and every gift, regardless of size, is important, some gifts seem to be the timely answers to prayer and address some immediate need. Sarah Ball's gift helped get the seminary off the ground. The $4,000 bequest from Frank R. Lubbock's will helped in the construction of Lubbock Hall, the seminary's refectory for many years.[3] Fred S. Robbins of Bay City contributed $15,000 toward the construction of the Seminary Chapel at a particularly critical time.

And mention should be made of Toddie Lee Wynne, who in 1954 purchased the land on which the Single Students' Dorm was eventually built, and of the McMillan Foundation, which provided funds for the construction of the McMillan Memorial Classroom Building in 1962, and of the Trull Foundation of Palacios, Texas, whose support led to the construction of the Trull Memorial Administration Building. Other financial contributions have helped to underwrite faculty endowments, scholarship endowments, and general endowments. Such generosity was often the result of tireless efforts of seminary officials and pastors who over the years cultivated relationships with faithful Presbyterians throughout the synod.

In August 1981 Miss Jean Brown of Hot Springs, Arkansas, died. Her will provided that Arkansas College (now Lyon College) receive $13.75 million and that Austin Seminary receive $11.25 million. The gift to the former school nearly tripled its endowment, while the seminary's endowment, or investment portfolio, virtually doubled. In addition to these gifts, Miss Brown "remembered 124 individuals and 34 charities in her will."[4] In 1981 the book value of Austin Seminary's investment portfolio was $12,493,494 and its fair market value was $13,047,619. In 1982 the book value was $25,146,670 and the fair market value was $24,072,711.[5]

Clearly, the Jean Brown gift was not the first association that family had with the seminary. Jean's younger brother, William Clark Brown, served on the seminary's Board of Trustees from 1934 until 1970, a tenure matched only by that of Robert Adger Law of Austin, who served from 1922 until 1958.[6] In 1940 three siblings—

W. C., Jean, and Josephine—made contributions to the Seminary "to assure the completion of the Seminary Chapel."[7]

The Brown family was in the lumber business in Hot Springs and had roots that went back to Orange County, North Carolina. The Brown siblings' father moved to Arkansas in 1869, eventually settling in Hot Springs around 1900. Of Scottish and Scotch-Irish descent, the Brown family members were strong Presbyterians, active in presbytery and synod activities and supporters of Presbyterian world missions. The Browns were active members of First Presbyterian Church in Hot Springs. In 1960 they became members of the Orange Street Presbyterian Church in Hot Springs which, two years later, changed its name to Westminster Presbyterian Church. Jean Brown died August 27, 1981; W. C. died October 1, 1989.

According to Catherine Sautter, registrar at the seminary from April 1958 to January 1990, "The Jean Brown bequest to Austin Seminary was a miracle from God [*sic*] which will be used for the future of the Church for years to come."[8] Herman Harren, vice president for business affairs at the time, has observed that the gift "saved Austin Seminary's life." Not only did the Brown bequest give the seminary exposure, but it provided a secure basis on which to grow.[9]

By 1999 the book value of the seminary's investment portfolio was $76,575,528, but the fair market value had grown to $95,450,381.[10] While this growth over eighteen years may be attributable to other generous gifts and wise investments, such growth is not as likely to have taken place without the Brown gift. It would also be fair to say that this gift enabled Austin Seminary to attain greater parity with its peers in terms of investments. The 1997–98 *Fact Book on Theological Education,* produced by the Association of Theological Schools in the United States and Canada, lists Austin Seminary as fourth among Presbyterian Church (U.S.A.) seminaries in terms of "long-term investments," behind Princeton Seminary, Union-Richmond, and Columbia Theological Seminary.[11]

In the November 19, 1981, minutes of the Board of Trustees is a tribute to James W. Mosley, pastor of Westminster Presbyterian Church in Hot Springs, and J. Gaston Williamson, a former seminary board member from Little Rock, Arkansas:

The Board of Trustees of Austin Presbyterian Theological

Seminary has heard with gratitude and joy the account of your assistance in obtaining for the Seminary the recent legacy from Miss Jean Brown—a gift which will dramatically affect the direction of this institution and of the Church in this region and beyond for years to come. Accordingly, The Board of Trustees extends to you its deep appreciation for your exemplary service to Austin Presbyterian Theological Seminary and for your devotion to its mission and ministry.[12]

At that same board meeting, the trustees established the Jean Brown Chair of Homiletics and Liturgics and elected Professor Robert Shelton to be the first incumbent of that chair. In addition, the board endowed the "Jean Brown Visiting Scholar Program," for which applications would be solicited. The successful applicant would be provided with a residence, an office, secretarial assistance, and a stipend for teaching "should the Faculty deem such an invitation to be appropriate."[13]

Also, as a result of the Jean Brown bequest, an "Enrichment Budget Program" was established by the Board of Trustees. Out of this fund, various projects were to be underwritten. In May 1982 the Board of Trustees authorized $58,000 to be distributed in the following way:

Christian Education Conference	$ 3,500
Center for Church Growth and Renewal	6,000
"Product" Evaluation	5,000
Minister-in-Residence	30,000
Crisis Intervention for Pastors	6,500
Special Events	3,000
Instructional Media Support Services	4,000.[14]

While this extraordinary and timely gift provided the basis for the seminary to grow, financially, it was not without its risks, the most prominent of which the perception by many that the seminary no longer needed money. That was one of the challenges faced by Dr. C. Ellis Nelson, who agreed to become the interim president in January 1984. In reflecting on this perception, Nelson observed:

It was during my first or second day in the president's office that a friend and former board member came by for a quick visit. After a few minutes of conversation he recalled the gift of 12 million dollars the seminary had received a few years earlier from Ms. Jean Brown. He then said, "Isn't it wonderful that the seminary is taken care of!" I knew about the gift, but the idea that "the seminary was taken care of (financially)" was a shock. As the weeks passed, I heard variations of this sentiment from enough people to cause a panic within me. The seminary was not "taken care of"—it was simply able to fulfill its mission more easily. Moreover, if that notion spread through groups and individuals who supported the seminary, there would be a constant reduction of gifts and bequests in the years ahead.

The mid-winter lectures were approaching, during which there was an Austin Seminary Association luncheon. At that time the president is expected to make a short talk on the state of the seminary. I used my time to start a campaign to stop "the seminary is taken care of" mentality. In jest I said I wasn't worried about my term as interim president—there was money enough for the next few years, but I was concerned about the future. I said that we needed to think in terms of improving the way we train candidates for the ministry and not to assume we had reached our goal. To enrich our educational work and better to serve the church would require constant financial support.[15]

While Austin Seminary had never been on better financial footing, the challenges it faced were immense. Leadership was required. Time for healing was needed. This community of the Word needed time to regroup and re-assess itself and its direction.

The spirit of generosity among friends of the seminary was witnessed again when, in March of 2001, Diane E. Buchanan, a member of the Board of Trustees, and her husband, Richard G. Andrew, made a gift of $1.2 million to endow a chair in pastoral theology in memory of Rev. William J. Fogleman, who died suddenly on May 24, 2000, in Wimberley, Texas. This gift was the largest of any living donor in the history of the school.

Fogleman, a graduate of Austin Seminary (M.Div. 1953), had served as pastor, general presbyter of Brazos Presbytery, and executive of the Synod of the Sun. He had also served as a mentor and friend to Buchanan, encouraging her to become more involved with the seminary.[16] Buchanan and Andrew live in Dallas and are members of Preston Hollow Presbyterian Church.

In response to the announcement of this gift, Scott Black Johnston, associate professor of homiletics, remarked: "Beyond honoring the life and ministry of a particular pastor—which this chair will do; and beyond helping this institution compete for faculty talent—which this chair will also do; the ultimate beneficiaries of this gift will be the students and the churches that they will serve. A gift like this has an incredible ripple effect as the teaching done by the professors who hold this chair enriches the lives of fledgling ministers who in turn touch the lives of thousands of faithful, and not so faithful, to whom they minister."[17]

Through such generous gifts as those of the Brown family and Buchanan and Andrew, the seminary has been able to take major steps forward in faculty development and greater institutional financial stability. But one would be negligent not to acknowledge the significant ways in which the more modest gifts of many faithful supporters also benefit the seminary. The consistent, selfless generosity of many faithful saints has, over the years, contributed in a powerful way to the training of men and women for the gospel ministry.

CHAPTER THREE

Regrouping and Reunion

If the Jean Brown bequest brought a sense of financial stability to Austin Seminary, then certainly the presence of C. Ellis Nelson in the president's office brought a sense of calm and stability after a particularly painful and stormy period in the seminary's life. Bruce Herlin, a seminary board member, has observed that Nelson was a natural, "at ease" leader who brought healing to the seminary constituency. Nelson's leadership at this time "saved the institution much trauma."[1] Trustee Emeritus Clarence Frierson described Nelson's presence as "providential."[2]

William Hedrick, former vice president for development, recalls: "The seminary was immensely blessed to have Ellis Nelson as interim president. "[3] George Stroup, professor of theology, adds his reflections on Nelson's role at this particular point in the life of Austin Seminary:

> Enormous credit should be given to Ellis Nelson for what he accomplished during his interim presidency. His humor, good sense, and wisdom restored confidence to the institution. I truly believe his interim presidency was the work of God's providence.[4]

A native Texan and a graduate of Austin College (1937) and Austin Seminary (1940), Nelson went on to earn the M.A. degree from the University of Texas at Austin in 1944 and the Ph.D. from Columbia University in New York in 1955. Nelson was ordained to the gospel ministry in 1940. In addition to serving as associate pastor and minister to students at University Presbyterian Church in Austin, Nelson also served as instructor in Christian education at Austin Seminary.[5]

In 1945 Nelson and his bride of four years, Nancy Gribble Nelson (daughter of Austin Seminary Old Testament professor Robert Gribble), left for Richmond, Virginia, where he served as director of youth work for the General Assembly of the Presbyterian Church, U.S. After three years there, the Nelsons returned to Austin, where he became professor of Christian Education and director of field education. Nelson's stint at Austin Seminary this time was nine years.

In 1957 the Nelsons went to New York, where Ellis became professor of Christian education at Union Theological Seminary. In 1960 he became Skinner and McAlpine Professor of Practical Theology. He served as dean of the seminary during 1969–70, a tumultuous year on many college, university, and seminary campuses across the country because of American military involvement in Vietnam.

In 1974 Louisville Presbyterian Theological Seminary called Nelson to be its president and professor of Christian education. After a very successful seven-year tenure as president, Nelson retired.[6]

In retirement, Nelson went to San Francisco to serve as visiting professor of Christian education and then returned to Austin. Nelson himself writes:

> My retirement in Austin was planned, but my becoming interim president was unexpected. The story in brief is as follows.
>
> I retired as President of Louisville Presbyterian Seminary on July 1, 1981, at age 65. Prior to that date Arnold Come, President of San Francisco Theological Seminary, invited me to be Professor of Christian Education for three years. During that time Come would retire and the new president would participate in the

selection of a new C.E. professor. Due to unplanned changes in the SFTS faculty, I was free to leave in December, 1983.

Several times before and during my stay at SFTS, Jack Maxwell talked to me about teaching at Austin Seminary when I retired. During visits to Austin in April and September of 1983, Maxwell, Shelton and I worked out a plan for me to teach about half time for three years while Laura Lewis was working on her Ph.D. degree.

Maxwell's resignation in early November of 1983 was a real surprise. The invitation from the Board of Trustees to become the interim president was even more of a surprise. The idea of taking hold of an on-going institution was not on my agenda. In fact, I was deeply involved with the Lilly Endowment in planning a "Faculty Seminar" on Christian Education that was to last for three years. After consultation with Robert Lynn of the Lilly Endowment and others, I accepted the board's invitation to be the interim president for one year.[7]

Clearly, Nelson's own personal and academic associations with Austin Seminary, his love for and appreciation of the school, and his considerable administrative experience elsewhere contributed to a calming effect and a renewed sense of confidence among the various Austin Seminary constituencies. Former president David Stitt has observed:

> He [Nelson] found, not a hemorrhaging of red ink as at Louisville, but of morale of students, faculty, trustees, and a disaffection of constituents, particularly clergy who knew and loved the school. Clergy, faculty, trustees, and students soon saw stability restored, rumors quelled, disaffections turned into enthusiasms, and the school momentum regained.[8]

As Nelson assumed his duties in the president's office, he discovered five areas requiring his attention: (1) public relations as a result of Maxwell's resignation, (2) issues related to faculty meetings and committee responsibilities, (3) board meetings and the issue of openness, (4) seminary financial support, and (5) renovation of the Single Students' Dormitory.

One example of the new spirit of openness under Nelson's

leadership that contributed to an atmosphere of confidence was the new approach to faculty meetings. Nelson recalls:

> I was told soon after I arrived that faculty meetings were brief. One was reported to have lasted less than 15 minutes. Faculty committees did not have regular, scheduled meeting times. Reports from faculty committees, even with policy issues up for vote, were not distributed in advance. The agenda for faculty meetings was not known in advance. These and other practices created discomfort for most faculty members.
>
> In conversation with the faculty I worked out the following plan for faculty meetings. An agenda for each faculty meeting would be in members' mail boxes no later than Monday prior to the Wednesday meeting of the faculty. All committee reports would be attached to the agenda. The agenda would indicate the status of committee recommendations so that professors would know if items were to be presented for discussion, information, or action.
>
> At the beginning of the 1984–85 school year I proposed that faculty members be on only two committees. We could then schedule all faculty committees on two Wednesday afternoons. The two Wednesday afternoons plus the Wednesday faculty meeting would simplify the schedule and eliminate the time wasted in finding a time and place for each faculty committee meeting. These suggestions were accepted and, I think, helped to use faculty time more efficiently.[9]

In addition to using faculty time more efficiently, Nelson's attitude of respect toward the faculty no doubt contributed to a healthier, more collegial environment.

Similar steps with regard to board meetings added a refreshing air of openness and cooperation that had been absent. Nelson recalls:

> Board meetings are controlled by the board; but under normal circumstances the president of the seminary and chairperson of the board work out the agenda and plan the style of the meeting. I learned that except for the Vice President for Business Affairs no other administrator attended board meetings, although they

filed reports. In conference with the board chair person and conversations with the Dean, and V.P. for Development, we invited the administrators who reported to the board to present their report in person and to respond to questions about their report. This process symbolized the team approach to leadership of the seminary.[10]

The unwritten rule—that there was to be no communication between board members and faculty without the president's knowledge and/or approval—clearly no longer applied. This kind of openness led to a fresh sense of trust and confidence in the leadership and the direction of the seminary.

Early on in his eighteen-month interim presidency, Nelson discovered plans for renovation of the dorm for single students, particularly to accommodate the growing number of women students. However, he also found no plan for funding this project. According to Nelson,

> The architect estimated that cost to be between $600,000 and $700,000. The contractor's bid was $1,000,000! Harren was able to locate about $400,000 held in a "maintenance and repair" account for major repairs. I decided that we needed to raise the $600,000 for two reasons. First, the normal way for institutions to improve their physical plant was to raise money for specific projects. Second, I wanted to break the psychology of "the seminary is taken care of." A campaign for the dormitory would focus attention on what the seminary needed rather than on what it had.[11]

While no faculty appointments were made during Nelson's tenure as interim president, Ross Dunn, a member of the Austin Seminary faculty in the field of Christian ethics since 1967, died of cancer on May 1, 1984. It was decided not to fill this position until the new president had arrived and could participate in the selection process. In addition, the "acting" was removed from Robert Shelton's title and he became the academic dean of the seminary.

During this period, Ann Hoch West, director of student services and admissions since the fall of 1979, resigned to enter a doctoral program. Nelson recalls:

> Since this administrator is essential for the steady stream of ap-

plicants to the seminary, we decided the position should be filled. We first moved this position from under the president's supervision to be under the V.P. for Development, Bill Hedrick. In consultation with Hedrick we called John Evans. This was the only change in administrative staff.[12]

While bringing a calming presence to the seminary community, in addition to renewing confidence among the school's constituencies, especially among churches throughout the synod, Nelson found time to pursue an interest and a concern he had, namely, the transition seminary graduates must make from student to leader of a congregation. While Pete Hendrick represented the seminary in a program designed by the synod, in 1990 Nelson secured the first of two successive two-year grants from the Lilly Endowment to fund a pilot project to help newly ordained ministers in their adjustment to ministry.

In the summer of 1983, the two major branches of the Presbyterian church were reunited when both General Assemblies met in Atlanta, Georgia. Bridging a gulf that had existed since the outbreak of the Civil War, this action represented the culmination of efforts in both branches of the Presbyterian church that went back at least fifty years. In fact, the third president of Austin Seminary, Dr. Thomas W. Currie, chaired a General Assembly committee that had labored for reunion as early as forty years before its realization. It was upon returning from a meeting of that committee in April 1943 that Currie was felled by a stroke that proved to be fatal. His successor as president, David L. Stitt, served as secretary of that committee. So, while reunion became a reality in 1983, there were many who had had that goal as a dream for a long time and had worked toward it, including representatives of Austin Seminary.[13]

As a faculty member and as a recognized authority in the field of Christian education, Ellis Nelson not only was familiar with both branches of the Presbyterian church that were now coming together, but for seven years he had served as president of the only Presbyterian seminary that belonged to, and was supported by, both branches—Louisville Presbyterian Theological Seminary.

At a meeting of the Executive Committee of the Board of Trustees on January 4, 1984, a presidential search committee was elected. Board members included Edward D. Vickery (ex officio as board chairman), Clarence N. Frierson, Joyce LeMaistre, Edwin W.

Stock, Jr., Stephen A. Matthews, Jerold D. Shetler, and Kenneth W. Whittington. Other members of this search committee were Rev. Taft Lyon (from the Austin Seminary Association), Rev. Allen Smith (representing the synod), George Heyer and Ralph Underwood (from the seminary faculty), and a student to be named later.[14]

Two months later, a meeting of the board was called, the primary purpose of which was to adopt the qualifications of the next president of Austin Seminary. There were ten qualifications which were deemed to be "essential" and six which the board considered "desirable." The ten "essential" qualifications were: (1) theological training and experience be in the Reformed tradition and, as the by-laws require, that the president be an ordained minister in the PC(USA); (2) "Be able to relate effectively with the entire constituency of the Seminary, and thus establishing confidence which will attract student, faculty, and support"; (3) ability to work with governing bodies of the church, and communicate the mission and the concerns of the seminary with vision and conviction; (4) possess a vision of, and commitment to, the seminary's dedication to provide the best possible theological education; (5) affirm the mission statement of Austin Seminary and support the covenant between the seminary and the Synod of the Sun; (6) understand and advance Austin Seminary's mission to multiple cultures; (7) provide leadership for Austin Seminary in the reunited church; (8) be competent in administrative and financial matters and in fund-raising activities; (9) "Evidence an open and concerned relationship with all members of the Seminary community, maintain collegiality with the Faculty, and nurture the spiritual life of the Seminary as a community of worship, learning, and fellowship"; and (10) "Be committed, as Chief Executive officer, to facilitate communication between the Board and the Faculty."[15]

The six "desirable" qualifications included the following: (1) have pastoral experience in a local congregation; (2) have an academic doctoral degree and have demonstrated scholarly achievement; (3) possess experience in administration of an educational institution; (4) be able to enhance relations with other educational institutions, especially the University of Texas and the Episcopal Theological Seminary of the Southwest; (5) be known to those who serve at the General Assembly level and be familiar with the programs and agencies of the General Assembly; and (6) have an appreciation for, and sensitivity to, the languages and customs of the multiple cultures related to the seminary.[16] At this same called meeting, Janis Smith, a student, was added to the Presidential Search Committee and Bob Shelton was elected to a three-year term as academic dean.

By September of 1984, the search committee was prepared to submit to the board the name of a candidate to fill the president's office. At a meeting on September 10, the board voted unanimously to elect Jack Levin Stotts to be the seventh president of Austin Seminary and professor of Christian ethics.

A native of Dallas and a graduate of Trinity University in San Antonio (1954), Stotts had grown up in the United Presbyterian Church in the United States of America, the "northern" branch of the two main strands of the Presbyterian Church. He received his B.D. from McCormick Theological Seminary in Chicago (1957), where he studied under such scholars as George Ernest Wright, Frank Cross, Ed Douey (chairman of the committee that wrote the Confession of 1967), and Hulda Niebuhr. In 1957 he began work on a doctorate at Yale Divinity School, where he studied under H. Richard Niebuhr, Hulda Niebuhr's brother. While a student at Yale, Stotts also served as assistant pastor of a congregation in Wallingford, Connecticut.

In 1958 Stotts went to the University of Tulsa, where he served as the first chaplain of that school. During his undergraduate years at Trinity, Stotts was one of several students (including Herman Harren) who expressed concern over the lack of black students on campus, especially in light of the United Presbyterian Church's statements favoring integration. Facing similar attitudes in Tulsa, Stotts invited Jim Lawson, a black United Methodist ministerial student at Vanderbilt Divinity School in Nashville, to come and speak. Lawson had been expelled from Vanderbilt for his leadership in nonviolent sit-ins as part of the civil rights movement. This invitation was not well received by the university administration. However, Lawson did in fact come to Tulsa and spoke twice—once to students and once to university faculty. On both occasions, Lawson spoke to a full house. The administration did not renew Stotts' contract for a second year.[17]

From 1961 to 1963, Stotts served as pastor of the First United

Presbyterian Church (now St. Paul Presbyterian) in San Angelo, Texas, where he had served a three-month interim pastorate in the summer of 1957. It was also the home church of his wife, Virginia, whom he had met at Trinity University and married two weeks after their graduation from Trinity in 1954. In 1963 Stotts accepted an invitation to join the faculty of McCormick Seminary, from which he had graduated only seven years before. He received his Ph.D. from Yale in 1965.

When he came to Austin in the summer of 1985, Stotts had been at McCormick Seminary for twenty-two years, the final ten years as president. He had become a recognized leader in the United Presbyterian Church, USA. In addition to numerous articles, Stotts published two books while at McCormick—*Believing, Deciding, Acting* (1968), which was designed to serve as an introduction of Christian ethics for laypeople, and *Shalom: The Search for a Peaceable City* (1973), which focuses on Christian social ethics. It should be noted that each book was published during particularly turbulent times in this country when ethical questions were being raised and heretofore accepted ethical assumptions were being seriously challenged—on seminary campuses as well as on college campuses, in the church as well as in society.

It may have surprised some that a person with such national standing as Stotts would come to a school that in many respects was still considered a predominantly regional seminary. Only one other Austin Seminary president had ever previously served as president of another school before coming to Austin. T. R. Sampson, the seminary's first president, had served as president of Austin College (1897–1900) before beginning the second effort to establish a Presbyterian seminary in Austin in 1900. Stotts offers the following thoughts on his acceptance of the call to return to Texas and become president of Austin Seminary:

> My coming to APTS in 1985 was, in my mind, important as a symbol of the new unity our predecessor denominations affirmed and celebrated in 1983. My history had been one of participation in the "Northern" branch of the church and by the school's invitation to me and my acceptance represented the oneness we had and the oneness we sought. Having had a visibility in the Northern church because of my presidency of McCormick, I believed

that my going to APTS, a former "Southern" seminary, was not unlike Randy Taylor's going to the presidency of San Francisco Seminary. Both demonstrated our oneness. I believe I brought with me some credibility in the Northern Church for APTS in the former precincts of the PCUSA.[18]

In his final report to the board as interim president, Ellis Nelson noted much of the work that had gone on at Austin Seminary during his eighteen-month tenure. But he opened this report with the observation that "Austin Seminary is the only one of the ten seminaries in the reunited Presbyterian Church (U.S.A.) that remains a synod institution."[19] Clearly, reunion would have an impact on seminaries as well as governing bodies of the church. Southern seminaries had always answered to their respective synods, while northern seminaries were responsible to the national office.

In the new design, all seminaries would be related to the whole denomination but would be allowed to maintain previous ties to other governing bodies. Among other things, for Austin Seminary, this meant that members of the Board of Trustees could come from outside the boundaries of the Synod of the Sun. The increased national exposure coincided with an expressed desire by some at Austin Seminary to recruit students from outside the borders of the Synod of the Sun.

Nelson also reported that, thanks to the efforts of Vice President for Development Bill Hedrick, a challenge grant of $250,000 had been received from the Mabee Foundation toward the $998,303 needed to renovate the Single Students' Dormitory ($466,000 had been found in a seminary building fund by Herman Harren). In response to a low-key campaign, the generosity of congregations, foundations, and individuals met the challenge grant. With about three-fourths of the necessary funds, Nelson reiterated his desire to halt the widespread perception that the seminary was "taken care of" financially because of the Jean Brown bequest.

Nelson closed his report with these words:

> This will be my last report. After commencement there is a certain amount of correspondence—especially about scholarships—which needs to be done; and there is the getting ready for the General Assembly. I have prepared and sent in a report on

Austin Seminary for the Standing Committee on Seminaries, even though we are a Synod institution. I thought it best to be cooperative; but I made it clear in the report that Austin Seminary is an institution of the Synod of the Sun. I will be a part of the General Assembly Standing Committee on Seminaries and I will interpret and explain Austin Seminary to that Assembly Committee. After the Assembly I will look forward to Monday, July 1. That will be the day a new president gathers up the hopes and ambitions of the Board, faculty, students, staff and our many supporters to improve and enlarge what is already an excellent seminary program. I will help Jack Stotts in any way he requests; but I expect to do what I came to Austin 18 months ago to do—teach half time and do research and writing the other half. So, I will not disappear: I will just enjoy the fellowship and stimulation of this wonderful community.[20]

With characteristic poise and humility, Ellis Nelson had returned a sense of stability and calmness to the Austin Seminary community. His devotion to Jesus Christ and his love for Austin seminary contributed mightily toward a healthy seminary that eagerly awaited new leadership.

CHAPTER FOUR

The Stotts Years
(1985–96)

Changes were afoot in this country in the 1980s. One development was the way in which women assumed more visible positions of leadership in the United States. In 1980 a conservative Republican, Ronald Reagan, was elected president. It was President Reagan who appointed the first woman, Sandra Day O'Connor, to the United States Supreme Court. In 1983 Sally Ride, whose sister is a Presbyterian minister, became the first American woman astronaut to travel in space. In 1984 Geraldine Ferraro became the first woman candidate to appear on a major party ticket when she was Walter Mondale's choice as candidate for vice president on the Democratic ticket.

Internationally, in 1985, the year Jack and Virginia Stotts moved to Austin, Konstantin Chernenko, leader of the Soviet Union, died and was replaced by a young, dynamic leader by the name of Mikhail Gorbachev. At fifty-four years old, Gorbachev was of a different generation than that of his predecessors and called for more openness through a policy called *glasnost.* Within four years, this policy would lead to the breakup of the Soviet Union and the rise of democracy in many former Soviet satellite countries.

The election of Jack Stotts as the new Austin Seminary president represented a new beginning of sorts for the institution. The steady and calming leadership provided by Ellis Nelson did much to create a sense of eagerness and goodwill as the seminary community anticipated the arrival of Dr. Stotts.

Although Stotts did not officially begin his duties as president of Austin Seminary until July 1, 1985, the wider seminary constituency was introduced to him in a limited way in an article he wrote for the April 1985 faculty edition of the Austin Seminary *Bulletin,* an issue that was devoted to "Presbyterians and Evangelism." His article was entitled "Evangelism As Recovery of the Gospel." In it, the president-elect of Austin Seminary reviewed, in summary fashion, the history of evangelism in the Reformed tradition, and particularly in the United States. As he looked at evangelism in the present day, Stotts noted how engaging in evangelism requires more than offering the gospel to others. It also requires an awareness of one's own constant need to be fed by that good news:

> So the initial question for those of us concerned for sharing the gospel is first to ourselves, *"Do we seek the gospel of Jesus Christ for our own lives?"* The self-righteous ask only about how they can communicate the gospel to others. The authentic evangelists test themselves by such questions as these: "Do we seek to be transformed by God's love?" "Do we seek to have the central principle of our lives become the love of God and neighbor?" And the focus for the evangelist is on what God has done. The proclamation is never, "I have found it!" It is always, "I have been found. I believe, help my unbelief."[1]

He concludes by pointing to the power of the gospel to transform lives—not only the lives of others, but our own lives as well:

> Thus we do not evangelize when we only repeat the formulae and carry out campaigns. When we share ourselves from the "inside out," from the heart, from the soul, we share in our Lord who lives in us and in whom we live. Evangelism so understood is a necessity for the Christian, not an option. The excitement of the future is really then an extension of the excitement of the present. It is not worlds out there to be conquered and to be changed. It is not people out there to be altered. It is simply the excitement

of God's love in us that empowers us to have compassion for all
people and to share with all people ourselves, and therefore our
Lord. The seal of John Calvin is a bush that burns but is not consumed. It is a bush that burns with the power of the spirit but is
not burnt up, for it is the spirit which gives life to all who see it.
I suggest that evangelism is being ignited by the spirit so that our
lives are not consumed but they are shared with a new power.[2]

The service of worship at which Stotts was inaugurated as president and professor of Christian ethics was held at Covenant Presbyterian Church in Austin on November 15, 1985. Participating in
this service were the fourth and fifth presidents of Austin Seminary,
David Stitt and Prescott Williams, respectively, along with the academic dean, Robert Shelton; the chairman of the Board of Trustees,
Edward D. Vickery; the stated clerk of the General Assembly of the
Presbyterian Church (U.S.A.), James E. Andrews; and the executive of the Synod of the Sun, William J. Fogleman. Other participants included Clarence N. Frierson, chairperson of the Presidential Search Committee; C. Harry Sarles, the former pastor of City
Temple Presbyterian Church in Dallas; Ilene B. Dunn, the executive
secretary of the Austin Seminary Association; Daryl E. Johnson,
the president of the Student Senate; R. Richard Baldwin, the pastor
of Covenant Presbyterian Church, Austin; and Stotts himself.

In his greetings from the General Assembly of the Presbyterian
Church (U.S.A.), Jim Andrews, member of the 1956 graduating
class of Austin Seminary, called on Stotts and the seminary to help
the church develop a responsible theology. Andrews observed:

We have a habit at the denominational level of solving great
problems with inadequate conceptional preparation. The last
General Assembly dealt with six matters related to ordination
without having the vaguest concept of a doctrine of ordination.
We are dealing with the problem of developing a new approach to
the life of the church in a mission design without ever having to
solve the problem of Austin Seminary course in Theology 101 and
the problem of authority. We do not know how to share power.[3]

Stotts' inaugural address was titled "All Things New?" Noting
America's "enchantment with newness," including new presidents

of institutions, he tempered that notion with an invitation to recall and appreciate those who went before. Stotts reminded his listeners that there are old and enduring values and convictions—both theological and institutional—to which the seminary was committed and which had served the seminary well. Theologically, the seminary affirmed

> the conviction of a sovereign God whose ruling is known in Jesus Christ as creating, redeeming and ordering all that is, including ourselves, but whose majesty will not be exhausted by our measurements, either of words or of piety; the simultaneous frailty and splendor of human endeavors; the confession of our self-inflicted woundings, individually and corporately, and of the wounded universe which yearns and groans for healing and completeness; the experiential necessity of our hearts being responsive to God's generous presence; the soaring power of scriptures rightly interpreted; the "willing service" we are called to render to God and neighbor; ...[4]

Institutionally, Stotts named four areas that are crucial for the long-term health, integrity, and viability of the seminary: a strong faculty and student body, a strong Board of Trustees and administration, a constructive relationship with the church, and a committed seminary staff.[5]

Stotts then cited three challenges he saw before Austin Seminary. The first was to provide "fresh understandings of our particular theological tradition" as well as "the 'construal' of reality that reflects and points to the one source of truth." In serving the source of truth, Stotts said, one of the seminary's tasks is to integrate into some meaningful whole the knowledge and information that is being accumulated in other areas of human life.

A second challenge that the new president put before the seminary community was "a renewed quest for a delayed ecumenical vision and practice." Closer relationships with its Episcopal and Lutheran neighbors should be cultivated. Stotts went on:

> The proposition is this: we can only be Presbyterian as we are ecumenical, for it is the one Church of Jesus Christ into which we have been elected and to which we have given our consent. To

confess that we are dependent for our own life on lively interaction with other faith communities is the proper stance. To admit that is a hard saying, offensive to our Presbyterian pride. But that way lies healing for our brokenness, enlivening of our ministry. Such a broadening church means as well a seminary curriculum that is open to various models of ministry, without denying what is deemed faithful to our own tradition.[6]

In his first year as president, Stotts set two main goals for himself—"becoming familiar with the internal life of the Seminary and getting to know, while representing Austin Seminary to, the external constituency."[7]

The matter of restoring trust between the seminary and its various constituencies was critical to the well-being of the seminary. One way in which this sense of trust could be measured is in the enrollment of the student body. In 1983 enrollment of Master of Divinity (M.Div.) students was down 23 percent since 1956, when there were 85 students, and 37 percent since its high point of 103 students in 1964. In the 1982–83 academic year, there were 65 students enrolled in the M.Div. program at Austin Seminary (of whom two were on leave of absence). But this trend was not unique to Austin Seminary. Between 1981 and 1982, Princeton, McCormick, Dubuque, Columbia, and Union-Richmond all showed decreases in enrollment. Louisville, Pittsburgh, and San Francisco reflected increases in the number of M.Div. students during this same period.[8]

In contrast, the number of Doctor of Ministry (D.Min.) students grew from the very beginning of that program in 1976, when there were 40 students enrolled. By 1981 there were 71 D.Min. students. By the next year, that number had jumped to 87. In fact, in 1981, D.Min students accounted for 43 percent of the total student enrollment at Austin Seminary, while M.Div. students represented 46 percent of the enrollment. The following year, the number of D.Min. students outnumbered the M.Div. students by 50 percent to 36 percent.[9]

In the spring term of Stotts' first year (1985–86), there were 149 students enrolled in M.Div. courses, more than 100 of whom were full-time students. This represented the highest enrollment in the M.Div. program ever at Austin. At the same time, there were 71 D.Min. candidates enrolled.[10] Much of the credit for this increase in enrollment is due to the aggressive recruiting efforts of John Evans, director of vocations and admissions. However, the anticipation of a new start for the seminary may have been an added attractive feature.

By the spring of 1986, a total of 55 students had already been admitted to the M.Div. program for 1986–87, in contrast to the 38 students who had been admitted by the same time in 1985. While, no doubt, this increase in enrollment in the basic theological degree program could be attributed to several causes, certainly one of them had to be the rise in confidence in the new seminary administration among alumni/ae, churches, donors, students, and faculty. By the end of Stotts' second year, he and John Evans projected an entering class of 44 students for the following fall in the M.Div. program, as compared to 42 who actually entered in the fall of 1986.[11]

By the time Stotts retired in May 1996, the enrollment of M.Div. students had reached 163, and the number of D.Min. students was 99. The total number of special students was 52, and there were 22 students enrolled in the Master of Arts program. Clearly, the growing sense of confidence in the seminary that was restored with Stotts' arrival in 1985 continued over the next eleven years, as the enrollment figures suggest.

Jim Andrews' call for theological leadership from the seminary in his remarks at Stotts' inauguration was not a hollow one. Although the issue was not directly related to ordination, Jack Stotts was called upon to provide theological leadership at the General Assembly level in a very significant way. With the reunion of the two main branches of the Presbyterian family in 1983, the moderator of that General Assembly, Dr. J. Randolph Taylor, appointed a "Special Committee to Prepare a Brief Statement of the Reformed Faith for possible inclusion in the *Book of Confessions* of the Presbyterian Church (U.S.A.)."[12] Taylor appointed Stotts chairman of this twenty-one-member committee. While representing a broad theological spectrum within the church, fourteen members of the twenty-one-member committee came from academia. In 1989 Joan Salmon-Campbell, moderator of the General Assembly, appointed a Committee of Fifteen to review the document and make recommended changes. Thirteen of the fifteen members were pastors and church members. The final product was an eighty-line document, Trinitarian in structure, entitled *A Brief Statement of Faith: The Pres-*

byterian Church (U.S.A.), which was approved for inclusion in the *Book of Confessions* by the 203rd General Assembly in 1991.

Jack Rogers, a member of the committee to draft this document, has written the following about the final product:

> "A Brief Statement of Faith: Presbyterian Church (U.S.A.)" in two pages confessed the faith of the church Catholic, Protestant, and Reformed. Without conscious intent, the committees, drafting and revising, had developed a document that contained the elements mentioned in Chapter II of the Form of Government, in *The Book of Order,* along with other traditional emphases. Additionally, A Brief Statement extended the Reformed tradition into new areas not previously articulated in *The Book of Confessions.* It provided a narrative of Jesus Christ's life and ministry, generally omitted from previous creeds. It unequivocally announced that God "makes everyone equally in God's image." For the first time, women were specifically declared equal to men and called to all of the ministries of the church. And, as no previous confessional document had done, it derived feminine as well as masculine images from Scripture to illustrate the love and faithfulness of God. Other nuances showed evidence of sensitivity to the concerns of women and racial ethnic persons. While the committees had concentrated on faithfully affirming the Reformed tradition, they had also faithfully applied it in new ways to the understanding of Scripture given by the Holy Spirit in their time.[13]

For years, the seminary had published the faculty edition of the Austin Seminary *Bulletin.* In the fall of 1990, the title was changed to *Insights: A Journal of the Faculty of Austin Seminary.* That issue was devoted to the *Brief Statement.* The General Assembly would not vote on it until the following summer, so the document was still under discussion throughout the church.

Stotts' leadership in the church had been acknowledged before reunion. The stature and respect that came with his work on the *Brief Statement of Faith* reflected well on Austin Seminary and, if only indirectly, contributed to more national exposure than it might otherwise have enjoyed. Stotts' leadership in this respect continued a pattern of national leadership in the church from Austin Seminary.

Faculty Development

During the years of the Stotts administration, the faculty grew as the student body grew. With that growth came inevitable changes. Continuity and change characterized the development of the faculty over the next eleven years. In the fall of 1985, George Stroup, associate professor of theology, resigned in order to accept a position as professor of theology with tenure at Columbia Theological Seminary in Decatur, Georgia. Stroup had been at the seminary since 1980. The resignation was effective December 31, 1985. The board authorized the administration to take steps to fill that vacancy as well as the one created in the field of Christian ethics by the death of Ross Dunn on May 1, 1984.

The sense of continuity and change in the faculty is seen in the actions taken by the board at its May 1984 meeting. Prescott Williams, at the seminary since 1959, continued teaching in the field of Old Testament. Robert Shelton, who came to the seminary in 1970, continued in the academic dean's office and in teaching homiletics. John Alsup, having come to Austin in 1975, continued teaching New Testament. And Ralph Underwood, who had been at the seminary since 1978, continued to teach in the area of pastoral care.

The contract of Dan Garza (employed in 1982) in the field of racial ethnic ministry was extended for three years beginning June 1, 1987. The contract of the minister-in-residence, C. D. Weaver (1983), was extended for three years beginning June 1, 1987. Cynthia Campbell (1981) was promoted to associate professor of theology and ministry with a three-year term beginning June 1, 1987. John R. "Pete" Hendrick (1981) was re-elected to a six-year term as professor of mission and evangelism beginning June 1, 1987. Robert Paul (1977) was elected to a one-year term as professor of ecclesiastical history and Christian thought, effective June 1, 1986. And C. Ellis Nelson, having originally come in 1983 as a visiting professor of Christian education and shortly thereafter served as interim president, was elected to a one-year term as visiting professor of Christian education.[14]

At the same meeting, the board elected Ismael Garcia to fill the position in Christian ethics. Born in Brooklyn, New York, and raised in Puerto Rico, Garcia received his M.A. and Ph.D. from the

University of Chicago and taught at McCormick Theological Seminary before coming to Austin. A layperson, Garcia's membership was in the United Church of Christ.[15]

Finally, the board authorized the administration to employ a visiting professor in the field of theology for the 1986–87 academic year. David Harned, a visiting fellow from Princeton Theological Seminary, lectured in the field of theology in 1985–86, while Thomas W. Currie III, pastor of Brenham Presbyterian Church, taught in that field in the 1986–87 academic year.[16]

In November 1986 the board elected Dr. Alan E. Lewis to the position of professor of constructive and modern theology, with tenure, effective July 15, 1987.[17] Lewis, a native of Belfast, Northern Ireland, had studied at Princeton Theological Seminary from 1971 to 1974 and then for five months at the University of Tuebingen in Germany. From 1975 to 1977 he served as assistant pastor in a Presbyterian church in Lergs, Scotland. He received his Ph.D. from Princeton in January 1977. For the ten years prior to coming to Austin, he taught theology at New College at the University of Edinburgh.[18] He, his wife, Kay, and their son, Mark, moved to Austin in the summer of 1987.

When Lewis underwent a physical examination for emigration purposes in August 1987, doctors discovered a tumor on one of his lungs. Around Christmas of that year, Lewis underwent surgery to remove the tumor at St. David's Hospital in Austin. The tumor, it was learned, was cancerous and attached to his lung and his heart. He was not able to deliver his inaugural lecture until the spring of 1988. The lecture was entitled "Apocalypse and Parousia: The Anguish of Theology from Now Till Kingdom Come" and examined the relationship between humanity and God in a nuclear age.[19]

In the fall of 1989 it was discovered that the tumor had grown again, and in October Lewis underwent surgery to have one lung removed. Over the next four years, Lewis endured many sessions of chemotherapy and radiation treatments. Kay Lewis describes 1992, their twenty-third year of marriage, as "a very good year."[20] Having entered the seminary's Master of Arts in Theology program, Kay wrote a paper called "My Theology of Prayer" which appeared later as an article in the journal *Theology in Scotland.* In that paper, Kay wrote the following about the experience of 1992:

Chemotherapy is over and appears to have been effective. Prayers of thanksgiving that Alan can resume teaching and that I can attend classes on 'Grief' and 'Pain.' 'Lord, thank you for opening up my world again, for the fact that I can be among other people and exchange ideas. Grant that what I learn in these classes may equip me for whatever may lie ahead.'

In the fall, I attend Alan's 'Introduction to Theology' class. 'Lord, please help him to get through this lecture, you know how worried he is that he will have one of his memory lapses during class. Thank you for letting me hear what I have worked to enable him to do.'[21]

After a long, painful, and valiant battle, Lewis died on February 19, 1994. A memorial service was held in the Seminary Chapel on February 23. The University of Edinburgh also held a May memorial service at the Greyfriars Church, which Kay Lewis attended. In his report to the board at the conclusion of the academic year, President Stotts wrote the following:

We at Austin Seminary are recipients and stewards of a good spirit that pervades our life together. This is a gift from God that is mediated through trustees who care even as they govern; by staff whose work is a vocation; by faculty and administrators whose teaching, research, and administering is lodged within the imperative to serve Christ's church; by students who find themselves—sometimes surprisingly so—enthusiastic about learning and its pertinence for their future ministries; and by graduates and friends who uphold Austin Seminary by their prayers and contributions. We are grateful for this good spirit which we dare to affirm is the graceful presence of God's Holy Spirit working among us.

It is this Holy Spirit which allows us to rage against and grieve the harshness of premature death while simultaneously clinging to and affirming the mercy and goodness of the God who gives us life in Jesus Christ. Such was the case with the death of Professor Alan E. Lewis. For six years he struggled physically and spiritually with cancer. In all of that time he witnessed by his teaching, colleagueship, and life a faith which indeed was a sign of the way God uses human weakness to be a witness to God's love and power.

Alan Lewis was spiritual leader while walking in the valley of the shadow of death, finally fearing no evil but walking by the light of faith, a light that illumines the way for all of us. He was finally defeated physically, as will each of us be. But by the power of God he was spiritually the conqueror of death. He resides with God and the communion of saints. His legacy to us endures.[22]

In addition, at that meeting the board agreed to the recommendation that the following resolution be spread on the minutes of the board and copies sent to Kay and Mark Lewis:

Alan Edmond Lewis

Whereas Alan Edmond Lewis was a faithful follower of Jesus Christ; a teacher whose passion for the truth was contagious; a faculty member who garnered the admiration and affection of his colleagues; a churchman who measured his actions by whether they helped to build up the Body of Christ; a witness to the light of the world and an advocate for the oppressed, whatever their condition; and a friend to all; and

Whereas we grieve his death on February 19, 1994 even as we are grateful to God for his life;

Whereas Alan leaves his wife Kay and their son Mark;

Therefore we the Trustees of Austin Presbyterian Theological Seminary do hereby record our gratitude to God for the life and ministry of Alan Edmond Lewis, affirm his contribution to Austin Seminary for almost seven years as Professor of Constructive and Modern Theology and extend to Kay Lewis and Mark Lewis our condolences on their loss, and assure them of our prayers that God's Holy Spirit may continue to sustain them now and into the future.

Given this 21st day of May, 1994.[23]

For some years, Lewis had cultivated a particular interest in "Holy Saturday," the day between Good Friday and Easter morning. He worked on a book-length manuscript which examined, both biblically and theologically, the notion of God's death in Jesus Christ on the cross, a notion that contemporary Christians wish to ignore as they move from the cross to the empty tomb. In 1993 Lewis wrote the following:

> For a considerable number of years now, beginning back in Edinburgh, I have been working on a fairly lengthy manuscript on the "theology of Easter Saturday." Its working title is *On the Second Day: God and Humanity between Cross and Resurrection.* It is in fact an attempt to interpret and contribute to the contemporary "theology of the cross," which has enjoyed some prominence, especially in Europe, primarily through the work of Jurgen Moltmann and Eberhard Jungel, both of them being influenced by their teacher Karl Barth. Their thought is not easy, and part of my aim is to render it somewhat more accessible to the nonacademic reader. The much-ignored theme of Holy Saturday seemed to me very helpful for this interpretative task, since it provides a unique boundary point from which to consider the interconnections between themes of Good Friday and Easter.[24]

Although he continued to work on and revise the text up to his death, Lewis did not see it published. After much labor of editing and seeking a publisher, Kay Lewis and her son, Mark, with the help of others, were able to see Alan Lewis's wish fulfilled in 2001 when Wm. B. Eerdmans Publishing Company published the book under the title *Cross and Resurrection: A Theology of Holy Saturday.* John Alsup, professor of New Testament, wrote the foreword.

Identifying the second day as both "a no-man's land" and "a boundary," Lewis writes that Holy Saturday must be examined and explored more fully and that not to do so would be to miss the power and the meaning of both the cross and the empty tomb.

> What is so lacking in the way that the church normally hears its [the story's] own decisive narrative is that Christians have forgotten, and make no effort to imagine, what the story is when freshly heard, without the benefit of hindsight and the drawback of familiarity. Yet the familiar rendering of the Easter story, heard as it were on "mono," is a hopeless distortion of its true sound. For the comforting joy of Easter morning already from the start anesthetizes Friday's pain; the anticipation of Sunday makes casual and phony the waiting of the second day, since there is never

any doubt that there is a new day coming, to be waited for. It is, we say again, only the "Stereophonic" sound of both the first-time story and the familiar which gives the narrative its quality of gospel Word, and its deepest meaning. Perhaps from this perspective the second-day boundary between the cross and the empty tomb is also the balance knob which secures equilibrium between novelty and familiarity, between the original story and the oft-repeated. For it is the grave of the second day which makes that original story what it is—a tale of contrast and reversal; of darkness, night, and finally light; of death and nothing, and only then life. But once we know about the light and life, the grave becomes the point not of antithesis only but also of unity, not of contradiction alone but of identity: an identity-in-contradiction. For by uniting the first day and the third in a single event, the second suggests that the darkness is itself illuminating, the defeat victorious, and death both the opposite and the source of life.[25]

At the same November 1986 board meeting that the election of Alan Lewis as professor of constructive and modern theology was announced, the seminary also learned of the retirement of Professor Robert Paul, effective the following June. In May 1987 the board announced that Ellen Babinsky, a Ph.D. candidate at the University of Chicago, would become assistant professor of church history beginning August 1, 1988. John Alsup (New Testament) and George Heyer (theology) were promoted to full professors, effective June 1, 1987. Andy Dearman was elected for a five-year term as associate professor of Old Testament, effective June 1, 1988. Fred Holper, who had come to the seminary in 1985–86 as assistant professor of homiletics and liturgics, received a three-year extension, effective June 1, 1988.[26]

The sense of change and continuity among the seminary faculty continued. Dr. John Jansen, a member of the seminary faculty since 1958 and retired from full-time teaching since 1983, died in his sleep in April 1987. In his report to the board in May 1987, Jack Stotts wrote the following:

> Professor Jansen, upon his retirement in 1983, had completed twenty-five years as a faculty member of this seminary. During that time he was Acting Dean for one term and on top of a busy

schedule of teaching, preaching and ecclesiastical assignments, wrote nine books and innumerable articles and reviews. He was well loved by students and colleagues and is sorely missed. His widow, Mrs. Mary Jansen, will continue to remain in Austin. Our common grief at our loss is, by God's grace, gradually being integrated within our gratitude to God for John Jansen's life and work, and by our hope that rests in God's resurrection of our Lord Jesus Christ from the dead.[27]

Jansen's ability to combine serious scholarship with personal integrity and self-effacing humor had a powerful impact on generations of seminary theologs. It was not unusual for seminary students to see him working in his office as late as midnight. Jansen seemed to enjoy telling stories of incidents of his own absent-mindedness. He was a popular preacher. He was scheduled to preach one Sunday morning at a church in Austin. When he arrived, he discovered the service already in progress. Embarrassed at being tardy, Jansen threw on his robe and dashed down the aisle, joining the worship leader. Upon seeing the surprise of his colleague, Jansen realized that he was in the wrong church.

On another occasion, Jansen misplaced a set of keys. He wrote about his experience:

WHERE'S MY KEY?

Omar Khayyam wrote:

"There was the Door to which I found no key; There was the Veil through which I could not see."

An absent-minded emeritus professor has had his own problems with a key.

Last Saturday I was getting more boxes from the liquor store on Mesa to get on with the job of getting our town house ready for rental—dishes, linens, clothes, etc. being stored in my seminary office (which is beginning to look like the Tower of Babel with over 50 boxes—and the end is not yet). Anyway, after parking the car back of the liquor store and filling it with empty boxes, I could not find my car key. Thinking it must have dropped from my pocket, and unable to find it, I called Mary, who came with her car and an extra key for mine. Some days later I found the errant key—it was in the lock of the car trunk.

The following Wednesday evenight [*sic*] we were filling out an insurance form that should have been sent long ago and which had to be in Philadelphia before the end of the month. Mary and I drove to the post office down-town. Needing to xerox one item, I was at the copy machine while Mary was weighing the envelope. I moved away when another lady came to xerox something. When we were ready to leave, I discovered to my dismay that my key book was gone. Sure that I must have left it on the copy machine, the only conclusion was that the lady must have taken it by mistake and dropped it in her purse—and she was already gone. My assumption, of course, was based on personal experience, for last year I had mistakenly taken Gene Luna's key book in the Library and I had not realized this for several days while she was frantically looking for her keys. And now the shoe (or the key) was on the other foot! We were left with the question not only of how to tell Herman Harren that I had lost four seminary keys, but also the practical question of how to get home. I had left three notices in the post office ("Will whoever took my keys call 345-9845") and then I discovered that I had an extra key in my pocket. That resolved the question about how to get home but not the embarrassment of confessing to Herman. We started home, returned to see if our lady had perhaps discovered her error and returned, to no avail. But, when we were home, there was my key book in the kitchen. I had used the extra key without ever remembering or realizing that I had left the key book at home. So I went back to post office to remove my signs! And so went one of our last evenings before departing for Britain. Those who know how upset I can get will understand why I was a nervous wreck—and why I'm writing this at 4:30 A.M. because I could not sleep. Maybe this will put me to sleep—as I'm sure it will put you to sleep as it's already too long a story!

Well, Shakespeare would say, "All's well that ends well," and as Charles Loomis said, "I am bigger than anything that can happen to me. All these things, sorrow, misfortune, and suffering, are outside my door. I am in the house and I have the key."[28]

In addition to the death of John Jansen, other changes affected the profile of the seminary faculty. After seven years on the faculty, Dr. Cynthia Campbell tendered her resignation in May 1988 in order to accept a call to become senior pastor of First Presbyterian Church in Salina, Kansas. In addition, Rev. Cal Klemt, seminary librarian since 1966, was given disability retirement in October 1988. In December 1988 Dr. Prescott H. Williams, having come to the seminary in 1959 and having served as professor of Old Testament languages and archaeology, as dean (1966–76), and as president (1972–76), announced his intention to retire, effective May 31, 1990. In his letter of resignation Williams wrote:

> We are grateful for the providence which brought us here, with our four children, and has kept us here through years of unexpected opportunities and developments. We have received encouragement, support, understanding and challenges as members of the seminary community during these years of many changes. When others have thanked me for believing in them and supporting their development, I have often said that this community has taught me the critical importance of sharing confidence, by placing it in me, often when I did not possess confidence on my own.
>
> The opportunity to enjoy being professor, dean, president in this place and with people who freely love because they are freely loved and freed in the gospel to love—and to seek others' wellbeing—has again and again provided surprises, a sense of achievement in meaningful work and joy in sharing the task of preparing others to serve. I have had innumerable occasions to thank our Father for bringing us here and giving us associates like you and your predecessors, like my colleagues and our friends among faculty, staff, administration and alumni/ae. Jane and I have often remarked that our engagement here, often viewed by others as "service," has in reality been providentially-given privilege.[29]

In recognition of Williams' devoted tenure at, and contributions to, Austin Seminary, the faculty edition of the seminary *Bulletin* in the spring of 1990 was a Festschrift of essays honoring him. Entitled "God's Steadfast Love," these essays came from current and past Austin Seminary colleagues, as well as from scholars at other institutions, including a former student, Pamela Owens, who was completing work on her Ph.D. in Old Testament at the University of Chicago Divinity School.

In the introduction to that collection, President Stotts wrote the following:

> There is a presence about Prescott H. Williams, Jr. It is strong, commanding attention. It is gentle, communicating concern. It is demanding, calling one to attention. It is direct, not even edged with guile. It is firm, suggesting stability. And more.
>
> But the wheel stops on stability for me. It is a standout characteristic, one that radiates from this multi-talented and very gifted person. For Prescott Williams is a steady person upon whom people lean, one whose teaching can be relied on, one who teaches so that what is learned endures. Stability.
>
> And stability has been one of Prescott Williams' gifts to Austin Seminary. It is not so much the length of time that Prescott has been here, though we are grateful for those thirty-one years. It is that he has been a reference point as other marks have shifted. He has been a representative through changes of Austin Seminary's substantial commitment to a theological education that was grounded in the Bible and had as its foundation the Lordship of Christ.[30]

Even though officially retired after thirty-one years (1959–90), Williams continued to teach an occasional class and to do research, remaining an integral part of the seminary community.

Catherine Sautter, registrar, tendered her resignation, effective December 31, 1989. While not a faculty member, Sautter had worked closely with faculty and students as counselor, confidante, and coordinator of schedules for thirty-one and a half years. In the 1989–90 Seminary Catalogue, which was dedicated to her, one finds the following words:

> Over the years, Cathy Sautter and the Seminary Catalogue have become synonymous. For twenty-five years she has served as the editor and given it birth each year. Hours and hours have been spent gathering, typing, arranging and proofreading diverse materials. For many the catalogue will long remain "Cathy's catalogue."

Indeed, it may not be too much to say that for many persons, Cathy Sautter and Austin Presbyterian Theological Seminary have become synonymous over the past three decades. Surely her commitment to Austin Seminary and her commitment to the Presbyterian Church (U.S.A.) are unsurpassed. She was not an employee of the seminary; she was a part of it. She always wanted the best for its students, its faculty and its programs. She has been fiercely loyal to the institution, an indefatigable worker, an unfailing advocate for the Seminary and a faithful servant of the church. She has been a counselor for students, a confidante for faculty and a reliable resource for the constituency.

This is her last catalogue; she has decided to retire at the end of 1989. It is highly appropriate, therefore, that it be dedicated to her. We do so with deep gratitude and appreciation. Of course, you do not replace a Cathy Sautter. You give thanks to God for her. And one thing is certain: her love for and contributions to Austin Seminary will continue to shape this school for years to come.[31]

Another staffperson, Jimmie Clark, announced her retirement after more than thirty years of service to the seminary, effective December 31, 1989.[32] Over those thirty years, Clark worked for Henry Quinius, Bob Shelton, Carter King, and Pete Hendrick. She stayed because "I loved it. I loved every day I worked there. I loved those students as if they were my own."[33]

The registrar's position was filled by Jacqueline Hefley, who had come to the seminary in August 1987 to work in the Office of Admissions and Financial Aid. A Presbyterian from Fort Worth, Hefley was an alumna of Austin College and had worked at Southwestern University in Georgetown as an admissions counselor for four years before accepting a position at the University of Texas in the Financial Aid Office in January 1987.[34]

While these developments represented change for the seminary, continuity among the faculty was reflected in the naming of C. D. Weaver as "Dean of Students and Campus Minister," the election of Lewis Donelson to a five-year term as associate professor of New Testament, the granting of tenure to Ismael Garcia as associate professor of Christian ethics, and the election of Laura Lewis to a three-year term as assistant professor of Christian education.[35]

In addition to searching for faculty and staff for existing positions, in February 1989 the board authorized a description for a new position—professor of comparative religions. The summer of 1989 saw the arrival of a new seminary librarian, Valerie Hotchkiss. Hotchkiss left in 1993 to become librarian at the Bridwell Library at Perkins School of Theology in Dallas. She was succeeded by Rev. Timothy Lincoln, who arrived in February 1994 and remains in that position today.

While Hotchkiss was at Austin Seminary, she oversaw at least two significant developments. The first was the computer automation of the entire library, making such tools as the card catalog a thing of the past. By May of 1991, the vice president for business affairs, Herman Harren, was able to report that "[t]he Library automation system has begun to take shape."[36]

The second was to work with the Presbyterian Historical Society of the Southwest and its executive director, Thomas W. Currie, Jr., in establishing the Stitt Library archives and the McCoy Historical Research Center. In May 1991 an eight-page document entitled "The Archives Project of the Stitt Library of the Austin Presbyterian Theological Seminary and the McCoy Historical Research Center: Declaration of Intent" was prepared by Hotchkiss, library interns Andrea Whitworth and Tim Young, and Professor Donald Davis, Jr., of the University of Texas. The report appeared in the minutes of the Board of Trustees. The introductory paragraphs state the purpose of the project:

> In the hopes of attracting more researchers and encouraging the study of Presbyterians and Presbyterianism in the southwest, the Stitt Library would like to renovate the archives area to provide more storage and work space, as well as a reading room for researchers. This is a major project requiring a complete renovation of the library basement, the purchase of shelving, furniture, computers, and archival storage supplies, and the addition of a staff position as Archivist.

Continuing, the report offers its hope for the McCoy Center:

> Working with the McCoy Historical Research Center we hope to become a center for research on all aspects of Presbyterianism

in the southwest. The McCoy Center is committed to encouraging the collection of church records in this geographical area for deposit in the national archives of the Presbyterian Church and in the Stitt Library Archives. Furthermore, the McCoy Center hopes to become involved in the production of oral histories. These histories would also become part of the research center at the Stitt Library.[37]

One of the goals in this cooperative effort was to hire an archivist, a position that became full-time in 1997. Bill Brock was the first seminary archivist and stayed until 2000, when he left for a position with the PC(USA)'s Department of History in Montreat, North Carolina.[38] Brock was succeeded by Kris Toma, who earned her master's in library information systems from the University of Texas and who came later that same year.

In the fall of 1989, Dr. Christine Blair came to the seminary as assistant professor of the church's ministry and director of the Doctor of Ministry and Continuing Education programs. The daughter of a worker in the foreign service, Blair was born in Morocco and was raised in Italy, India, and France. She was confirmed in the Anglican Church of Old Delhi when she was eleven years old. She was ordained as a minister in the Presbyterian Church in 1982 after receiving the equivalent of a master of divinity degree from the Claremont School of Theology (she had received a master's in religious education in 1975 from the American Baptist Seminary of the West). While working on a doctorate at Claremont, Blair also served on the staff of a Presbyterian church in the area. She received her Ph.D. in 1988. Although she had no prior acquaintance with Austin Seminary, she responded positively to a call from Jack Stotts to consider coming to Austin.[39]

According to Blair, the Doctor of Ministry program had its origins, nationally, when San Francisco Theological Seminary, the Claremont School of Theology, and the Chicago Divinity School began a program in 1970. Austin Seminary began its program in 1974, offering it both to those in the M.Div. program ("In-Sequence D.Min.") and to those already in the ministry ("In- Ministry D.Min."). In 1976 the first candidates received their doctor of ministry degrees from Austin Seminary: Ray Chester, John Danhof, Arthur Jones, and James Mosley.[40]

Initially, Dick Junkin, academic dean, directed the program out of his office with administrative assistance from Catherine Sautter (registrar) and Fern Chester (secretary). John R. "Pete" Hendrick and Cynthia Campbell preceded Christine Blair as directors of the program. Eventually, the "In-Sequence D.Min." was eliminated as an option. In the 1980s the program underwent an evaluation and restructuring under the advice and counsel of Seward Hiltner, professor of pastoral care at Princeton Seminary. According to Blair, Austin's Doctor of Ministry program is rated among the top four in the country, with students coming from the United States, Canada, and Cuba, and representing many different denominations.[41]

While continuing education for pastors and educators had been available at Austin Seminary for some time, it first received serious attention from Jack Maxwell, when Jerry Tompkins was asked to oversee it. Under Tompkins and his successors, the program received more organization, more intentionality, and more coordination.

With the announced retirement of Prescott Williams, a search for someone in the field of Old Testament began. In July 1990 Dr. Stephen Breck Reid arrived to fill that position and began teaching that fall. A member of the Church of the Brethren, Reid had earned his doctorate at Emory University, where Andy Dearman, the other Old Testament professor, had also received his Ph.D.

In the fall of 1990, the search for a professor of comparative religion culminated with the appointment of Dr. Terry Muck to that position. Muck, who at one time had been a world-class handball player, was a native of St. Paul, Minnesota, and had been a member of the Baptist General Conference, which was made up primarily of those of Swedish extraction. In 1993–94 he went through the necessary process to become a minister in the Presbyterian Church (U.S.A.). After earning his Ph.D. in comparative religion at Northwestern University, Muck worked at the journal *Christianity Today*, where he stayed for ten years. He knew of Austin Seminary because of his visits to the campus of the University of Texas for handball tournaments. Since Princeton Seminary was the only other seminary he knew of which had a world religions department, he was intrigued that Austin was advertising for just such a position.[42]

Changes continued when Fred Holper, who had taught worship and liturgics at Austin since June of 1988, announced that he was leaving in 1991 to teach at Union Seminary in Richmond, Virginia.

Bill Hedrick resigned as vice president for development in November 1991 to accept a call as pastor of Second Presbyterian Church in St. Louis. John Evans, director of vocations and admissions, moved into the development office, succeeding Hedrick in May 1991. Eleanor Cherryholmes was named director of vocations and admissions the following November. She remained there until her retirement in May 1997.

Within a year, the endowment of two chairs was announced. First, in May 1991, the First Presbyterian Church, Shreveport, D. Thompson Chair of New Testament Studies was established. John E. Alsup was named as the first occupant of that chair the following November. A year later, in May 1992, the John and Helen Lancaster Chair of Mission and Evangelism was established in honor of the recently retired pastor of First Presbyterian Church, Houston, and his wife. John R. "Pete" Hendrick was named the first occupant of that chair and was installed at a service at First Presbyterian Church on January 31, 1993.

Robert Shelton, academic dean, had been at the seminary since 1971. In May 1992 he was reappointed by the board to a five-year term as dean, effective June 1, 1993. At the end of that term, in May 1998, he would be granted a terminal one-year sabbatical, at the end of which, according to the plan, he would retire.[43] Those plans, of course, changed. But for the time being, the sense of continuity in the dean's office was preserved.

Many changes were about to take place in the makeup of the faculty. In coordination with the Synod of the Sun, in May 1992 the seminary board established a position in the area of the church and higher education. The title of the position would be: "Lecturer in the Church's Ministry in Higher Education."[44] Michael N. Miller filled that position in 1993.

William Stacy Johnson, who had earned a law degree at Wake Forest University before going to Union Seminary in Richmond to receive his M.Div., was called to fill the position in systematic theology left vacant by Alan Lewis's death. Initially appointed as a lecturer, Johnson would be promoted to assistant professor upon completion of his Ph.D. at Harvard Divinity School. His was a five-year appointment beginning August 1, 1992. At the same time, Stanley R. Hall was called to be professor of liturgics, filling the vacancy left by Fred Holper's departure for Union Seminary, Richmond.[45] The position, which had included responsibilities for both liturgics and homiletics, was divided, and in 1993 Scott Black Johnston, a Ph.D. candidate at Princeton Theological Seminary, was elected instructor in homiletics for a three-year renewable term, advancing to the position of assistant professor upon completion of his doctorate.[46]

With the retirement of Pete Hendrick came the need for a director of the Supervised Practice of Ministry (SPM) program, as well as a replacement in the field of mission and evangelism. Michael Jinkins, pastor of the Presbyterian church in Brenham, accepted the call to serve as director of the SPM program. Having earned a doctorate in theology at the University of Aberdeen in Scotland, Jinkins was also named assistant professor of the church's ministry. The three-year appointment became effective August 1, 1993. The search for a professor of evangelism and mission was not successfully completed until August 1996, when Dr. Sherron Kay George was appointed to a five-year renewable term as assistant professor of evangelism and missions. George came to the seminary after having served as a missionary in Brazil for over twenty years.

George Heyer, who had been at the seminary since 1964, announced his intention to retire December 31, 1993. He was named emeritus professor of Christian doctrine.[47] A replacement did not arrive until August 1995, when Cynthia Rigby, a candidate for the Ph.D. degree from Princeton Theological Seminary, accepted a three-year renewable appointment.

Heyer's retirement, along with that of Prescott Williams and the retirement and death of John Jansen, represented the passing of the torch from one generation to another. Each had taught at Austin Seminary for twenty-five years or more. The spring 1994 issue of *Insights* (formerly the faculty edition of the seminary *Bulletin*) was a Festschrift in honor of Heyer. Contributions came from Robert Shelton, Alan Lewis, Rebecca Weaver (Union Seminary, Richmond), and Thomas Torrance (emeritus professor of church dogmatics, University of Edinburgh, Scotland). In the introduction, President Stotts noted Heyer's contribution to Austin Seminary:

> George Heyer, to whom this issue of *Insights* is dedicated, has marked the character of this school by his joint commitment to

teaching and to those he has taught for the past 30 years. The theme of a rigorous and caring professor runs through several of the articles that follow and saturate the oral comments made about him. The fact of the matter is that George Heyer has influenced generations of Austin Seminary students by the courses he led and by who he is as a person. He has been enormously important to the character of this school because he has embodied the values of Austin Seminary as intellectually demanding and personally caring. He has by his tenure among us both passed on the tradition and contributed new dimensions to who we are as a community of faith and learning. We are all—individually and corporately—in his debt.[48]

These were the last appointments of new faculty in the Stotts administration. At the May 1995 meeting of the Board of Trustees, Stotts submitted a letter indicating his plans to retire on or about July 1, 1996, giving the board more than a year to complete the search for a new president.

According to the 1986–87 Seminary Catalogue, issued after Stotts had been president one full year, there were fifteen faculty members. That included Stotts himself as president, Cal Klemt as librarian, and C. Ellis Nelson as visiting professor of Christian education. By the time Stotts retired in July 1996, the faculty numbered twenty-two members. Several observations can be made about the development of the faculty during Stotts' tenure as president. First, the number of women faculty members increased significantly. In 1986 there were two women on the faculty: Cynthia Campbell and Laura Lewis. While Stotts was president, that number grew to five: Lewis, Ellen Babinsky, Christine Blair, Cynthia Rigby, and Sherron George.

Second, when approached with offers from other theological institutions, faculty members increasingly opted to stay at Austin. The seminary seemed to become less and less a stepping-stone to more prestigious positions. It became at least as attractive to stay at Austin as it might be to move to another school. When asked why this was so, faculty members offered a variety of answers: collegiality among faculty members, the absence of a politically charged atmosphere, the freedom to exchange ideas, the support and encouragement of the administration.

Third, while teaching continued to have a very high priority for Austin Seminary faculty, scholarship and publications were not ignored. The faculty journal *Insights,* appearing twice a year, afforded faculty opportunities to publish articles. But, more and more, articles and books appeared that indicated that Austin Seminary was firmly grounded both in the church and the academy.

Finally, Austin Seminary faculty remained committed to and active in the church, particularly at the local level. From the beginning, Austin Seminary has emphasized its relationship to the church at every level. In order to prepare its students for the parish ministry, the faculty has understood the importance of its own involvement in the life of the local congregation. While emphasis on parish experience among faculty members was not what it had once been, involvement in the life of the church continued to be valued during Stotts' administration.

The Physical Plant

Just as a seminary is no more solely bricks and mortar than the church is, it is also true that adequate facilities enhance a seminary's and a church's ability to carry out its purpose. In 1908 Sampson Hall, which housed the library, classrooms, administration offices, and faculty offices, and Lubbock Hall, which provided food services, were constructed. Aside from faculty homes and student housing, there were no physical additions to the campus until the Chapel was built in 1941–42. With the end of World War II and the arrival of David L. Stitt came many changes to the campus: a library (1949–50), Single Students' Dormitory (1955), married student apartments on University Avenue and Thirtieth Street (1951–52 and 1957–58), and the Trull Administration Building and the McMillan Memorial Classroom Building (1962). During this time, other properties were purchased, particularly ones that enabled the seminary to offer housing to married students.[49]

As was seen in chapter one, during Jack Maxwell's tenure, most of the improvements to the seminary's physical plant came in the form of renovation and expansion of existing buildings, with the notable exception of new married student housing on the north side of Waller Creek. The Stitt Library was expanded in a significant way. The organ in the Chapel was upgraded. The Single Students' Dormitory was renovated and was dedicated on April 21, 1986.

In anticipation of the largest enrollment in the history of the seminary in the fall of 1986, the Board of Trustees voted to accept a recommendation by John Evans, director of vocations and admissions, that a twelve-unit apartment/condominium building at 402 East Thirtieth Street be purchased for $774,000. Of that amount, $700,000 was to be financed for five years.[50] A year later, the board authorized the purchase of two more apartment houses, at 404 East Thirtieth Street and 406 East Thirtieth Street, at a cost of $685,000.[51]

In May 1988 the Single Students' Dorm became "Currie Hall," named for the seminary's third president and his wife, Thomas White Currie and Jeannette Roe Currie. The plaque that was affixed to the building read:

CURRIE HALL

DEDICATED TO MEMORY OF
THOMAS WHITE CURRIE 1879–1943
Professor of Bible and Church History; President of Austin
Presbyterian Theological Seminary 1922–1943

AND TO HIS WIFE
JEANNETTE ROE CURRIE 1883–1946

Their fidelity to Jesus Christ nurtured this Seminary;
Their lives made apparent the cost and the glory of discipleship.
Matthew 16:24

AND TO THEIR CHILDREN

Thomas White Currie, Jr.	David Mitchell Currie
Stuart Dickson Currie	Elizabeth Jeannette Currie

Sometime after Stotts' arrival at Austin Seminary, he became aware that there was no common place on campus for people, especially large numbers of people, to gather. Churches have fellowship halls. There was nothing similar at the seminary. Such a place would promote a greater sense of community and would accommodate conferences and assemblies. The rise in numbers of students and faculty also pointed to the need for more office and classroom space. Stotts also recognized that the construction of a campus community center would give the seminary a much-needed sense of success in terms of its ability to raise money. It would give the seminary increased visibility, both to the Austin community and to the seminary community, particularly the alumni.[52]

At its meeting on May 23, 1992, the Board of Trustees approved the recommendation of the Institutional Development Committee that the following provisions be part of a capital campaign:

1. That the Board of Trustees approve, in principle, the architect's conceptual design for the proposed Campus Center, as presented by the architectural firm of O'Connell Robertson & Associates, with the proviso that the administration give attention to concerns for continuing long-range plans for physical plant needs including adequate faculty space, and consideration to cost effectiveness for on-campus lodging accommodations for campus guests.

2. That the Board of Trustees approve the Campaign Objectives and Goals for Testing for the capital funds campaign, as submitted:

Campus Center	$3,500,000
Endowment for Campus Center	500,000
Scholarship Endowment for Need-Based Award	1,000,000
Endowed Faculty Chairs	2,000,000
1 chair at $1,000,000	
2 chairs at $500,000	
Stitt Library: Modernization &	
Archival Development	750,000
International Scholarship Endowment	250,000
Total Campaign Objective & Goal for Testing	$9,000,000

3. That the Board of Trustees approve proceeding with a pre-campaign Feasibility Study, assisted by the consulting firm of Dini and Associates of Houston, Texas, with a Feasibility Study Report to be presented to the Board of Trustees and acted on at the November, 1992, meeting of the Board.

4. That the Board of Trustees approve proceeding with a joint project to raise $400,000 in cooperation with Louisville Presby-

terian Theological Seminary for T. Watson Street Endowed Scholarships for International Church Leaders at APTS and LPTS, contingent upon the results of the pre-campaign study.[53]

The following October, Mr. Larry Vaclavik and Ms. Elaine Welborn of Dini & Associates presented the results of a feasibility study regarding a capital campaign. Their recommendation was that Austin Seminary could embark on a $4 million campaign to "fund the construction and endowment of a proposed campus center." They also recommended, however, that the preliminary goal be $5 million, which "would include projects for scholarships and faculty support and would be used in initial meetings with prospective donors who might wish to contribute to projects other than a campus center."[54] Eventually, the goal became $4.5 million. The campaign would run from May 1993 to May 1995.

By November 1993, board member Jo E. "Jed" Shaw could report that 100 percent of the trustees, administration, and faculty had pledged to the Capital Funds Campaign. Drawings for this new facility, which would be located between Currie Hall and the McMillan Classroom Building on the hill sloping north toward Waller Creek, were authorized in November as well.[55]

In February 1994, $2,645,000 had been received in gifts and pledges.[56] By the following November, $4,427,000 had been pledged or given toward the $4.5 million goal, and the board entered into a contract with American Constructors Company as the contractor/consultant for the new campus community center. Construction began on March 1, 1995. By the May 1996 meeting of the Board of Trustees, over $5 million dollars in gifts and pledges had been raised.

After eighteen months, the new building was completed. It was dedicated October 19, 1996, and named "The James I. and Hazel McCord Community Center" as a way of honoring "the memory of a former professor of systematic theology and academic dean of Austin Seminary (1946–59)."[57]

This three-floor structure contains a dining room that is large enough to accommodate a crowd such as that which traditionally gathers for the Alumni Luncheon at the conclusion of the Mid-Winter Lectures. In it also are classrooms, the Continuing Education and Doctor of Ministry offices, technological capabilities such as those that are used in distance learning, and overnight accommodations for guests.

The campaign was clearly a team effort. Board of Trustees chairman Ed Vickery asked fellow board member Jed Shaw to chair the campaign. He described his role as helping to "steer things." Shaw recalled that other board members who were significantly involved in the campaign were Bessie Lou Doelling and Louis Zbinden. Robert Bohl, pastor of First Presbyterian Church in Fort Worth, played a key role in securing a gift from the Luce Foundation.[58]

By all accounts, the success of this capital campaign was largely due to the organization and direction of John Evans, vice president for seminary relations and development. His knowledge of the seminary constituency and his ability to cultivate relationships with potential donors were crucial to the campaign's success. According to Stotts, Evans was "the pivot" around which everything else revolved.[59]

With the successful completion of the McCord Center, there was no longer any need for the oldest building still on campus, Lubbock Hall, which was constructed in 1908. In October 1996 the board voted "to confirm Executive Committee action to remove Lubbock Hall at an estimated cost of $25,000–$30,000. These monies would come from the capital reserves fund.[60]

As mentioned earlier, in May 1995 President Jack Stotts announced to the board, in executive session, his plans to retire on or about July 1, 1996. The board accepted his letter with regret and granted him a twelve-month terminal sabbatical, beginning on or about July 1, 1996. A presidential search committee was authorized.[61]

At its May 18, 1996, meeting the Board of Trustees adopted the following resolution of appreciation of the service to Austin Seminary of Jack Stotts:

> *Whereas* Jack Leven Stotts, B.A., B.D., M.A., Ph.D., D.D., has completed eleven years of extraordinary service to Austin Presbyterian Theological Seminary as its seventh president, culminating an illustrious career of over 30 years in theological education; and
>
> *Whereas* President Stotts has provided wise and perspicacious leadership for Austin Seminary and its constituencies, resulting in increased seminary enrollment, enriched educational opportuni-

ties and environments, and improved institutional financial stability; and

Whereas his genuine caring for and sensitivity to students, staff, administrators and faculty have constituted a standard and an exemplar which have ennobled, empowered and brought healing and hope to many; and

Whereas his gentle spirit and friendly manner have been an enduring gift to all who have come in contact with him; and

Whereas his acumen and discernment have instructed and challenged all who have worked closely with him; therefore,

Be it Resolved that Austin Presbyterian Theological Seminary—its Board of Trustees, its Faculty, its student body—give thanks to Almighty God for the life and ministry of Jack and Virginia Stotts among us; and

That we express our deepest, heartfelt appreciation to Jack and Virginia for all they have meant and mean to us; and

That on the occasion of this milestone in their lives we commend them and their future to God in the certain confidence that God will continue to use them for God's purpose in this world.

The resolution was signed by Jo E. "Jed" Shaw, chairman of the Board of Trustees.[62]

Stotts' contributions in the area of ecumenical relations are reflected in another document, dated May 19, 1996, coming from Austin Seminary's neighboring school a couple of blocks to the east. It read:

The Board of Trustees, Administration and Faculty
of the
Episcopal Theological Seminary of the Southwest
salutes

The Rev. Dr. Jack L. Stotts

on the occasion of his retirement as President
of the Austin Presbyterian Theological Seminary.

His vision of the ecumenical dimension
of theological education has enhanced

the relationship between our seminaries and the
Lutheran Seminary Program of the Southwest.

Because his exemplary tenure and service in Austin
have benefited not only his seminary
but ours as well,
we hereby convey to him our deeply felt
admiration and appreciation.

May 19, 1996   Austin, Texas[63]

At the same meeting at which it passed the resolution honoring
Jack and Virginia Stotts, the Austin Seminary Board of Trustees appointed Academic Dean Robert M. Shelton acting president, effective August 1, 1996, "until the next president takes office."[64]

Summary

Recalling the atmosphere of low morale in virtually every constituency of the seminary prior to Jack Maxwell's resignation in
November 1983, there was a new confidence that emerged under
the leadership of Jack Stotts. The transition from Maxwell to Stotts
was made much smoother by the calm and stable interim presidency of Ellis Nelson. Nevertheless, Stotts' national stature in theological education brought a fresh awareness of new possibilities.
As president of McCormick Seminary and as chair of the committee to draft a confession for the newly united Presbyterian Church
(USA), Stotts brought attention to Austin that would inevitably
enhance the school's image across the country.

In his final report to the Board of Trustees, Stotts reviewed
some of the accomplishments of his eleven years as the president of
Austin Seminary. For example, enrollment in the M.Div. program
grew from 90 in 1985 to 180 in 1995. The D.Min. enrollment grew
from 73 students to 94 students. The faculty grew by five permanent positions and one lecturer, and two faculty positions were endowed by congregations in the Synod of the Sun. The budget increased from $2,600,000 in 1985–86 to $5,000,000 in 1996–97. The
endowment almost doubled, from $31 million to $60 million. Com-

pensation for faculty and staff exceeded the average of other Presbyterian theological institutions. And, of course, the addition of the McCord Center, along with the renovation of Currie Hall and the purchase of three apartment buildings for student housing, contributed to an enhanced sense of community.[65]

Stotts helped shift Austin Seminary from being a regional school to one that drew students from across the country. Increased attention was given to the "Texas to Montana corridor" as attempts were made to draw students from the Synods of the Southwest, the Rocky Mountains, and Mid-America, as well as from the Synod of the Sun.

At a time when some churches were dividing or withdrawing from the denomination over theological matters, and at a time when some seminaries (including some Presbyterian ones) found themselves caught up in bitter and divisive controversies over theological issues, Austin Seminary seemed to be a remarkably harmonious community. Much of the credit for this has been attributed to Stotts' style of leadership, one that encouraged conversation and debate, but which also encouraged collegiality. Freedom to disagree, theologically, among faculty members while remaining colleagues and friends has been cited by many faculty members as an important reason they have stayed and as a factor that has strengthened the sense of community.

Linda Cunningham, who has worked with and for Presidents Maxwell, Stotts, and Shelton as well as Interim President Nelson, observed for eleven years that Stotts was consistently able to heal old wounds and take the seminary to a higher level, and that his churchmanship, nurturing character, and open style inspired a new sense of trust within the seminary community and beyond to its various constituencies.[66]

John Evans, who graduated from Austin Seminary in 1968, came back to work at the seminary in 1984 as the director of vocations and admissions, and became the vice president for development and church relations in 1991, points to Stotts' integrity, accessibility, and concern for people as critical characteristics that led to his effectiveness as a seminary president.[67]

Clarence Frierson, a member of the Austin Seminary Board of Trustees for twenty-two years and elected a trustee emeritus in May 1994, observed that during his tenure on the board there were two major turning-points. The first was the Jean Brown gift, which doubled the endowment. The second was the election of Jack Stotts to be president. "People liked, trusted and respected the president of Austin Seminary! Jack possesses personal and political skills, integrity and has the respect of the entire church. His record as president speaks for itself."[68]

At its meeting in October 1996, the Board of Trustees honored Stotts by electing him president emeritus.[69]

Again, the pattern of continuity and change continued. The search for a new president to lead the seminary began again. This time, however, the new president would find a seminary that had grown in several ways—in numbers of students and faculty, in financial strength, in expanded national exposure, and in support from and confidence of its constituency. The seminary community was changing, but remained a community nonetheless.

CHAPTER FIVE

The Shelton Years
(1996–2002)

With the announcement of Jack Stotts' intention to retire on or about July 1, 1996, the Board of Trustees authorized the incoming chairman, Jed Shaw, to appoint a presidential search committee. That committee consisted of ten persons, six of whom were trustees: Louis Zbinden (chairman), Peggy Clark, Ted Hartman, David McKechnie, Sydney Reding, and Max Sherman. In addition, serving on the committee were: Robert Shelton and Andy Dearman (representing the faculty), Elizabeth Pense (representing the Austin Seminary Association), and Gary Oliver (representing the student body). By virtue of his office as chairman of the board, Jo E. "Jed" Shaw also sat on the committee.[1]

Attached to the November 1995 minutes of the Board of Trustees is a position description for the position of president of Austin Seminary and the essential qualifications for that position. Not substantially different than the qualifications listed in previous presidential searches, this list indicated the desire for the next president to be an ordained minister in the Presbyterian Church (U.S.A.) whose faithfulness to Jesus Christ as Lord and Savior was clear and who, equally clearly, was committed to the Presbyterian Church (U.S.A.) and the Reformed tradition. Furthermore, the next president needed to possess the ability to work with, encourage, and support the faculty. In addition to being a sound administrator, the president of Austin Seminary needed to be able to raise funds for the school, both for the present and for the future in the form of increasing the endowment. The new president needed to be someone who both recognized "the Seminary's location among diverse cultures of the Southwest and who seeks to advance the seminary's mission in its location" and who "has the ability to guide and direct the seminary to new horizons and singular distinction."[2]

The Presidential Search Committee had been formed in May of 1995, giving the committee a year's head start before Stotts' resignation took effect July 1, 1996. Because the search committee was still in the process of seeking a new president after a year's work, Robert Shelton was appointed acting president August 1, 1996. The search committee interviewed several candidates. In fact, on two different occasions the committee offered the position to persons who subsequently declined.

After two years, the search committee felt that perhaps the best candidate was in their midst. At the May meeting of the Board of Trustees, the committee recommended that Robert M. Shelton be named president of Austin Seminary for a designated term of two years, effective June 1, 1997. This term would be subject to renewal by the board.[3] Shelton agreed to become the eighth president of Austin Seminary.

Shelton had come to Austin Seminary in June 1971. Born in Karnak, Illinois, in 1934, he was the son of an ordained minister in the Cumberland Presbyterian Church. He earned his bachelor's degree from Maryville College in Maryville, Tennessee, in 1955 and his bachelor of divinity from Memphis Theological Seminary in 1958. In the fall of 1958 he went to Princeton Theological Seminary to begin work on a Ph.D. in homiletics. He received the master of theology from Princeton in 1959 and his Ph.D. in 1965. His dissertation focused on the preaching of Harry Emerson Fosdick.[4]

Shelton came to Austin after having served as a pastor and teacher in the Cumberland Presbyterian Church. He was teaching at Memphis Theological Seminary when he accepted the call to teach at Austin Seminary. When asked why he came to Austin Seminary, Shelton mentioned two main reasons: a sense of call and a personal enthusiasm for the work that was being done there.[5] He recalled that he had known about Austin, at least in part, through the writings of Dietrich Ritschl, a German theologian who had taught at the seminary as a visiting professor in 1958 and had delivered the Thomas White Currie Lectures in 1965. But he also heard more of Austin Seminary through acquaintanceships with Walter Johnson, Carlyle Marney, and Jim McCord.[6]

There is perhaps no one person who has both witnessed and influenced the life of Austin Seminary in the past thirty years more than Bob Shelton. One example is provided by Andy Dearman, academic dean and professor of Old Testament:

> Bob has been a member of virtually every faculty search committee for the last 30 years. Indeed, it is possible that he has been either an elected or ex officio member of every search committee during that time, save when he was on sabbatical. In any case, by virtue of longevity on the faculty and by sheer persuasive influence, he has had the major role in shaping the faculty in recent decades.[7]

As professor and as academic dean, Shelton has either taught or advised virtually every student who has matriculated at Austin Seminary since 1971. He has served as advisor to Austin Seminary presidents and to faculty members. When appropriate and when needed, he has served as pastor to anyone connected to the seminary—faculty, students, staff, administration, alumni and their families. He was on the handball court with Stuart Currie when Currie suffered a fatal heart attack. A trusted friend of Ross Dunn, he preached at the memorial service after Dunn died of a lengthy bout with cancer, a disease with which Shelton himself was all too familiar, as he watched his first wife, Barbara, die of it in 1980. Having preached at the installation service of Austin Seminary graduate and friend Bobby Graham at the Presbyterian church in Helena, Arkansas, in September 2000, Shelton witnessed Graham's death at the close of that service as he collapsed of a heart attack. Within the week, Shelton preached at the memorial service for Graham at First Presbyterian Church in Little Rock.

He witnessed the expansion of the Stitt Library, the building of new married student apartments, the campaign for and construction of the McCord Center, the razing of Lubbock Hall. He was present to celebrate the news of the Jean Brown bequest and was named the first holder of the Jean Brown Chair of Homiletics and Liturgics.

He has served under four of the seminary's seven presidents (Stitt, Williams, Maxwell, and Stotts) and one interim president (Nelson). He has also witnessed the downfall of a seminary president and both the pain and the relief that accompanied it. He was part of the process of restoring the confidence of the seminary's constituencies. It is not, therefore, too much to say that Bob Shelton understands, has participated in, and has contributed to the sense of community that has pervaded the life of Austin Seminary over the past quarter-century as much as anyone.

Ironically, in spite of his longevity at, and faithfulness to, the seminary, he became the only president-elect of Austin Seminary who was not a member of the denomination to which the seminary belonged. Because of the requirement of the by-laws that the president be an ordained minister in the Presbyterian Church (U.S.A.), Shelton offered to move his membership from the Cumberland Presbyterian Church. Instead, the Board of Trustees waived that requirement in this particular instance.[8]

Interviewed for the seminary publication *Windows* following his election as president, Shelton observed, "I'm sure there have been Austin Seminary presidents with greater ability than I have, but I think there's never been one who loves Austin Seminary more or desires to serve it more." In that same interview, Shelton indicated the theme that he wanted to strike for his administration: "If I have any theme, it's going to be to reestablish that notion of the 'school of the church,' and expand and stretch that notion. Being a responsible and effective school of the church is the greatest opportunity."[9]

The inauguration of Shelton as president of Austin Seminary took place in the sanctuary of Covenant Presbyterian Church in Austin on November 14, 1997. That morning in the Seminary Chapel, George Stroup, professor of theology at Austin Seminary before moving to Columbia Seminary in Decatur, Georgia, presented a lecture that addressed the theme of the relationship between the academy and the church. Entitled "A Lovers' Quarrel: Theology and the Church,"[10] Stroup's presentation examined the way in which the academy and the church have often viewed each other with suspicion, and yet, how each is integrally related to the other. Each has its shortcomings and each can point out, legitimately, the flaws of the other, Stroup says, but

> [w]hat has bound the church and its theologians together in the past has not always been their affection or even their respect for each other, but a shared commitment to the God they know in Jesus Christ. It may well be that the future of their relationship is not so much a question about their commitment to one another as it is a question about their respective commitments to God.[11]

In his own inaugural address, Shelton again took up the theme of the seminary as "a school of the church" and as a part of the larger Christian community.[12] Describing the relationship between the church and the seminary as a symbiotic one, Shelton offered three characteristics of a seminary if it is to be a healthy partner in this symbiotic relationship: (1) the seminary must be "a doxological community, a group of believers active and intentional in rendering praise to God";[13] (2) "the seminary as a school of the church is called to serve the church—to be a servant of the church—in order that the church can faithfully serve God and the world. ... Without the church a seminary by definition has lost its fundamental *raison d'etre*";[14] and (3) members of the seminary community must believe the church, that is, "participating faithfully in the life of the church, the church's worship and mission. ..." and "genuinely loving the church with all its problems and shortcomings and with all its imperfections."[15]

Shelton concluded with a stirring call for the "school of the church" to look backward with gratitude and to look forward with hope and a passion for its calling:

> To be a school of the church, a seminary must be a place which graciously welcomes the faith and tradition of the saints who have established it and have gone before. A place where those who teach, learn, and worship are judged and graced by that God who came to us in Jesus Christ. It is a place where, like the church which has given it birth, its inhabitants strive ever to be not disobedient to that heavenly vision which Isaiah described poetically and graphically as waters breaking forth in the wilderness and

streams in the desert. It was a vision of a time when the eyes of
the blind are opened and the ears of the deaf are unstopped. A vision of a time when the speechless sing for joy and the full glory
of God is manifest. A vision of a time when everlasting joy and
gladness will be pervasive in all creation, and sorrow and suffering
will be banished. A school of the church engenders and presents
a passion for that vision and a passion for Jesus Christ who gave
his life for that vision, a passion which is contagious and com-
pelling, a passion which inspires women and men to proclaim and
work for that vision with hands ever strengthened and knees
made firm through the power of God's spirit in the church and in
our lives.[16]

An awareness of the seminary not only as a community within itself but as a part of the larger community of faith and exploring
what that means was at the heart of the inaugural festivities.

Shelton brought to the office of president the kind of energy
and enthusiasm that he brought as a professor and as academic
dean. After suffering heart attacks in 1985 and 1990, he became an
avid jogger, but he continues to describe himself as "an unrepentant
workaholic."

When Shelton became acting president in August 1996, the
campaign for the McCord Center had been successfully completed
and the building was to be dedicated the following October. There
was increased awareness that the school would celebrate its centennial in 2002. It seemed an appropriate time to examine the organizational structure of the seminary administration and, at the same
time, to develop a long-range plan for the future of the school.

At the October 18, 1996, board meeting, not only was the Mc-
Cord Center dedicated and Jack Stotts named president emeritus,
but the board agreed "to employ the Dini Partners to conduct a development assessment and organizational study at a cost of
$20,000."[17] Out of this two-year study came a master plan which the
board adopted in May 1999. It consisted of a vision statement and
nine strategic goal areas. Distinctive about the vision of the seminary is an explicit goal to make much more than a regional appeal:

Building on its tradition of excellence in theological education,
Austin Presbyterian Theological Seminary will become nationally

recognized for the high quality of its education, formation, and training of pastors and other church leaders.[18]

While Austin Seminary has always offered a high quality of education, and while it has provided an extraordinary number of nationally prominent church leaders, its primary goal has also always been to train pastors for the Presbyterian church in the Southwest. Under Jack Stotts, the seminary intentionally began recruiting students beyond the Synod of the Sun. Now, however, it appears that nationwide recognition was to be the goal.

Beneath the vision statement were nine "strategic goals," ranging from issues related to "increased academic excellence/enriched curriculum" to "development of fiscal and human resources" to "physical plant and grounds" to "institutional technology development."[19]

Because the student body has become more diverse, denominationally, one of the strategic goals (number 6) stated: "Austin Presbyterian Theological Seminary will clarify and strengthen its relationships with the Presbyterian Church (U.S.A.) and other denominations, particularly the United Methodist Church." Due to the relatively large number of United Methodist students, the seminary hopes to endow a chair in Methodist studies.

The next goal acknowledges the broader range of relationships the seminary has enjoyed over the years, namely, continuing to cultivate relationships with the Episcopal Seminary of the Southwest, the Lutheran Seminary Program in the Southwest, the University of Texas at Austin, seminaries and theological schools in the Council of Southwestern Theological Schools, and other Presbyterian Church (U.S.A.)–related seminaries.[20]

Strategic Goal 3 had to do with the development and strengthening of the seminary's fiscal and human resources. Toward that end and in connection with the celebration of the seminary's centennial in 2002, work began on exploring the possibility of a capital campaign. At a meeting on March 3, 2000, the Executive Committee of the Board of Trustees authorized the administration to enter into a contract with the firm of Marts & Lundy "to conduct a feasibilty study for a capital campaign."[21] Among the purposes of the campaign were funding for new student housing and a parking garage, a child-care center, an addition to the Stitt Library, six endowed professorships (at $1.2 million each), endowed scholarships for students, endowed technology, "smart" classrooms, renovation of the Chapel, and renovation of the ground floor of the McMillan Building.

The following fall, President Shelton recommended to the board approval of "the designing and implementing of a Centennial campaign in the amount of $15 to $16 million, to begin in June 2000 and conclude in December 2005."[22] One significant part of this campaign was achieved when it was announced on March 7, 2001, that board member Diane Buchanan and her husband, Rick Andrew, gave $1.2 million to endow the William Jethro Fogleman Chair of Pastoral Theology.

When Shelton was elected president of Austin Seminary for a designated term of two years in May 1997, the seminary's investment portfolio was approximately $76 million. By the fall of 1999, that figure had grown to more than $95.4 million. This growth coincided with an expanding economy in the rest of the country. Prospects for the success of the Centennial capital campaign remained bright in spite of a much more sluggish economy in 2001 and economic uncertainty brought about by terrorist attacks on September 11, 2001, that destroyed the twin towers of the World Trade Center in New York City and a portion of the Pentagon in Washington, D.C.

Faculty and Staff Development

At the same meeting in which Bob Shelton was elected president of Austin Seminary, the Board of Trustees also promoted Ismael Garcia to full professor of Christian ethics, effective June 1, 1997. In addition, Stanley R. Hall was promoted to associate professor of liturgics and elected to a five-year term, effective June 1, 1998.[23]

By its November 1997 meeting, the board received a letter from Herman Harren, vice president for business affairs. It announced Harren's intention to retire, effective July 31, 1998. A search committee was authorized to find a successor. On April 12, 1998, Harren had a stroke. He had recovered sufficiently to make an appearance at the board meeting in May 1998. In gratitude for his twenty-seven years of service to the seminary, the board gave him and his wife, Margaret Harren, funds for a trip of their choice.

On August 1, 1998, Catherine (Cathy) Civiletto succeeded Harren and assumed the duties of vice president for business affairs. She came to the seminary after four years at Texas A&M University in College Station, "where she was the manager of financial planning in the Office of Treasury Services."[24]

Upon entering the Office of Business Affairs, Civiletto discovered that Harren had laid a very firm foundation, both in terms of business practices and investment practices. Improvements that were needed, according to Civiletto, included modernizing relationships with banks (such as electronic banking and direct deposit of the payroll) and dividing the business office responsibilities into accounting and operations. With the growth of the seminary, the emphasis needed to be placed on the organizational system rather than an individual who would be responsible for the day-to-day operations.[25]

At the same meeting in which Shelton's term as president was extended until June 2002, on the recommendation of Shelton, J. Andrew Dearman was elected to a five-year term as academic dean. Dearman had been at the seminary since 1981 and had served as acting academic dean since 1997.[26]

In January 1999 the Rev. Dr. Jerold D. Shetler became the new vice president for institutional advancement. Shetler had served on the seminary's Board of Trustees from 1980 to 1989 and as chairman of the board from 1985 to 1989. During those years he served as pastor of Preston Hollow Presbyterian Church in Dallas. Having served that pastorate for thirteen years (1975–88), Shetler moved to Greensboro, North Carolina, where he served as pastor of First Presbyterian Church from 1988 to 1998. Shetler had served pastorates in Covington, Virginia; Raleigh, North Carolina; and Lynchburg, Virginia, prior to moving to Dallas in 1975.

A graduate of Union Theological Seminary in Richmond, Virginia, Shetler brought with him a strong commitment to theological education. In addition to his service on the Austin Seminary Board of Trustees, he had served on the Council on Theological Education (C.O.T.E.), an organization in the Presbyterian Church, U.S., that was formed to foster a sense of unity among southern Presbyterian seminaries and was designed with reunion in mind. While in Greensboro, Shetler also served on the board of Union

Theological Seminary in Richmond. So, as he retired from the pastorate, he brought a wealth of experience in the church, knowledge of Austin Seminary's own history, and awareness of the importance of theological education to this new position at Austin Seminary.

In the fall of 1998, the seminary's Development Office was strengthened with the arrival of John C. Wilton, Jr., as the director of annual giving. Wilton, a 1993 graduate of the University of Texas at Austin, came to the seminary after having served as director of development and alumni relations at Schreiner College in Kerrville, Texas.[27]

The biblical departmental faculty expanded by one member when, in the fall of 1998, Dr. Kathryn L. Roberts was appointed as assistant professor of Old Testament. An ordained minister in the Reformed Church in America, Roberts received her M.Div. from Colgate Rochester Divinity School/Bexley Hall/Crozer Theological Seminary in 1988. From 1992 to 1994 she served as assistant pastor of the Community Reformed Church in Feasterville, Pennsylvania. She earned her Ph.D. in Old Testament from Princeton Theological Seminary in 1996. Roberts is married to J. J. M. "Jimmy" Roberts, William Henry Green Professor of Old Testament Literature at Princeton Seminary.[28] In the spring of 2000, Roberts was reappointed for a second three-year term, effective July 1, 2001.[29]

At the same time that Roberts was elected to the faculty, Lewis Donelson was promoted to full professor of New Testament, Scott Black Johnston was promoted to associate professor and elected to a five-year term as associate professor of homiletics, and Michael Jinkins was promoted to a five-year term as associate professor of pastoral theology and director of the Supervised Practice of Ministry (SPM).[30]

In the spring of 1999, four faculty members were promoted. Laura Lewis achieved the rank of full professor of Christian education; Stephen Reid became full professor of Old Testament studies; William Greenway was elected to a tenure-track position as assistant professor of Christian studies for a three-year renewable term, beginning June 1, 1999; and Michael Miller's title was changed from lecturer in the church and higher education to research professor in the church and higher education.[31]

The continued growth in the size of the student body demanded a growing faculty. Joining Scott Black Johnston in the area of homiletics in the fall of 1999 was Carol Antablin Miles, a Ph.D. candidate from Princeton Seminary. She was elected to serve a three-year term beginning in August 1999 while she completed work on her dissertation and completed the process for ordination. That dissertation was completed and the Ph.D. awarded in May 2000. The Austin Seminary publication *Windows* reported that while she was a student at Princeton, "Miles was awarded a Princeton Doctoral Fellowship and received both the Edward Howell Roberts Scholarship in Preaching and the Frederick Neumann Prize for Excellence in Greek and Hebrew."[32] She was ordained as a minister in the Presbyterian Church (U.S.A.) on March 19, 2000, at First Presbyterian Church in Berkeley, California.

Her husband, David Miles, also an ordained minister in the Presbyterian Church (U.S.A.), was called to serve as interim pastor to the seminary community and dean of student life. Prior to this appointment, David Miles had served as senior pastor to the Lamington Presbyterian Church in Bedminster, New Jersey, where one of his parishioners was the governor of the state of New Jersey, Christine Todd Whitman. In the Winter 2001 issue of *Windows*, he wrote of that experience:

> One of the most challenging questions before me as a preacher was whether or not I should intentionally aim my sermons at her. While some of my parishioners and many of my pastoral colleagues urged me to use the pulpit to preach her a sermon about this issue or that, I tried my best to resist the temptation. Those of us who preach always have our congregation in mind when composing a sermon, and certainly particular people appear in our mind's eye as we imagine how they might react to a particular thing we might say. While Christie often came to mind when I was preparing to preach, I would inevitably zoom out in my imagination and remind myself that it was my responsibility to preach to the entire congregation.
>
> I believe that the gospel itself is politically charged. My philosophy about preaching on political issues is that one must begin, not with the political issue, but with the gospel. I know that if I am faithful to the gospel, it will inevitably lead to particular political issues relevant to the day. And given the generally conservative, affluent, and politically powerful nature of my congregation

at Lamington, I know that my preaching—to the extent that I remained faithful to the gospel—challenged their social and political convictions, by and large.[33]

In the summer of 2001, Westminster Presbyterian Church in Austin called David Miles to become its pastor, and he accepted that call. In July he and Carol, their two sons, and David's parents planned a vacation at a family cottage in Maine. After making preparations to move into a new house in Austin, David and his father flew to Maine, where the rest of the family had already gathered. The rental car they were driving was struck by another car, and both David and Tom were killed. Memorial services were held in Lamington, Princeton, and Austin.

Once again, the seminary community experienced the sense of change as it grieved the death of one of its members. The apostle Paul's charge to the Christian community in Rome, that they "rejoice with those who rejoice, weep with those who weep" (Romans 12:15), was heeded as it had been so many times before. There were other changes among the faculty as well. Terry Muck announced his resignation, after ten years at Austin, in order to accept a call as professor of world religions at Asbury Theological Seminary in Wilmore, Kentucky. Sherron George was promoted to associate professor for a five-year term, beginning July 1, 2001. But before that new term began, George announced that she believed God was calling her to return to Campinas, Sao Paolo, Brazil, as a theological consultant to the Presbyterian Church (U.S.A.).

In May 2000 John Evans, vice president for development and church relations, announced that he was leaving the seminary to work for the Presbyterian Church (U.S.A.) Foundation as the Texas regional development officer.

Having received his B.A. from Austin College, Evans entered Austin Seminary in 1964 and received his M.Div. in 1968. His first charge had been as associate pastor at Westminster Presbyterian Church in Austin. After working for the Synod of the Sun, Evans returned to the seminary in 1984 as the director of vocations and admissions. He served in that office until July 1991, when he was named vice president for development, filling the position vacated by Bill Hedrick. His sixteen-year tenure at Austin Seminary was distinguished first, during his leadership in the admissions office, by a significant increase in the size of the student body, and second, as vice president for development, by the successful campaign which resulted in the construction of the McCord Community Center. Furthermore, it was while he was in the development office that Austin Seminary tied for second place in the nation among all U.S. seminaries in alumni giving. Fifty-seven percent of all alumni contributed to Austin Seminary in 1996–97.

At the 2000 Alumni Luncheon at the close of the Mid-Winter Lectures, Evans was reminded of the words of the medieval mystic Meister Eckhart, whom he often quoted: "If the only prayer you say in your whole life is 'thank you,' that would suffice." Evans began his final report to the Board of Trustees with those same words.[34] Surely, Evans' own sense of gratitude to God awakened in others a similar awareness of God's goodness. One way they were encouraged to express it was by supporting Austin Seminary.

In seeking a replacement for Evans, Shelton and the Board of Trustees re-arranged some titles and administrative responsibilities. Jerry Shetler became vice president for church relations and planned giving. Evans' replacement would have the title of vice president for institutional advancement. In the summer of 2000, Timothy A. Kubatzky accepted the invitation to serve the seminary in that capacity. A graduate of the University of Missouri at Columbia, Kubatzky came to Austin Seminary from Southwestern University in Georgetown, where he had served as vice president for development since 1995. He also had worked at Rice University in Houston and for the University of Houston system. He is an elder in First Presbyterian Church in Georgetown, Texas.

In the fall of 2000, Ralph Underwood, professor of pastoral care, announced that he intended to retire in December 2001. The first member of the United Methodist Church on the faculty or staff of Austin Seminary, Underwood had taught at Austin Seminary since 1978. Quinn Fox, who had served as director of vocation and admissions since 1997, submitted his resignation, effective December 31, 2000, so that he could accept a call to become associate pastor of First Presbyterian Church in Colorado Springs, Colorado.

Bill Brock, seminary archivist, left in April 2000 in order to accept a position as collection management archivist with the Presbyterian Historical Society in Montreat, North Carolina. He was succeeded the following fall by Kris Toma, whose arrival coincided with preparations to celebrate the seminary's Centennial in 2002.

Stacy Johnson resigned as W. C. Brown Professor of Theology in the summer of 1999 to join the faculty of Princeton Theological Seminary. In May 2001 President Shelton announced that the seminary had hired David H. Jensen as assistant professor of Reformed theology, for a three-year renewable term, effective July 1, 2001. Jensen earned his Ph.D. from Vanderbilt University in 1999 and had come to Austin from Manchester College in North Manchester, Indiana, where he had taught religion and philosophy.

In December 1999, Daryl Johnson, a 1986 graduate, returned to the seminary campus to serve as the operations manager. He came to Austin having served as pastor of First Presbyterian Church in McAllen, Texas.

When Quinn Fox left the office of vocation and admissions, Ann Fields, a 1998 graduate of Austin Seminary who held doctorates from the University of Texas at Austin and Southwest Texas State University, was appointed interim director of the Office of Vocation and Admissions. In the summer of 2001, the position of vice president of student affairs was created, subsuming within it the duties and responsibilities of the previous position of dean of student life and pastor to students. A member of the United Methodist Church, Fields was appointed to this new position. Sam Riccobene, a 1991 graduate of Austin Seminary, became the new director of vocation and admissions in September of 2001. He returned to Austin after pastorates in Pennsylvania and Oklahoma.

Another sign of change and growth in the administration was the establishment of the Office of Supervised Practice of Ministry as a full-time position. Previously, it had been combined with other responsibilities, most recently with those assigned to Michael Jinkins, who also taught pastoral theology. In October 2001, David Johnson arrived on campus to fill this new full-time position. Having served pastorates in Galveston and Irving, Texas, Johnson had also taught at the Brite Divinity School in Fort Worth. He earned his M.Div. from Yale Divinity School and his Ph.D. from Princeton Theological Seminary.

But continuity within the community contributed to a sense of stability. Stan Hall and Michael Jinkins were granted tenure as a new academic year began in the fall of 2000. Tina Blair was re-appointed associate professor of practical theology and director of the D.Min. program for a five-year term. Cynthia Rigby was promoted to associate professor of theology for a five-year term. Bill Greenway continued to teach at the seminary, but under a new title—assistant professor of philosophical theology.[35]

Hispanic Ministry

Well documented is the fact that many efforts have been made over the years to cultivate a relationship with the Hispanic community. Such efforts met with varying degrees of success, usually halting and temporary. Exploratory efforts were made to see if Austin Seminary, the Episcopal Seminary of the Southwest, and the Lutheran Seminary Program in the Southwest could combine resources toward establishing a center for Hispanic ministry.

Ismael Garcia, professor of Christian ethics, was at the center of these and other efforts. A major development that represented the seminary's desire to demonstrate its commitment to ministry in the Hispanic community was the invitation to the Asociacion para la Educacion Teologica Hispana (AETH) to relocate its administrative offices to the Austin Seminary campus.[36]

According to Garcia, AETH is a professional, interdenominational organization of Hispanic theological educators. It was founded in 1989 in Atlanta, Georgia, and was housed at Columbia Theological Seminary. Among other things, AETH provides educational materials to those engaged in theological education in the Hispanic community.[37] Professor Ebenezer Negron was elected as the chief administrator of AETH.

One of AETH's responsibilities is the administration of a two-week summer program which is held at the Oblate School of Theology in San Antonio. It is accredited by the Association of Theological Schools and enjoys the support of more than fifty theological schools and seminaries. In 2001 Garcia was the director of this program.

These efforts by Shelton and Garcia, among others, to identify Austin Seminary with Hispanic ministry are significant. If the gospel is to be proclaimed in and to a world where linguistic and cultural borders are becoming more diffuse, then such efforts must become more intentional. Garcia suggests that, given the growing Hispanic population in Texas and throughout the Southwest in general, and given the relatively homogeneous character of the student population at Austin Seminary, perhaps non-Hispanic students should be taught about Hispanic cultures rather than insisting that Hispanic students be taught about non-Hispanic culture. He wonders if Hispanic issues should not be incorporated into more seminary courses.[38]

Summary

Any summary of the work of a seminary president while he is still in the office is inevitably incomplete, but certain observations can be made. First, it can safely be said that over the past quarter-century no one has had more influence on the shape of the faculty and administration of Austin Seminary than Bob Shelton. Andy Dearman's observation was accurate: The combination of longevity and personal persuasiveness ensures that Shelton's legacy will have a lasting impact on the life of Austin Seminary.

Second, Shelton's presence and leadership since 1971 have provided a sense of continuity in the midst of changes which inevitably have an impact on any institution. With the exceptions of Prescott Williams and George Heyer, no other person currently associated with the seminary has maintained a longer, more active relationship with Austin Seminary than Bob Shelton. His presence over that time period represents a stability that has been healthy for the seminary.

Third, his gifts as teacher, colleague, and administrator have contributed to a sense of confidence among students, faculty, board members, and the broader constituency of the seminary. Not only does Shelton embody the recent history of Austin Seminary, but his ability to put others at ease cultivates the sense of community that has characterized Austin Seminary throughout its history. Over the years, he has been an effective spokesperson and a strong advocate for the seminary.

Fourth, although he was elected president "for a term" and expects to retire at the end of the seminary's centennial year in 2002, his presidency has not been a caretaker one. He has been aggressive in recruiting faculty to meet the needs of a growing student body; in expanding an administration that can be more effective as it seeks to be a nationally recognized theological school; in raising funds for a capital campaign that will meet the physical as well as the educational needs of the seminary in the twenty-first century. In the seminary's longstanding desire to cultivate a relationship with the Hispanic community, Shelton's leadership in AETH has brought a visible presence of Hispanic ministry to the campus.

Several persons have offered their evaluations of Shelton's presidency. Pete Hendrick points to the master plan for the twenty-first century adopted by the Board of Trustees, the reorganization of the seminary administration, the empowerment of the Board of Trustees, the increased efforts to develop an emphasis on Hispanic ministry, and the establishment of two endowed faculty chairs as significant milestones during Shelton's six years as president.[39]

Board member Bessie Lou Doelling writes the following about Shelton's tenure:

> Bob is a dreamer and also a "doer." He dreams of the things that are good for the Seminary and then gets busy with the right people to put these dreams into effect. He has my highest regards as a person and as a leader. It has been one of the most inspiring and emotional experiences of my life to serve as a Trustee of the Seminary under Bob Shelton. . . .[40]

Jed Shaw, member of the Board of Trustees from 1990 to 1999 and chairman from 1995 to 1999, was an attorney from Houston and moved to New Mexico in 2001. He writes of his surprise at Shelton's emergence as a potential candidate for consideration as president during the search process following Jack Stotts' retirement:

> As dean, Bob had the character traits and actions of a loyal, supportive second-in-command. . . . I witnessed Bob's year as interim president, slowly integrating into the job, not pushing the envelope nor upsetting the apple cart, more or less passive in nature, much like his job in supporting Jack Stotts.
>
> Along about mid-year, Bob slowly introduced "his plan" and "his vision." I watched in mild amazement the transformation of

this wonderful man into "His job." I was fortunate to be able to spend time and be closely related with Bob during this time. Not only did Bob impress me, but the Presidential Search Committee, under the able leadership of Louis Zbinden, had its eyes opened.

With little reservation, the Search Committee unanimously approved Bob as the person to lead us to the next level. For the next two years as chair, I found myself "hanging on" to the train that Bob was engineering. In addition to his wide range of ideas and inspiration to the faculty and staff, I was especially impressed with the energy of the President's office. ...

As I reflect over the last six years, one year as interim president and five years as president, I feel blessed to have witnessed the dedication and development of a man I call a good friend.[41]

Jerry Tompkins, a historian in his own right and former vice president of Austin Seminary, offers an appreciation for the Cumberland heritage that Shelton brought both to Austin Seminary and to the presidency:

Bob Shelton is—always was—a Cumberland Presbyterian, and wherever I have heard him speak, preach or just converse, I've heard the faint chorus of that heritage in the background. Those voices are in his blood, and they are there to stay.

The Cumberlanders had been the ecclesiastical leading edge of America's westward migration for a hundred years, arriving before the Methodists and Baptists and certainly before any other Presbyterians. These sturdy Presbyterians valued, above all else, Biblical preaching tied securely to evangelistic fervor.

Then came troubled times in 1906, when two-thirds of them merged with what had become the Presbyterian Church in the United States of America. There followed years of litigation over church property and institutions, in which the Cumberland Church usually lost. The prize lost in Texas was Trinity University.

The continuing church held fast to its heritage of Biblical preaching and evangelism, and that heritage predestined—or at least predisposed—Robert Shelton to homiletics by the time he entered the Cumberland seminary at McKenzie, Tennessee. But the inheritance proved not to be a boundary for Shelton: his doctoral dissertation at Princeton Theological Seminary, where he went for graduate work in 1958, was about Harry Emerson Fosdick, the nation's premier popular, modernist, urbane preacher from 1920 to 1945, and who was also a pioneer in radio preaching. ...

Cumberlanders are a gentle but stubborn lot. They are somehow equipped for long journeys, which is what Shelton has taken at Austin Seminary. He has been around since 1971—more than 31 years. He is the eighth president in the Seminary's 100-year history, yet he was hired by the fourth president, David Stitt.

Shelton has given every president he has served under the opportunity to request he leave the Cumberland Church for the Presbyterian Church (U.S.A.) or one of its predecessors. None ever suggested he leave his church. So Shelton has continued the Cumberlander that he is to the core, attending presbytery meetings, serving on Cumberland church committees at every level, serving a year as the Cumberland General Assembly's moderator, even once considering—years ago—the opportunity to become president of the Cumberland seminary, now moved from McKenzie to Memphis.

In his youth, Shelton excelled in various athletic endeavors and is honored at his alma mater in Maryville College's Hall of Fame. He is capable of raucous laughter but there is a pervasive melancholia about the man. Across the years, most of us who know him have observed the wrenching events in his life which account for this fact.

Yet somehow he makes even his sometime somber introversion work for him. One Sunday several years ago, I sat in a pew of a church where Shelton was the preacher of the day. As the notes of the prelude died away, Shelton ambled forward—he does not make a regal entrance—to the center of the chancel, and stood there silently for several seconds, his hands clasped behind him. He began quietly to recite the call to worship. A hush spread over the sanctuary. It was evident that he had memorized what turned out to be a rather long call, and yet he made frequent eye contact around the sanctuary as he spoke. I remember feeling that he had not just memorized the verses, but had inwardly digested them, and what came forth was from deep within him. It was one of those timeless moments which I will remember.

I am not nominating Shelton for sainthood. We are good friends but not close friends, and therefore I make no claim to knowing his heart. But there is something about him which often demonstrates those old Cumberland qualities: simplicity, endurance, quiet confidence in matters of consequence, and a strong belief in the power of words in the service of Christ's church.

Shelton's pervasive presence and achievements at Austin Seminary for almost a third of a century are not likely a surprise to Cumberlanders.[42]

In short, in seeking what he believes to be the best for Austin Seminary, Shelton labored tirelessly. This is perhaps best reflected in the celebration of the seminary's Centennial in 2002, which he envisioned and over which he presided. More than a celebration of an institution's hundredth anniversary, it was a celebration of the life of a community of the Word that is devoted to preparing men and women to proclaim that Word to a world desperately needing to hear it.

Alan E. Lewis, professor of constructive and modern theology, 1987–94.

Edward D. Vickery, chairman, Board of Trustees, 1983–85; 1989–94.

Jack L. Stotts, president, 1985–96.

Rev. Jerold D. Shetler, chairman, Board of Trustees, 1985–89.

Robert M. Shelton, president, 1997–2002.

Jo E. "Jed" Shaw, Jr., chairman, Board of Trustees, 1994–99.

C. Ellis Nelson, acting president, 1984–85; research professor of Christian education, 1987–present.

Genevieve "Gene" Luna, assistant librarian, 1968–2000.

Jean Brown

John F. Jansen, professor of New Testament interpretation, 1958–83.

Atrium of the McCord Community Center.

*President Stotts, Board Chairman Jed Shaw, Professor George Heyer, and In-
augural Heyer Lecturer Robert Berdahl, president of the University of Texas
at Austin.*

George S. Heyer, Jr., professor of the history of doctrine, 1964–94.

Clarence N. Frierson, chairman, Board of Trustees, 1978–83.

Jack Hodges, superintendent of buildings and grounds, 1955–94.

Jimmie Clark, secretary, 1958–89.

Fern Chester

Catherine Sautter, registrar, 1958–89.

Rev. Louis H. Zbinden, Jr., chairman, Board of Trustees, 1999–2002.

CHAPTER SIX

Lectures

As a school of the church, a seminary belongs both to the academic world and the world of the church. Its faculty has a responsibility to prepare students for the pastoral ministry. It also has a responsibility to the academy, that is, for research and publishing. It has a responsibility to set the example for the church of the cultivation of the mind in the service of Jesus Christ, to provide opportunities for the larger church to learn and grow in the faith, to provide opportunities for the church to engage in the activity of faith seeking understanding.

While the faculty has always sought to publish both articles and books, in the past twenty-five years there has been a heightened emphasis on doing so, both as a responsibility to the academy and a service to the church. Virtually in every field represented by Austin Seminary faculty, impressive publications have been produced.

The seminary faculty has sought to live as a school of the church over the years in a variety of other ways as well: through continuing education opportunities for clergy and layfolk; by providing classes that will enable Christian educators to become certified by the denomination; by individual involvement in the life of congregations throughout Austin and around the synod.

But one of the ways in which these two worlds have coincided over the years at Austin Seminary has been through public lectures, some of which have been endowed. Such lectureships provide occasions for the seminary to bring scholars and churchmen of note to the campus. This has the twofold benefit of providing a public and ecclesiastical forum before which the scholars may present their recent theological work, and an opportunity for the larger church and the public to be exposed to the academic life of the church. Bringing outstanding scholars to the campus can have the added benefit of enhancing the stature of the seminary. And, in some cases, some very significant contributions have been made both to the church and to scholarship as a result of these lectureships.

The Mid-Winter Lectures, usually held the week following the last Sunday in January, have over the years produced some important contributions which transcend denominational ties. According to one source,

> In 1945 the Alumni Association and Board of Trustees of Austin Presbyterian Theological Seminary established a lectureship, bringing distinguished scholars to address an annual mid-winter convocation of ministers and students on various phases of Christian thought.
>
> Since that time the Seminary has had the privilege of presenting to its students and alumni at these convocations the reflections of leading Christian thinkers on important issues and, in part, of stimulating the publication of these reflections for the benefit of a wider audience.[1]

In 1945 Homer Price Rainey, president of the University of Texas at Austin, delivered a series of lectures on "Spiritual Foundations of Democracy." Also delivering lectures that year were Ernest Trice Thompson of Union Seminary in Richmond ("Christianity and World Order") and Gonzalo Baez-Camargo of Mexico City. Those early years saw such eminent scholars come to Austin Seminary as Josef Hromadka, a guest professor at Princeton Seminary from Czechoslovakia (1946), Paul Scherer of Union Seminary in New York (1947), D. Elton Trueblood of Earlham College (1948), and H. Richard Niebuhr of Yale Divinity School (1949). Niebuhr's lecture series, "Christ and Culture," was published in 1951 by

Harper and Row under the same title. Former president Jack Stotts identifies that project as a "kind of crown on the series in terms of impact and enduring importance."[2]

In 1949 two Mid-Winter lectureships were endowed. The E. C. Westervelt lecture series was established by Mr. and Mrs. Edwin Flato of Corpus Christi to honor her parents; the Robert F. Jones Lectures in Christian Education were established by the Women of the Church of the First Presbyterian Church in Fort Worth. Jones served as pastor of that congregation from 1944 to 1978.

A third Mid-Winter lecture series was established in 1952 by the Tom Currie Bible Class of Highland Park Presbyterian Church in Dallas. The endowment honored the third president of Austin Seminary, who also served as stated supply of the Highland Park Church from December 1932 through the summer of 1937. While the Jones Lectures are concentrated on some aspect of Christian education, the Currie Lectures may cover theology, church history, biblical studies, or ethics. The emphasis of the Westervelt Lectures has been on preaching, pastoral care, biblical studies, ethics, or some other aspect of the church's ministry. The variety of subjects and speakers have contributed to this annual intellectual and spiritual feast that has become known as the Mid-Winter Lectures.

In 1963, for example, over the course of three days one heard Krister Stendahl of the Harvard Divinity School lecture on "Paul among the Jews and Gentiles" (later published under the same title), Carlyle Marney, pastor of Myers Park Baptist Church in Charlotte, North Carolina, address the theme "The Tragic Sense of Hope," and Orval Mowrer of the University of Illinois speak on "Religious Faith and the Counseling Arts."

The following year brought James Barr of Princeton Theological Seminary ("The Old and the New in Interpretation"), Rachel Henderlite, director of curriculum development of the Presbyterian Church in the United States ("The Holy Spirit and Christian Education"), and Roland Mushat Frye of the Folger Shakespeare Library in Washington, D.C. ("MacBeth: Mirror of the Disintegration of Modern Man") to the Austin Seminary campus.

The past twenty-five years have seen prominent scholars in the field of Christian education deliver the Jones Lectures: Sara Little (1975), John Westerhoff III (1976), Maria Harris (1982), Dorothy Jean Furnish (1983), James W. Fowler (1985), Craig Dykstra

(1986), Richard Osmer (1996), and Dorothy C. Bass (2001). In 1998 Katherine Paterson, winner of the Newbery Medal and National Book Awards for Children's Literature, spoke as the Jones lecturer on "From Story to Stories," which encompassed stories that shape our faith, the image of God in human creativity, and reclaiming the nature of wonder.

Some of those who have delivered the Jones Lectures have also had ties to the seminary. For example, after she delivered the Jones Lectures in 1964, Rachel Henderlite returned to Austin Seminary in 1965 to serve on the faculty. David Ng, a professor in Christian education at the seminary from 1975 to 1981, was the Jones lecturer in 1991. C. Ellis Nelson holds the distinction of being the only person to be invited to deliver a series of lectures during the Mid-Winter Lectures on three different occasions. On all three occasions he was the Jones lecturer. In 1959 his topic was "Communication of the Biblical Faith"; in 1978 it was "Don't Let Your Conscience Be Your Guide"; and in 2000 he spoke on "Childish Religion: What You Should Do About It."

Regarding the Jones Lectures, President Shelton avers that the "names of the lecturers read like a 'who's who' in the field of Christian Education during the last half of the 20th century. . . . The many publications by these authors have given direction to the field of Christian Education in the mainline denominations."[3]

The Currie lecture series brought to the campus such prominent scholars as John Mackay, president of Princeton Theological Seminary (1952), George Hendry, professor of theology at Princeton Seminary (1955), James Muilenburg, professor of Hebrew and the cognate languages at Union Seminary in New York (1956), John Dillenberger of Harvard Divinity School (1959), James Hastings Nichols of the Chicago Divinity School (1960), Paul Lehmann of Harvard University (1961), Dietrich Ritschl, who at the time was teaching the history of doctrine at Pittsburgh Theological Seminary (1965), and Robert McAfee Brown of Stanford University (1966).

Among some of the more distinguished Currie lecturers in the past quarter-century have been Jim Gustafson in the field of Christian ethics (1975); church historians Martin Marty (1977), Sydney Ahlstrom (1979), and George Marsden (1999); biblical scholars Eduard Schweizer (1980), Paul Hanson (1981), Walter Brueggeman (1983), Elaine Pagels (1994), and Patrick Miller (1998); and theologians Shirley Guthrie (1985), John Leith (1986), George Lindbeck (1988), Brian Gerrish (1992), and Robert Jensen (2001).

Two sons of the Austin Seminary president for whom the Currie Lectures were named delivered those lectures: Stuart D. Currie, professor of New Testament languages and exegesis at Austin Seminary, in 1973; and Thomas W. Currie, Jr., church historian and pastor of Oak Cliff Presbyterian Church, Dallas, in 1978.

Among the distinguished deliverers of the Westervelt Lectures have been Wallace Alston, president of Agnes Scott College, who spoke on "The Cross in the Straits of the Soul" (1949), William Elliott, Jr., pastor of Highland Park Presbyterian Church in Dallas, whose series bore the title "Called to Preach" (1954), Frank Caldwell, president of Louisville Theological Seminary, whose lectures were entitled "Preaching the Seasonal Word" (1957), David H. C. Read, pastor of Madison Avenue Presbyterian Church in New York City, who spoke on "In Quest of Particularity" (1962), and Hendrikus Berkhof, professor at the University of Leiden in the Netherlands, whose addresses focused on "Present-Day Problems of Eschatology" (1967).

In the past twenty-five years, other distinguished Westervelt lecturers have included Jack Rogers (1977), who at the time was professor of theology at Fuller Theological Seminary and would be elected moderator of the General Assembly of the Presbyterian Church (U.S.A.) in 2001; the German theologian Helmut Thielicke (1978); Browne Barr, dean of San Francisco Theological Seminary (1982); Fred Craddock, professor of preaching at the Candler School of Theology in Atlanta, Georgia (1983); Jurgen Roloff, professor of New Testament in Erlangen, Germany (1987); Peter Gomes, chaplain at Harvard University (1989); William Willimon, professor and dean of the Duke University Chapel (1991); Eugene Peterson, pastor for twenty-nine years of Christ the King Presbyterian Church in Bel Air, Maryland, and professor at Regent College in Vancouver, British Columbia (1992); James Forbes, pastor of the Riverside Church in New York City (1994); Ellen Charry, professor of theology at Princeton Theological Seminary (1998); and Ralph Wood, university professor of theology and literature at Baylor University (2000).

One of Austin Seminary's own graduates (1951) and former

professor of Old Testament, James Wharton, delivered the Westervelt Lectures in 1999.

In addition to the wealth of scholarly research that is shared, the Mid-Winter Lectures provide an opportunity for reunion of seminary alumni and fellowship among supporters of the seminary. Normally opening with worship on Monday night, the opening lecture is held in the sanctuary of University Presbyterian Church. All other lectures are held in the Seminary Chapel. Former president Stotts observed:

> I think they have been very important to Austin Seminary and the broader community over the years. There have, of course, been some lectures more important than others. ... I believe that one gift of the lectures has been to stimulate younger scholars to get on paper what they are thinking. The PR was very good as both alums and others came together. Sometimes the fellowship among the alums was the most important thing that happened.[4]

In reflecting on the Mid-Winter Lectures, President Shelton wrote:

> I know of no other seminary which can claim such an academic feast for its alums, its faculty, its students and its larger constituencies. In my opinion the establishment of these lectures was critical for moving the seminary from a little-known, provincial school to one which was recognzed beyond a four-state region, as well as a seminary which thought of itself as no longer narrow and provincial. The lectures and lecturers brought new and challenging ideas to the campus and enriched greatly the educational environment of the school.[5]

Thomas White Currie, Jr., offered the following thoughts on the significance of the annual mid-winter gathering in Austin to hear a variety of scholars:

> Roland Mushat Frye delivered the Westervelt Lectures in 1964. They concerned Shakespeare's *Macbeth.* He had annotated copies available for a nominal cost. He led us from the witches' brew to Duncan's death. We saw Banquo's ghost. Like with a tarbaby, each

effort of Macbeth to extricate himself from his fate fastened him more securely. Until, "by the grace of Grace" Malcolm was crowned at Scone. We saw ambition descend into depravity. We saw evil its own destruction.

A voice from afar may bring a fresh note. As I recall, Ellis Nelson helped initiate the Mid-Winter Lectures. One of the first was Gonzalo Baez-Camargo from Mexico [1945]. The idea of bringing a person from an Hispanic culture was new to me. There was T. Watson Street on the world mission of the church. I remember George Arthur Buttrick and Thomas G. Long on preaching and Shirley C. Guthrie on theology. Who can forget James Wharton on Old Testament or Helmut Thielicke on the bombs over Germany?

To name a few is to omit the many. These men and women have opened windows into vistas, uncovered treasures, lit searchlights. One of the delightful accompanying results is the fellowship among the alumni/ae and the scholarly books that have come forth.[6]

Another series of lectures was established in 1947 when "Mrs. W. R. Settles of Big Spring, Texas, in 1947 pledged $10,000 to establish this series to be offered each January. The subject of the Settles Lectures would alternate year to year between missions abroad and missions at home."[7] The first Settles lecturer was James Finley Hardie, pastor of the Broadway Presbyterian Church in Fort Worth, who spoke in 1949 on "The Christian Message in the Modern World." The following year brought to the campus the eminent church historian Kenneth Scott Latourette of the Yale Divinity School, whose address was "The Expanding Church in an Age of Storm."

T. Watson Street, who had taught at Austin Seminary (1947–61) and then became the executive secretary of the Board of World Missions for the Presbyterian Church, U.S., returned to the campus in 1963 to deliver the Settles Lectures on "Missions in the New Era." John Knox Press published those lectures in 1965 under the title *On the Growing Edge of the Church*. Street returned in 1974 to deliver the Settles Lectures yet again.

In 1973 John R. "Pete" Hendrick, Austin Seminary graduate and a once and future faculty member, delivered these lectures. In 1977

John Knox Press published these lectures under the title *Opening the Door of Faith: The Why, When and Where of Evangelism.*

Others who have delivered these lectures over the past quarter-century include the liberation theologian Gustavo Gutierrez (1983), Samuel Moffett of Princeton Seminary (1985), Bishop Mortimer Arias, president of the Seminario Biblico Latinoamericano in San Jose, Costa Rica (1986), Gayraud S. Wilmore of New York Theological Seminary (1987), James H. Cone of Union Seminary in New York (1988), James H. Costen, president of the Interdenominational Theological Center in Atlanta, Georgia (1989), Sang Hyun Lee of Princeton Seminary (1991), Austin Seminary graduate Jorge Lara-Braud (1992), and Mukome L. Tshihamba of Zaire (1994).

George Heyer retired as professor of Christian doctrine in December 1993. He had taught at the seminary since 1964. In May 1995, the Board of Trustees established the George S. Heyer, Jr., Distinguished Lectureship. Its purpose was to be:

1. To honor George S. Heyer, Jr., for his thirty years as a valued member of the Austin Seminary faculty.
2. To reflect the values of academic excellence and vigor associated with Professor Heyer.
3. To symbolize and advance the important relationship between the academy and the church.
4. To represent the strength of the resources of the University of Texas at Austin for Austin Seminary's program.
5. To recall the long-lasting cooperation between the university and the seminary.
6. To encourage the positive relationship between faith and knowledge.[8]

The first Heyer lecture took place in 1996. Because this lectureship was intended to emphasize the relationship between the seminary and the University of Texas, it was appropriate that the first lecturer be the president of the university, Robert Berdahl. In 1997 Robert H. Abzug, professor of history and American studies and director of the American Studies program at the University of Texas, delivered this lecture. The 1998 Heyer lecturer was Douglas Laycock, professor at the University of Texas law school. In 1999 the new president of the University of Texas and member of

Covenant Presbyterian Church, Larry R. Faulkner, crossed the street to deliver the Heyer Lecture. An astronomer, William H. Jefferys III, was invited to be the George Heyer lecturer in 2001. Another member of the university's astronomy department and director of the MacDonald Observatory in the Davis Mountains, Frank Bush, was invited to deliver the Heyer Lectures in April 2002.

In addition to all these lectureships, the Hoxie Thompson Lectures have enabled various scholars to come to campus from time to time over the course of the academic year to deliver a lecture on a particular topic of interest. These lectures "were begun in 1961 by the late Hoxie H. Thompson of Trinity, Texas. Gifts from his family and friends augmented the original donation."[9]

As a school of the church, the seminary has a responsibility to both the academy and the church. This is reflected not only in the classroom, but it is made most visible when alumni/ae, pastors, church members, and members of the community come together with members of the seminary community to hear scholars address matters that are of interest to both communities. All of the endowed lecture series provide stimulating opportunities to cultivate a sense of community beyond the campus, but the Mid-Winter Lectures have been the occasion for the seminary community to be expressed most visibly.

CHAPTER SEVEN

The Seminary
Beyond the Seminary

In addition to publications and involvement in the life of the church, the seminary administration and faculty faced in the 1980s a new challenge and opportunity that took them beyond the Austin campus. One of the growing phenomena in theological education was older students, that is, students who responded to a call to enter the ministry and attend seminary, having already spent several years in another field of work. These "second career" students often had families and financial liabilities.

Another growing phenomenon was an interest among Christian educators in taking courses that would enable them to become certified with the Presbyterian denomination. Thirdly, there seemed to be an increased desire among many laypersons in taking seminary courses simply to continue their own growth and education.

In an attempt to address these needs, various seminaries began to establish satellite programs that would enable interested persons to take courses without having to move immediately to the main campus. Fuller Seminary, for example, located in Pasadena, California, established a satellite campus in Seattle. Other satellite campuses followed.

Houston Extension Program

In the spring of 1983, representatives of New Covenant Presbytery, located in Houston and the surrounding area in southeast Texas, approached Austin Seminary about the possibility of offering extension courses in Houston. The Rev. Robert H. Fernandez, associate executive of New Covenant Presbytery, invited Academic Dean Robert Shelton to Houston to discuss with him and representatives of the Adult Education Committee what might be possible.

In a report on the subject, Shelton wrote:

> In August 1983, Jack Maxwell and I drove to Houston and visited with Bob Fernandez and David Stitt, who had previously expressed the view that Austin Seminary should consider offering courses in Houston. During the visit that day considerable interest and enthusiasm were expressed on the part of both Stitt and Fernandez.
>
> Different approaches were discussed. Fernandez stated he had also invited PSCE [Presbyterian School of Christian Education] to send representatives to explore their offering courses. We explored the possibility of working with PSCE. We also discussed location and schedule. Bob Fernandez said we could use the Presbytery office at 41 Oakdale. We also talked about First Presbyterian Church just across the street.
>
> At the close of the meeting it was decided that Bob Fernandez would make a survey in Houston under the auspices of the New Covenant Adult Education Committee to determine if there were sufficient interest to warrant offering courses.
>
> Jack and I contacted Marvin Taylor [representative of ATS, the Association of Theological Schools, the body that grants accreditation to theological schools] before we went to Houston and after. Marvin told us that Southwestern Baptist Seminary in Fort Worth presently conducts a full M.Div. degree program in Houston which had been sanctioned by ATS. This meant, among other things, that the availability of adequate library facilities had been

confirmed. Marvin suggested that we establish a minimum number of students necessary for us to offer a course, announce a course or two and see what happens.[1]

In an undated memo to himself regarding "Theological Education by Extension," President Maxwell wrote the following:

> I talked with Marvin Taylor on August 16 concerning the possibility of a satellite program in Houston, particularly with respect to the amount of an M.Div. degree which could be offered by extension. He says that it is theoretically possible to offer the entire program by extension, noting the standard which reads: "A significant portion of an extension degree program must be taken on campus or in classes taught by regular faculty." He says that there will be proposal to the next biennial meeting of ATS which, if adopted, would require at least one-half of the program to be taken at the parent school or at a satellite which is identical in every respect to the parent institution. Of course, he does not know whether this will pass.

Maxwell included further details of his conversation with Taylor:

> He told me that Southwestern Baptist Seminary [in Fort Worth] presently conducts a full M.Div. Degree program in Houston. The arrangement is that regular faculty commute there on Mondays. That program has been sanctioned by ATS, which means also that the availability of adequate facilities has been confirmed.
> In addition to the obvious questions—facilities, market, library, etc.—he suggested that we need to explore the willingness of our faculty to be involved over a long period of time.[2]

After receiving encouragement from the Board of Trustees at their meeting in May 1984, Shelton met again with Fernandez and other representatives of New Covenant Presbytery on February 28, 1985. Enthusiasm for a presence in Houston by Austin Seminary had not abated. It was hoped that courses could begin as early as the fall of 1985.

Out of these conversations came the following recommendations from Dean Shelton in May 1985:

(1) THAT Austin Seminary commit itself to offering one course in Houston each Spring Term and Fall Term for a period of two years, beginning with the 1986 Spring Term.

(2) THAT after two years the program be evaluated by a committee of Teaching Faculty and the Administrative Staff.

(3) THAT the four courses taught during this two-year period be as follows:

Spring 1986: *Reformed Theology*
Fall 1986: *Interpretation of Scripture*
Spring 1987: *Presbyterian Polity*
Fall 1987: *Methods of Teaching in the Church*

(4) THAT a Director for the program be employed for one year to begin work June 1, 1985.

(5) THAT the Director be paid a stipend of $1,500 for the year, and that $500 be allocated for the Director's secretary help and supplies.

(6) THAT $500 be budgeted for advertising the course offerings the first year.

(7) THAT the above funds be taken from Educational Miscellaneous in the Seminary's operating budget.

(8) THAT the courses be taught in the First Presbyterian Church of Houston if possible; if not, that they be taught at the Office of New Covenant Presbytery.[3]

Dean Shelton also proposed certain guidelines for the program, among which were: persons taking Houston extension courses would be registered as "special students"; the courses taught by extension would be of the same quality as those taught on campus; satisfactory completion of extension courses could apply toward an M.Div. degree at Austin Seminary; approximately 75 percent of the extension courses would be taught by resident faculty of Austin Seminary, the other courses being taught by adjunct faculty; courses would be taught one day per week.[4]

In the spring of 1986, Dr. John F. Jansen taught the first Austin Seminary course in Houston. It was TH.212, a course in Reformed theology. The following fall, Dr. Lewis Donelson taught a course in the interpretation of scripture. "Church Polity and Administration" was taught jointly by Dr. Cynthia Campbell (polity) and Dr. William C. Poe (administration) in the spring of 1987. Poe, pastor of Braeburn Presbyterian Church in Houston, was also the first director of the extension program. The Rev. Laura Lewis taught "Methods of Teaching in the Church" in Houston in the fall of 1987, concluding the two-year trial period.

After the spring of 1988, when Dr. Andrew Dearman taught "The Interpretation of the Psalms," the seminary began offering two courses each semester. The two-course-per-semester pattern continued through the fall of 1997. Most courses were first- or second-year courses, maintaining a balance between required courses and electives. In the spring of 1998, "Elementary New Testament Greek" was offered for the first time in Houston. In addition, "Introduction to Pastoral Care" (Dr. Ralph Underwood) and "The Church as a Worshiping Community" (Dr. Stan Hall) were also offered. The Greek course was taught by Dr. John Baker, an Austin Seminary graduate and a Houston resident with a Ph.D. in linguistics from Rice University and extensive graduate work in ancient and Near Eastern languages.

In the fall of 1998, four courses were offered for the first time: "Selected Readings in Hellenistic Greek" (Dr. Baker), "The Government of the Church" (Rev. Clark Chamberlain), "Introduction to Christian Ethics" (Dr. Ismael Garcia), and "Religious Pluralism and the Christian Faith" (Dr. Terry Muck). Also for the first time, classes were not held at First Presbyterian Church in Houston, due to renovation of existing buildings and construction of new buildings. Two classes were held at Memorial Drive Presbyterian Church, and two were held at Grace Presbyterian Church.

One ongoing issue for the Houston Extension Program, in general, has been the lack of access to adequate theological library facilities. St. Mary's School of Theology, a part of the University of St. Thomas, extended borrowing privileges to those persons enrolled in the program. But in order to broaden access to other library facilities in the Houston area, in 1998 Dean Andy Dearman successfully negotiated agreements with Rice University and Houston Baptist University that allowed Austin Seminary students to have borrowing privileges there as well.

In the spring of 1999, Austin Seminary and the Houston Extension Program participated in a new technological experiment, namely, distance learning. With two-way audio and two-way video capabilities in both Austin and Houston, Dr. Andy Dearman stayed in Austin and taught some of his Houston classes "live" by way of this technology. That same semester, Dr. James Currie taught a church history class from Houston, with students in both locations. While the system has not been without its shortcomings, it will, in all likelihood, be one that will continue to develop and be used.

Over its lifetime, the Houston Extension Program has seen four directors. They have included Dr. William Poe (1986–88), Rev. William Proctor (1988–91), Rev. G. R. M. (Bob) Montgomery, Jr. (1991–96), and Dr. James S. Currie (1996–present). While serving as director, each has also served as pastor of a congregation. The task of the director has been to work with the academic dean of Austin Seminary, to administer and promote the program in the Houston area, to advise students regarding courses, and to serve as liaison between the Houston students and the seminary administration.

Sun City and West Texas

During the 1980s, two other extension programs were also developed by Austin Seminary. According to a proposal by Jack Stotts to the Executive Committee of the Board of Trustees in February 1989,

> In November 1984 Austin Seminary received a proposal from Faith Presbyterian Church, Sun City, Arizona, outlining a variety of ways that congregation was prepared to provide learning opportunities in the area of ministry with older adults for seminary students, seminary professors and pastors. The proposal was made because of the conviction of the pastors and the session that Faith Church is especially, if not uniquely, constituted to provide such opportunities.[5]

Because of the size and age of the congregation (more than 2,000 members, the majority of whom were over sixty years, with many in their seventies and eighties), and because this represented the fastest-growing group of citizens in the United States, and be-

cause there seemed to be a growing "need for ministerial compe-
tence in the area of ministry with older adults," this kind of setting
seemed to be ideal for a relationship with a theological institution.

In contrast to the Houston Extension Program, in which students in Houston would take courses in Houston with the view of
eventually moving to Austin to complete a degree, Faith Presbyterian Church would be the setting for theological education during
January for those students already enrolled at the Austin campus,
whether in the M.Div. or the D.Min. program. The Rev. Francis
Park, pastor of Faith Church, would direct the program.

The Board of Trustees approved the proposal, and the program
began in January 1990. Park, who graduated from the College of
Wooster and Pittsburgh Theological Seminary, served churches in
Ohio and New York before moving to Arizona in 1984. He also
served on the church's Vocation Agency for nine years and the
General Assembly Mission Council for eight years. He reflects on
how the seed for the extension program germinated and eventually
took root:

> When I arrived to become pastor of Faith Church on Jan. 1,
> 1984, it was very apparent that there was no current preparation
> for ministers in regard to ministry with older adults. Thus, late
> that year, I asked Session if they would be willing to engage in a
> program that would bring in students/ministers to experience
> what life in a retirement community was like. We could use our-
> selves as a laboratory and share what we had learned with others.
> They responded very willingly. Sun City is a unique community
> in all the world and Faith Church is a key leadership element in
> the community. ...
>
> At about that time the first Clerk of Session of Faith Church
> died and left about $50,000 to the church for the on site training
> of seminary students at Faith. She was a Godsend. As a result the
> program has had minimal impact on the budget and now is a
> flourishing self-sustaining program. ...
>
> At some point, Bob Shelton as Dean took the program before
> the Faculty and Board and received approval for accreditation.
> Then he proposed a common program with all our seminaries to
> receive credit by working through Austin's Jan Term program.
>
> All told there have been about 175 students to benefit from the

program and it is still an active program of both the Austin Seminary and the Faith congregation.

As Dean, Bob was an ardent supporter of the program, participating in many ways and traveling to Sun City frequently to oversee developments. As President, Bob has not had the time to be as personally involved but he certainly has made it known that from his perspective the ACT [Aging Creatively Today] program is significantly beneficial. There just aren't enough students or pastors taking advantage of the opportunity that is presented.[6]

Park goes on to point to the benefit, both to the church and to the retirees, of taking advantage of the gifts and abilities of older adults:

We tried to identify that the aging process is a very upbeat, positive and creative experience. It vitalizes and enables people to be enthusiastic about life and daily living. My analysis is that if people say that someone is older, retired, and over the hill then they are committing homicide. But if an older, retired person says "let the younger people do it—I've done that before," then they are committing suicide. We need to help the Church see that we can turn the Church around simply by using our older adults who have the time, treasure, and talent to make it happen. We also need to let the world know that retirees have the skill and experience to make available to every conceivable cause and concern and make a difference.[7]

The program continues under the leadership of Jerald B. Landrey, Faith Church's current pastor.

At about the same time the Sun City program was beginning, inquiries were arriving at the seminary from persons in West Texas regarding the possibility of courses being offered in the Midland-Odessa area. In March of 1988, the Rev. Al Moreau, pastor of Trinity Presbyterian Church in Midland, submitted the draft of a proposal to Dean Shelton. According to this proposal, interest in such a program reflected two perceived needs:

1. These persons wish to secure a seminary degree, but because of family and job commitments cannot at this time in their lives leave home for extended periods of time to be resident in Austin.

2. The other persons wish to upgrade their skills academically in Christian Education and Presbyterian theology and Presbyterianism in general.

These are primarily married women, college graduates, with children at home who are now working in their churches in nurture roles and who see in the future a call to be more involved and professionally trained in local church Christian Education.[8]

Classes would meet at First Presbyterian Church in Odessa and Trinity Presbyterian Church in Midland. The design of the program was similar to that being used in the Houston Extension Program. A combination of seminary faculty and adjunct faculty taught the courses, beginning in the summer of 1989, when Alan Lewis taught Reformed theology. They continued through the spring of 1994, the last course being "Theology in the Modern World" and taught by Thomas W. Currie III, pastor of First Presbyterian Church in Kerrville.[9] The program was discontinued in 1994 because the number of students taking courses for credit had dropped to four and no other prospective students could be identified.[10]

Al Moreau recalls:

> The impetus for the West Texas Extension of Austin Seminary was the fact that there were several adults interested in taking seminary courses, but who could not at that point in their lives pick up and move to Austin. In fact, one of them ... was flying to Austin each week for classes. ... We offered one course during each school semester and one intensive course in the summer. At least 5 of the students eventually enrolled at Austin full time and graduated and have since been ordained.[11]

San Antonio

Almost since its beginning, Austin Seminary has tried to address the issue of ministry to, with, and among the Spanish-speaking population, especially in Texas. In 1921 the Rev. Antonio Horatio Perpetuo, a native of Brazil and a graduate of the College of Wooster (1909) and Princeton Theological Seminary (1912), came to Austin Seminary to teach Hebrew. He also was "responsible for preparation offered for the Spanish-speaking candidates. Mr. Perpetuo left the Seminary after two years."[12]

The program that was begun by Perpetuo continued, primarily through the efforts of Dr. Robert Gribble, professor of Old Testament languages and exegesis. In the 1930s and 1940s, Dr. O. C. Williamson and Dr. R. D. Campbell also taught in this department. When the presbytery that consisted of Spanish-speaking churches was dissolved in the early 1950s, the seminary's Spanish department was also discontinued. In the mid-1960s, a new effort was made to connect with the Hispanic community. An ecumenical agency, the Hispanic-American Institute, was formed and housed at the seminary campus. Jorge Lara-Braud, an Austin Seminary graduate, was the director. It "lasted until the mid-seventies, when each ecclesiastical group went its separate way."[13]

President Jack Stotts saw theological education among the Hispanic community as an ongoing, unmet need—and an opportunity. In March 1995, a group of Presbyterians interested in establishing an extension program in San Antonio met there to discuss the feasibility of such a program. After a couple of more meetings, Stotts began exploring the possibility of making this effort an ecumenical one. To that end, a meeting was hosted by Austin Seminary that included representatives from Perkins School of Theology in Dallas, the Oblate School of Theology in San Antonio, the Episcopal Seminary of the Southwest in Austin, the Lutheran Seminary Program at Austin Seminary, and Austin Seminary. Several different possible directions for the projects were discussed, including having as one of its major emphases the recruitment of Hispanics to the ministry. A possible joint relationship with Trinity University was also discussed.[14]

In September, another meeting was held, at Northwood Presbyterian Church in San Antonio. Those present were Angela Abrego (director of Hispanic ministries of the Synod of the Sun), Andy Anzaldua (member of the synod's Hispanic-American Ministries Council), Frank Seaman (pastor of Northwood Presbyterian Church), Dan Garza (director of racial ethnic ministries at Austin Seminary), Jack Stotts, and Bob Shelton. While contact with the Methodists would be maintained, clearly, the program would be supported by and aimed at Presbyterians. A luncheon was to be held in San Antonio for all interested persons in the San Antonio area on November 10. The following week, on November 17, there was to be a luncheon for Hispanic pastors and interested persons from other denominations.

A program of study was designed, various questions were anticipated and addressed, and a timeline was put forward. It was to be a three-year pilot program with classes originally planned to begin in September 1995. A minimum enrollment of ten students was needed for the program to survive. In addition, there needed to be "[e]vidence of progress toward completion of study program for majority of students" and "adequate funding in place to cover direct costs of the program."[15]

This proposal was submitted to the Board of Trustees at its November 11, 1995, meeting. The board granted its approval. Unfortunately, while interest in an extension program in San Antonio was expressed among Anglo Presbyterians, no more than a handful of Hispanic persons signed up for classes. The program never got off the ground.

Extension Program Reflections

Charlsie B. Ramsey, now the pastor of two Presbyterian churches in Arizona, was an early participant in the Houston Extension Program. A member of New Hope Presbyterian Church in Katy, Texas, Ramsey eventually matriculated at San Francisco Theological Seminary and received her M.Div. from that school. Of her experience in the Houston program, she writes:

> The Extension Program was the catalyst for me to seek ordained ministry. I took a total of thirteen courses beginning in the Fall of 1985 [*sic*] through the Fall of 1992. Every course was an adventure, and I learned so much. The professors were interesting, more than qualified to teach, and took a genuine, pastoral interest in us as students and people. ...
>
> I had become a Presbyterian in 1979, joining Memorial Drive, and was a lukewarm member. In 1983, I found New Hope and began a deliberate spiritual quest. My knowledge of my new denomination was sparse. I took my first course with the idea (which was correct) that I needed more knowledge of the Pres-

byterian Church and the Reformed Tradition. This first course was The Theological Task in the Reformed Tradition, studying Calvin's Institutes, taught by Dr. John Jansen. Dr. Jansen had to be frustrated with me, because I could never understand his answers to my questions. He tried to answer me, assuming I knew of the Reformed tradition, but the terminology was foreign to me. However, despite a grade of C in the course, which was probably more than I deserved, I continued taking courses and gradually began to realize I would like to get a degree.

As I continued studying, I discovered a reason for doubting the literal interpretation of the Scripture when I took The Interpretation of Scripture, taught by Lewis Donelson; then Andy Dearman affirmed it for me in Topics in Old Testament Theology, 8th Century Prophets. When I took Church and State from a Reformed Perspective, ... it was like a breath of fresh air to realize that the Presbyterian Church took Christ into culture, and this was not considered to be sin or too worldly (I had come from a fundamental background). I remember those remarkable tables and charts that Ellen Babinsky gave us to help us learn Christian history. She was a wonderful teacher; I loved her stories. Laura Lewis and Christina Blair both had such a passion for teaching children and youth. Dr. Cynthia Campbell and Jack Stotts both taught with such a humble spirit and yet had so much knowledge. I had never had any contact with religions other than Christianity and some Judaism, so Introduction to World Religions, taught by Terry Muck, was a welcome course. He taught each religion so objectively and with no criticism whatsoever. We did not find out what he really believed until the end of the course. ...

As you can see, I love my experience at the Austin Extension Program. It prepared me for Seminary. With my lack of Reformed tradition knowledge, it was important for me to have this kind of foundation in order to get the most out of Seminary.[16]

Harry Slye, associate pastor at Grace Presbyterian Church in Houston, began his studies in the Houston Extension Program after having served on the staff of Young Life for twenty-seven years. He had taken some courses at Fuller Theological Seminary while working for Young Life, but had been unable to complete his theological studies.

He joined the staff of Grace Presbyterian Church as the director of congregational life and felt called to the ordained ministry in the Presbyterian Church (U.S.A.). He graduated from Austin Seminary in 1994 and recalls his experience the Houston Extension Program:

> The first course I took in Houston was Mission and Evangelism from Professor Pete Hendrick. He graciously assured me I could handle the work ahead on the Austin campus.
>
> I completed 6 courses in the Houston Extension Program before beginning two years of travel weekly between Houston and Austin. The academic expectations were rigorous and the instructors topnotch. I loved the combination of work and study because the latter became a form of retreat and refueling which was often squeezed out in the crush of responsibilities at a church of 3,000 members. I found immediate application for the study in the extension program, and most of the courses fulfilled requirements for the M.Div. In addition to the Mission and Evangelism course, I completed the required course on Reformed Theology taught by Thomas Currie III, the required course in worship taught by Fred Holper, the required course in World Religions by Terry Muck, and two elective courses.
>
> When I began my commuter routine in the summer of 1992 with the six-week Greek intensive, I ran into other Houston students from the extension program. We were all grateful for the chance to study so much in Houston in order to minimize the dislocation in our family and economic situations.[17]

Shelley Craig graduated from Austin Seminary in 1998. A member of the Woodlands Community Presbyterian Church north of Houston, she served on the Advisory Committee of the Houston Extension Program and moderated it for a time as well. Upon graduation from Austin Seminary, she received a call to serve on the staff of First Presbyterian Church in Muncie, Indiana. For her, the Houston Extension Program "was a window of opportunity to 'try on' theological education to see if it might fit my desire to learn more than was currently available in my congregation." She continued:

> My initial yearnings were for more education in any area related to Bible or church or theology. Geographical/marital/parental con-

straints meant that I did not have the option of traveling to a Presbyterian seminary campus. ...

The Houston Extension Program was an initially low-commitment (I audited my first class), low-cost, minimally threatening entry into an arena of fellow seminary students, inquiring congregational laypersons, and helpful faculty. This arena and affirmation from my congregation were the foundation for the evolution of my vague sense of call into God's demanding call to Ministry of Word and Sacrament. It was a frustratingly slow process of balancing motherhood, full-time volunteer work in my church, study, and prayer. It allowed God time to work on my fears of the ramifications of ministry and to work within my family as they too grew into my sense of call. This process also gave me time for an active church life where I matured in my faith, practiced ministry in a wide array of circumstances, and was mentored by my pastor, who heard my call. Many, many times I chafed at being a part-time student. But now, in full-time ministry, I am grateful that Extension Program limitations matched God's timetable for me so that I am more prepared academically, experientially, and in my family situation for the demands of the parish.

Craig notes that the extension program had both advantages and disadvantages. Among the disadvantages she notes three principal ones: (1) limited library access, (2) limited time with professors and hence a lack of a sense of community, and (3) "some of the relationship and interdependence of learning among subjects in different classes is lost as seminary education is strung out over many semesters."

Among the advantages Craig lists the following: (1) "Students can maintain income-producing jobs and/or ministry in their local congregations and/or time for family and other interests while progressing toward an M.Div. degree"; (2) the ability to relate "academic or practical issues" to their home congregations; (3) "Because most Extension Program students tend to be second-career persons, their life experiences, motivation, and critical approaches enliven and challenge all class discussions"; (4) "Extension Program students remain engaged in the realities of life in the world outside campus as they must take more initiative to pursue seminary education"; and (5) "For potential M.Div. candidates who are not ready or able to travel to Austin, the extension program is a blessing for beginning exploration into their call to ministry."

Craig concludes her thoughts with the following:

> I have been asked, "What if the Houston Extension Program had not existed?" Such a question brings tears to my eyes, because for me, it means that I would not have the incredible blessing of being a Minister of Word and Sacrament and being able to serve God in this particularly challenging, life-giving, wonderful role. It has not been a stepchild experience for me, but a rewarding threshold toward my M.Div. degree and the many possibilities of ministry.[18]

Some who take courses in the extension program have no intention of working toward ordination or even a degree. They are there simply for the love of learning. One such person is Walter Faulkenberry, who retired from a career in the petroleum industry in 1993, lives in Kingwood, Texas, and is a member of First Presbyterian Church in Houston. He writes:

> My wife and I had raised two sons in the church and had been "active" members all of our lives. As ordained elders in the Presbyterian Church USA, we had served on almost every committee in the church at least once. I was involved in adult church school classes, attended lectures and seminars and was interested in broadening my perspective and understanding of my Christian heritage. I was actively looking for educational opportunities and was offered a brochure about the Houston Extension Program through my local congregation in Houston.
>
> My introduction to the Houston Extension Program came in the fall of 1993 when I audited a class on Christian ethics taught by Dr. Jack Stotts. I found the class work and the reading to be interesting and quite challenging for someone who had never taken a seminary class.
>
> I was particularly fortunate to have had Dr. Stotts since it was to be the last extension class he would teach before he retired. He is indeed a gifted and talented man. Since that first class, I have audited classes every semester through 1999, sometimes taking more than one class per semester.

I have found all of the courses offered a wide range of opportunity for growth and development not only intellectually, but also emotionally and socially. Logistically, I learned that it was wise, as a beginner, to pay attention to the course level. I inadvertently took Dr. Tom Currie's 200 level course, "The Theological Task in the Modern World" before his 100 level course, "Introduction to Theology"! By the time I took "The Theological Task in the Reformed Tradition" two years later, I was infinitely more prepared to experience the depth of thinking and processing that was required. Dr. Laura Lewis put students in touch with dynamics of maturing faith in her class as we examined contemporary theories of human development, as well as biblical and contemporary models of religious experience nurtured in faith communities. Dr. Stanley Hall's class, "The Church as a Worshiping Community," gave dynamic presence to the communal nature of the church universally and our group of students particularly. We examined historical and theological developments that have shaped and misshaped the church, the relationships between worship, belief, and human experience. I gained skills for the ministry of planning, leading and educating in my local congregation. Terry Muck opened the doors of my mind regarding religious pluralism and Lewis Donelson and Andy Dearman made the Old and New Testaments come alive. Ellen Babinsky shared Christian history non-stop for 2 hours every week for one seemester and I was fortunate to revisit Christian ethics with Ismael Garcia. ...

Another fascinating dimension to the Houston Extension Program is the makeup of the student body in each of the individual classes. The class profile generally included several people auditing the courses, who were exploring their interest further, and some were students pursuing a degree and some ordination as ministers of the word. It also tended to provide a broader understanding of fundamental beliefs and practices of other denominations. Our typical class included Presbyterians plus 5-7 other denominations such as United Methodists, Southern Baptists, Disciples of Christ, Muslims, and Mennonites to name a few. Being aware of their perspective and listening to the discussions between these groups added to my understanding of not just our differences but also our many similarities.

Faulkenberry concludes:

> As I reflect on my choice to become involved in the Houston
> Extension Program, I have been blessed beyond my expectations
> by the experience. It is my hope that the mission and ministry of
> Austin Presbyterian Seminary Houston Extension Program con-
> tinues to grow, evolve, and meet the needs of other seekers in the
> Houston area.[19]

Jim Gresham graduated from the University of Texas at Austin
in 1959 with a degree in chemical engineering. Born and raised in
the Presbyterian church, Gresham had lived in Texas, Louisiana, and
California. While he was in California, he was called to be an elder.

> I was invited to be an elder in 1992 at the age of 57 and ac-
> cepted after prayer and self-evaluation. During the ordination
> process, I realized that many of the duties of office required a
> greater knowledge of the history and traditions of the church. I
> had questions about the logic of some of the religious teaching. I
> really did not understand the meaning of some of the rituals.
> Then it happened, a quiet voice calling me to learn more about the
> Bible, read more, study the history and scripture. I considered
> going to Fuller Seminary in California at night, but before the de-
> tails for enrollment could be worked out I was transferred to
> Houston in 1994.
> We joined the First Presbyterian Church of Houston, the same
> church I attended as a youth. The Austin Seminary offered ex-
> tension classes at night at this church. This allowed me to attend
> classes and not conflict with my work. Classes started in the af-
> ternoon and met once a week.
> The first course was a challenge but I was hooked; the course
> was interesting and extremely gratifying. These classes opened
> the door to many evenings of enrichment, new knowledge, ful-
> fillment and comfort in my personal spiritual growth. I have con-
> tinued taking one course each semester. ...
> The teachers are excellent and the interface with other Christ-
> ian students builds new and lasting friendships. The thrill of read-
> ing the classics of literature from authors like Martin Luther,
> Jonathan Edwards, John Calvin, Karl Barth and Augustine is an

enduring experience. Contemporary authors like Walker Percy, John Irving, Anne Tyler, Annie Dillard and Flannery O'Connor increase your understanding of the experience of others in the pursuit of salvation.

The extension program has caused some frustration to those who cannot afford the cost of tuition, books, and spare the time necessary to study. The Seminary Extension courses are considered to be affordable to many, but some cannot stand the budget strain caused by yearly increases in tuition cost. The new television classroom is of interesting impact on the student. I feel that some of the important personal contact is lost in the classroom when the teacher is not present. The student needs to have a majority of the classes in personal contact with the teacher. Once the student and teacher are acquainted, additional lessons could be taught over TV, but the personal contact is important for nurturing the new student.

Overall the Houston extension program will thrive and grow in the future. The program attracts students who are willing to work and sacrifice for a single purpose to glorify God and reach for a goal others think is impossible. The program will achieve widespread impact and lasting value to it's students and teachers.[20]

In the fall of 2000, Gresham began commuting to the Austin campus in order to complete work on a master of arts in theological studies.

Marialice Billingsley, a member of Grace Presbyterian Church in Houston, began taking courses in Houston in the spring of 1994. She has since gone on to become a full-time student in the spring of 1996 on the Austin Seminary campus as a candidate for the M.Div. degree. About the Houston Extension Program she writes:

The APTS Houston Extension program has provided for Houston a great resource for individuals to seek a greater theological understanding of God that is beyond the congregational level. It has provided a safe intimate atmosphere to seek God's call and develop leaders for the church. Theological study continues to be extremely expensive. The extension program allows students to be employed so they can care for their families and pay for theological classes. This is a great benefit to many students and is a practical approach to furthering one's education in the turbulent economy we live in today. The greatest benefit the Houston Extension Program has is its outstanding faculty. The Austin Presbyterian Seminary faculty challenges students academically. The faculty not only represents the Reformed tradition but also is dedicated to the universal church. The Houston Extension program produces communication and enthusiasm between the local congregation and the seminary. It is a recruitment vehicle for the seminary as well as an educational tool for members of Houston congregations. The lack of the seminary community in the Extension program forces students to become self-reliant students. The Extension student faces the reality of pastors, who must continue education independently while pursuing a full time vocation. In this respect, the Extension student is faced with the reality of a pastor's role.

I feel very blessed by the Houston Extension program. It is the greatest secret in the Houston area! It has changed my life and opened new avenues for me to answer God's call.[21]

How has the seminary faculty viewed these extension programs? Many note the difficulty of traveling and returning in time for classes on campus the next day. In addition, when teaching in an extension program, there is not as much time for contact with the students as on campus, because of the travel logistics.

Scott Black Johnston notes that, while initially the idea of traveling back and forth to Houston once a week seemed something of a "hassle," he found teaching in Houston "exciting and invigorating."[22] While Terry Muck admitted that the experience was tiring, he considered the Houston Extension Program "an asset" and felt that the seminary should explore ways of strengthening it.[23] Lewis Donelson thinks that the institution going out among its constituency is "a wonderful idea." The different student profile in extension programs is fun and stimulating, in Donelson's view.[24] Stephen Reid commends the high quality of students who have come out of both the Houston and the West Texas programs.[25]

Laura Lewis, who has taught four times in the Houston Extension Program, has also had good experiences teaching there. Overall, the classes have been effective and the students involved, although one concern is maintaining a graduate school quality of classwork. As is true for other professors, one of Lewis's frustrations has been less time to spend with the students in Houston.[26] Cynthia Rigby has expressed the concern for the strain on faculty members which teaching in Houston causes, principally the strain of travel to and from Houston. Increasing the size of the faculty would enable faculty to feel more comfortable about teaching in Houston.[27] According to Ismael Garcia, the seminary faculty is generally supportive of the extension program. Indeed, he maintains that the faculty would like more ownership of the program in terms of determining course offerings and academic control, and argues that a closer relationship between permanent faculty and adjunct faculty could be cultivated. He sees Houston as being a feeder school for students coming to Austin and resists the idea of establishing a satellite campus.[28]

One adjunct faculty member who taught both in the West Texas and Houston extension programs was Thomas W. Currie III, pastor for thirteen years in Brenham and eleven and a half years in Kerrville. He reflects on his experience of teaching in West Texas:

> As near as I can recall, I taught two classes in Midland, one in 1991 and one in 1994. Both were theology classes, "Introduction to Theology" and "Modern Theology." The students were, for the most part, active laymen and laywomen in Presbyterian congregations in Midland, Odessa, Big Spring and even Lubbock. We had one or two Episcopalians and one or two Methodists, I believe. The classes were usually about 65% women, 35% men, and nearly all of them were actively employed as teachers, engineers, counselors, or some other occupation. A very few were homemakers. As I recall the Midland classes were held on Sunday evening. . . . Classes would begin at 7 and we would go to a little after 9:00. Most of the students had taught Sunday School that morning or had responsibilities that afternoon or simply had had to drive a good ways to come to class. It was kind of fun. We all had made an effort to get there and everyone was eager to learn. . . .
>
> I must confess that I loved going to Midland for at least a couple of reasons. First of all, it was a delight to teach folk who had made such an enormous sacrifice to be in the position to learn. They were like sponges, soaking up what you had to offer. They

were also demanding. Precisely because they had sacrificed much, they expected much. But also it was a joy to teach folk who were so deeply rooted in the church, in the life of their local congregations. Theology was not some exercise in abstraction for them but had a direct bearing on the way they taught Sunday School, planned for worship, thought about the purpose of the church. I enjoyed those Sundays flying all over Texas to teach in Midland on Sunday evenings. ...

Currie taught in the Houston Extension Program six different times, the first of which was in the fall of 1988. Of his Houston experience he writes:

We met at First Presbyterian Church and I taught the introductory course in theology. The last time I taught in Houston was in 1999, by which time the class had moved to Grace Presbyterian Church. The Houston extension was bigger and better organized. There were more men in the classes, probably around 40 to 45%. The classes averaged about 15 students, many of whom were professionals of one sort or another (lawyers, teachers, engineers, counselors). Obviously, 60 to 65% of the class were women, and many of these were homemakers. As was true in Midland, nearly all of the folk who came to class were active in their congregations, and most of them were Presbyterian, though there was also a number of Methodists.

We usually met on a weeknight. The Houston extension would offer 6 hours a semester, so usually there were two classes each night. A few of the folks took both classes, which must have made for awfully long days since many of them had already worked that day. Like their Midland counterparts, the Houston students were eager to learn and had high expectations for the class. Many of them were very, very bright. All of them were hardworking. I never had to cajole or plead with them to get their papers in on time. They liked discussion and some of the best times came when the reading had struck home and they were eager to reflect on it verbally. They were a joy to teach. Some of them went on into the ministry. Many of them attended Austin Seminary, but I know of at least one who went to San Francisco and another who went to Princeton.

The Houston extension was notable also in having a number of folk who wanted to be theologically trained but who had no intention of being ordained. They wanted to be better teachers or elders or worshippers. Their faith sought understanding. These folk were also a delight to teach because they were truly interested in theology for its own sake, that is, not as a means of getting some kind of degree, but for what insights it could offer in understanding their own faith.

Currie, currently serving as the dean of the newly created campus of Union Theological Seminary–Presbyterian School of Christian Education at Charlotte, North Carolina, offers some thoughts on the advantages of an extension program over against the disadvantages of the traditional academic setting of a seminary campus:

It was a delight to teach such folk. They were highly motivated students of theology who loved the church and yearned to "work out their own salvation" in the company of Christ's people. In some ways, teaching in an extension program has limitations. We never had enough time. The library facilities were inadequate at best. There was not the richness of conversation and interdisciplinary life that a campus affords. Yet the extension programs had gifts that a more academic setting lacks. There was the most wonderful urgency. The sacrifice, the commitment, even the lack of time all put an enormous premium on the learning experience. Moreover, the closeness of the church, the reality of the Christian community shaping lives and questions, was more palpable in the extension programs than in a more academic setting. That too was a gift. Finally, the extension programs, perhaps because they were places of struggle and hope and sacrifice and work, were also places of laughter and even joy. In any case, they were not stuffy places, nor were they dead. I have come to think that teaching theology in an extension program may come closer to the way it ought to be taught than anything else. I wonder if the close proximity to the life of the church does not enrich the experience and sharpen the questions. I wonder, for example, if Bonhoeffer's work at Finkenwalde might best be understood as a kind of extension program that illustrates the possibilities here. In any case,

I remain grateful to Austin Seminary for inviting me to be a part of the extension programs in Houston and Midland.[29]

The Sun City and Houston extension programs continue to offer educational opportunities beyond the traditional campus setting. The Houston program provides a way for those who wish to test a calling to the ordained ministry to do so. Those who are unable to move to Austin to begin their studies immediately can begin their seminary education in Houston. Christian educators can work toward certification by taking courses offered in Houston. Finally, the Houston Extension Program provides laypersons opportunities to discover the joy of learning and growing in the faith as they explore that faith.

While other seminaries have been bold in establishing extension programs, Austin Seminary has been more cautious, even in building on the ones already in existence. One of the challenges for the twenty-first century may be exploring bold and creative ways in which Austin Seminary can strengthen its presence beyond its own traditional campus.

Chapter Eight

From the Students

Apart from the trustees, the administration, and the faculty, the story of Austin Seminary would be incomplete without some memories and reflections by those who have formed the student body. While all members of the community contribute to the overall purpose of preparing persons to enter the gospel ministry, the students bring a unique perspective to the nature of that community. Their recollections of individuals, events, and experiences give life to a story that might otherwise remain a history of official actions and developments of an institution. Humor as well as serious thought are incorporated here and reflect the personal side to the community that has been Austin Seminary.

Ted Foote graduated from Austin Seminary in 1979. A native of Gatesville, Texas, and a graduate of Baylor University, he has served pastorates in San Antonio and Henderson, Texas, as well as Tulsa, Oklahoma. Of his years at Austin Seminary, Foote writes:

> Hard work. Laughter. Developing friendships. Growth in the knowledge and trust and love of God, in the knowledge and trust of self, and in the knowledge and trust and love of others. Hard work. Relaxation. Laughter. Developing friendships. Hard work.

The words of the preceding paragraph characterize something of life for many, if not most, students in the A.P.T.S. dormitory from 1975 to 1979.

There are many memories, but hard work and laughter stand out for me. While not the only qualities on which, across the years, a "spiritual life" for discipleship can be built, I'm convinced that, for some, these two elements are key components.

Foote recalls Jack Maxwell as a person who clearly had a troubled presidency, but also as one who had gifts he shared with some students, including Foote:

> Dr. Maxwell could pray. As Professor of Homiletics and Liturgics, and as a solid a preacher as he ever was, his ability to craft and give voice to prayers was as great an ability as I have known. . . .
> . . . [T]here should never be any doubt about the facile nature of his mind and the breadth of his knowledge (and skill, for example, at photography and piano) in areas interesting to him.
> Prayer was no exception, and his respect was unquestionable for the depths of anguish persons could, would, and needed to express from their respective experiences of trauma and affliction.[1]

For Jack Robinson, another member of the Class of 1979, academics and the sense of community stand out as particularly important:

> In 1975 Austin Seminary was, and continues to be, an academic institution—an institution of the church—but academic nonetheless. Your survival depended upon your academic ability. Spirituality existed amidst the community, as evidenced by the importance Chapel services held for students, staff, and professors; nevertheless, you sometimes felt the feelings of spirituality were buried beneath the books, the classes, the papers, and the studying.
> One student, who later left the seminary, asked me—as an upperclassman—"Where is the spirituality here?" I responded that it was in the seminary community, just not the way you think. It is a spirituality found amidst the academics, the books, and the classes.
> I, for one, appreciated that spirituality because it helped me to

mature theologically. Theological formation was important to me. To venture to a seminary where "Presbyterian" and "Theological" were part of its official title, meant something to me then and now. It meant I was part of a particular tradition that understood the Christian faith in a particular way, and was not ashamed to say: "This is who I am, this is my heritage, this is where I came from. ...."

As Dr. Dick Junkin walked us through the library stacks that first semester at seminary—pointing out the books of the "giants" of the theologians—I, at 22 years of age, felt insecure and intimidated. I was filled with awe. Who was I to be here to take up where they had left off? Who was I to walk in their footsteps? Yet, it was Dr. Bob Shelton who saved my sanity by his off-hand but well-timed pastoral remark to me (and other students) that: "Your mind is as good as theirs"—meaning Barth, Brunner, Bonhoeffer, Augustine, Calvin, and others. The truth of his statement can be debated; the good intentions cannot.

However, amidst the academic atmosphere that was ever present—often oppressively—there was the sense of community that held us together as individuals and as a body of students, staff, and professors. I often experienced genuine affection there—from an encouraging word from Dr. Gene March; to a simple thank you from Dave Ng; to helpful advice from Ross Dunn; to a simple acknowledging of my presence by Dr. John Jansen. ....[2]

Robinson himself went on to earn a Ph.D. from St. Louis University while serving pastorates in Florissant, Missouri, and later in Lexington, Kentucky.

Holly Heuer came to Austin Seminary with a degree from Southern Methodist University and some experience as a teacher in the Dallas Independent School District. She entered the seminary in 1976 and, after an intern year at Bellaire Presbyterian Church under former seminary president David Stitt, who was pastor there, graduated in 1980. Heuer recalls some of the highlights of her years in Austin as a roll call of faculty members:

Dick Junkin was a very important influence on me. I liked his intense style, his counseling "manner" and his ability to quickly understand my concerns. He was approachable as Dean of Students, and as a teacher was provocative, creative and affirming. Later, in his role as "Spiritual Mentor" of the denomination, I was able to see him as a passionate advocate for developing the interior life of faith. He has always been genuine.

John Jansen was like a kind grandfather. He, too, was deeply faithful, and reverent. His New Testament lectures were simply a witness to Jesus Christ. He was not critical or harsh, but always encouraging. He seemed so pleased when a student came by to visit. . . .

Ross Dunn was an enigma. He was rarely really prepared for class, but seemed to have a naturally theological and inquisitive mind. He was best at the beer garden, where, with students, he would engage us in conversations about ethical matters, or rather, we would talk about anything, and he would help us see things in a completely different light. I wasn't ever sure, though, exactly what he believed.

Gene March was a real favorite. I never knew if I just loved Hebrew, or simply thrived with Gene's teaching. His prayers before class were legend. He wrote the most beautiful, thoughtful, and inspiring prayers. I think that I gained from his invitation into God's presence, a sense of how to pray with others. He was humble, and at the same time, confident. He expressed a profound faith, which was engaged with constant inquiry. He actually seemed to love Scripture. He was always doing research, and manifested such authenticity, that I was at times, awestruck.

Bob Shelton was, and remains, my most important teacher. From serious reflection, I suspect that what I resonated with was the professor, who had been a pastor. His years in the pulpit shaped a man who understood and loved the church. He taught out of that rich experience and provided the most practical advice that I received. He understood me, my gifts, along with my laziness and pride, and spoke to me out of that knowing. He could be very encouraging, and yet, was always pushing me to the edge of my ability. I think I absorbed his way of seeing the church and seminary and world without even being aware of it. Preaching is a very important part of my ministry, and his style of teaching certainly shaped my practice.

Heuer went on to become a member of the Board of Trustees,

serving from 1990 to 1996. She reflects on some of the changes in the seminary from her student years to her years as a trustee:

> The seminary has grown from my student days into a big business. And in some ways, that shows. Certainly we have a larger faculty. Obviously, we have nicer buildings. We have a big budget, and lots of endowment. But I regret that this "establishment mentality" has made the seminary more conservative. It is less able than in earlier years to be a witness to the full spectrum of the gospel.
>
> My one major and consistent disappointment in the decisions of the Board during my tenure, is that we have hired faculty who have had no experience pastoring a church. When I say NO experience, sometimes I mean just that, no time as a paid member of a church's staff. Often, folks say they have been in the church, when they may have spent a year as visiting something or other. But consistently, we have hired folks who have never been a pastor. So, as a result, we really are training men and women in academic exercises of the faith. Oddly enough, when Bob Shelton talks about the seminary as the "school of the church," maybe he alone has actually served the church.[3]

Another member of the Class of 1980 was Steve Plunkett, a native of Fort Smith, Arkansas, and a graduate of Austin College. Two professors in particular stand out in his memory.

> Bob Shelton and George Heyer are the two professors who, more than anyone else, challenged and nurtured me. I always had the sense that Bob was about the business not just of leading us through required material, but of equipping us for ministry in the real world of the church. He had been a pastor before coming to Austin Seminary, and his identity as a pastor shaped the way he taught; it shaped his expectations of us; and, it shaped his evaluation of our work which could be both critical and compassionate at the same time. With Bob, there always seemed to be a higher purpose than the required reading or an assigned paper. To this day, I remember things which Bob said in class and, from time to time, I am struck with how Bob's influence still shapes the way I do my job.

I have never heard a finer lecturer than George Heyer. His ability to make complex theological issues accessible is amazing. His lectures were always crystal clear, as well as intellectually engaging and challenging. I still look back on occasion to my notes from George's class, particularly the one on Reformed theology.

Austin Seminary prepared me well for the ministry. I look back on those years with fondness and gratitude.[4]

Upon graduation, Plunkett went to Rusk, Texas, where he served as pastor of the Presbyterian church there. From there he went to Paducah, Kentucky, to serve First Presbyterian Church. In 1989 he accepted a call to be the senior pastor at St. Andrew Presbyterian Church in Denton, Texas, where he continues to serve.

Ken Peters came to Austin Seminary in 1980 with a Ph.D. in American history and having served on the faculty of Texas A&M University. He recalls being a part of a student movement to reform the curriculum at the seminary.

My years at the Seminary were from 1980–1983. Enrollment was low, and morale was lower. Student resignations, especially from the middler class, were happening frequently. The curriculum, we believed, seemed onerous for a three-year program, but our "revolt," if that is what people persist in calling it, would never have succeeded had it not been for a deep feeling of faculty disaffection about the life of the institution. When I and four of my middler peers went to talk with Dick Junkin about revising the course load we were not, contrary to the mythology that seems to have grown up around this event, carrying guns or threatening violence. What I expected from the Dean was a polite hearing, ending with the suggestion that maybe we ought to go back to class. His reaction, and that of the faculty, surprised me. Suddenly classes had been cancelled, a week was given over to a very public institutional self-study, and the curriculum was reduced by how many credits? I don't remember.

There was very little in this that helped the middler class. We were nearer the end than the beginning, so that when the end came, any interest we had in a big pay-off was hardly worth the effort. What I had not reckoned completely, however, was the extent to which this episode was to become part of a much larger movement that would end with Jack Maxwell's resignation as President. Students had less to do with that than the Seminary's much broader constituency, and to blame (or to credit) five middlers for effecting such an important change in the history of the institution is not realistic, in my opinion. Of course I could see that Dr. Maxwell was not a popular figure, and I'm sure I intuited that his tenure would end unhappily, but I did not hate him, and to suppose the Middler Revolt represented some kind of brilliant (or as some insist, arrogant) student conspiracy to topple him from power simply cannot be supported by any objective evidence.

May I say parenthetically that it would be a serious misjudgment to make Jack Maxwell the sole explanation for that troubled era, if that is how it is interpreted. Scapegoats are convenient, but rarely are they sufficient for explaining complicated issues and absolving people of their own responsibilities. The fact is that many people had many reasons for reacting to developments as they did.[5]

Upon graduation in 1983, Peters went to Dalhart and served as pastor of the Presbyterian congregation there. In 1989 he moved to New Braunfels to become pastor of the New Braunfels Presbyterian Church.

Kenneth Jatko entered Austin Seminary in 1983 when he was sixty-one years old. His recollections focus on the sense of community that he experienced there:

> To me, the atmosphere of the Seminary was encouragement of learning, a collegiality, that I appreciated. I think again, for me, that this was shown in the behavior of people such as Andy Dearman, Laura Lewis and C. D. Weaver. Somehow, they encouraged me to persevere and to hang in there. Dearman and Lewis were demanding but fair and sometimes I needed to be shown the error of my ways. I found the staff helpful and accommodating in making repairs or changes in the apartments. The campus was small enough so that, in some respects, it was like an extended family. We made some lasting friendships there and got insights into differing theological views. I was 61 at the time I entered seminary, so I didn't participate in some of the theological discussions that

some students did, as I needed more rest. And I think I probably missed something in my theological growth.[6]

Sallie Sampsell Watson entered Austin Seminary in 1983. There were five women in her class (out of a total of about twenty-five persons in her class) and five single women living in the dormitory. It was no longer unusual for women to be part of the student body; Watson recalls experiences that reflect both the acceptance of women on campus and their unique status:

> One of the fun things about being among the first "numerous" women on campus was that we got to be part of some of the first "all-women" events. The planning was neither intentional nor exclusive; it just happened that way. I believe that our trip to Central America in January 1987 was the first all-female-student January trip. Ann Rosewall, Dawn Herron, Cheryl Kirk-Jones, Teresa Sauceda and myself were sponsored (coincidentally) by the Presbyterian Women Birthday Offering and led by Ismael Garcia. In spring of 1985, I also found myself to be one of what Prescott Williams later called "The Seven Sisters." As it so happened, seven women students (and no men!) signed up to take Prescott's Hebrew Exegesis of Isaiah class. The variety of viewpoints, as well as the creativity exhibited in the final projects, was fascinating. Though we took note of these two all-women gatherings, I must say that by 1985 such gatherings felt more routine than remarkable. . . .
> . . . Having absorbed from seminary the notion that male-female differences were a non-issue, I was able to treat it as a non-issue with the various congregations I've served. Instead of training me to be a "woman minister," I'm grateful that Austin taught me to be the best minister that I could be—one that happens to be a woman, and who gratefully brings those gifts and differences to the ministry.[7]

Watson graduated with an M.Div. in 1987. Among her memories is one about Robert Paul that reflects his British humor, which endeared him to so many.

> One day in Dr. Paul's class (as a junior), he was lecturing as the middler class next door (I think it was Ralph Underwood's Pas-

toral Care class) stepped out in the hall for a break. They got rather chatty and noisy, even with the door shut. So Dr. Paul stepped over, opened the door, and in his charming British accent said, "Would you pleeeese be quiet?" They toned down for about two minutes. Then the din rose again. So he went back over and said, "Would you PLEEEESE be quiet?! Thank you!" I don't guess it was two minutes more before it got pretty loud again. This time he went over to the door, opened it, and at what seemed like the top of his lungs, said, "SHUT UP!" You could have heard a pin drop, both in the hallway and in our room. He came back to the lectern, looked at us with twinkly eyes and a grin, and said, "Ex cathedra!" (What the pope says, goes!) We howled.[8]

Watson also collected quips of some of her instructors, finding such sayings sometimes humorous, sometimes profound, sometimes both. The following aphorisms are attributed to Prescott Williams, professor of Old Testament:

"Hope is being drawn toward that fulfillment which you would never have generated yourself."

"It is the true prophet who asserts in times of crisis that all belongs to Yahweh."

"You only see Providence looking in your rear-view mirror."

Summarizing the story of Jonah, Williams is recalled as having said, "If you want to limit the grace of God, you just left yourself out."

According to Watson, the following are "Sheltonisms," statements attributed to Bob Shelton, professor of homiletics:

"People that always have to be right are both boring and dangerous."

"The place where people will get angriest with you is when you mess with their liturgy. And that's appropriate!"

An aficionado of Willie Nelson, the country-western singer, Shelton credits him with: "You never create out of opulence. You create out of the desert."[9]

And finally, Watson recalls Robert Paul as suggesting, "It's much harder to be a Christian witness than a Christian advocate."[10]

Clay Brown came to Austin Seminary out of the Cumberland Presbyterian tradition. He was at the seminary from 1986 to 1988. He recalls:

Overall, my experience while a student at Austin was quite positive. My vantage point is perhaps a little different than that of most students, for at the time I was a candidate for ministry in the Cumberland Presbyterian Church. In the Cumberland church, a candidate can serve as stated supply of a congregation; thus I was the full-time stated supply pastor of St. Paul CPC while attending Austin as a full-time student, a rare double given both PCUSA polity and the personal masochism needed to attempt two such commitments simultaneously.

The theological education I received at Austin was first-rate. No, I didn't agree with a lot of the statements uttered by my professors, for my personal theological convictions tended to be more conservative than those of most faculty members at the time. Yet with very few exceptions, the professors treated me and my opinions with grace and understanding. (Sometimes we students were not as graceful and understanding with each other— seminarians can be rather intemperate at times!) I did not sense great pressure to conform to their theological expectations. Instead I was encouraged to come to my own conclusions after diligent study; to back up my opinions intelligently, appropriately, and lovingly; and to listen to other viewpoints with charity, honesty, and openness. Quite a gift, I dare say. ...

A number of professors and administrators touched my life for good while I attended Austin. Chief among them, in no discernable order, are John Evans, Jack Stotts, Pete Hendrick, Lewis Donelson, Fred Holper, Andy Dearman, Prescott Williams, and Bob Shelton. I appreciate to this day their sense of vocation, their combination of the intellectual and the relational, and their expertise in their chosen fields. ...[11]

Kathy Neece was at Austin Seminary from 1985 to 1989. A native of Victoria, Neece recalls events in her first and her final semesters as being particularly important:

Seminary's impact on me was strong from the very beginning. At the convocation of the seminary students and faculty in September of 1985 the Reverend Dr. Cynthia Campbell delivered a paper entitled something like "Ministry as Imago Trinitatis." I was struck by her discussion of relationship within the Trinity, and relationship as being part of the essence of the Trinity, the essence of god-ness. I suppose I ought to check out the facts behind that memory, but truly, if seminary didn't begin that way, it should have. Then, a highlight of my last semester of seminary, Spring of 1989, was studying mystic Richard of St. Victor's writings concerning the Trinity. This was done at the insistence of Dr. Ellen Babinsky. And I do mean "insistence." I didn't want to read it. Ellen kept saying that I "needed" Richard of St. Victor, and she was right. Seminary from first to last required me to take seriously the doctrine of the Three in One, and since I have begun preaching, the sermon for Trinity Sunday has been among my very favorites to prepare.[12]

Upon graduation, Neece accepted a call to serve the Presbyterian churches in Caldwell and Somerville, Texas.

Barbara Farwell came to Austin Seminary primarily due to the influence of President Jack Stotts. Having heard him speak at a presbytery meeting in Boulder, Colorado, Farwell sought him out to make further inquiries about the school. She entered in the fall of 1988 and graduated in 1992. She recalls being impressed with the fact that, from the very beginning, the seminary staff seemed to know all the students, the new ones as well as the old ones.

> I loved Austin (the city) as well as the seminary. I was impressed on my first day on campus to find that everyone, from Dr. Stotts on down, knew the names of the new students. They had obviously studied our photos very well, but it was still impressive.

Farwell goes on to describe those persons who were particularly important in her theological education.

> What professors were influential for me? Certainly Dr. Stotts had an influence; I took two courses from him and loved every moment of his classes. He is a fine professor with a wry sense of humor. I also found him to be very gracious, a most caring individual in his role of seminary president. And Virginia Stotts is equally gracious, and a delight.
>
> Dr. Alan Lewis was one of my favorite professors, and his untimely death was a great loss for the seminary. I took basic theol-

ogy from him, and the beginning of Christology (he was unable
to complete the semester). His opening prayers for classes were
practically legendary; they were always moving and heartfelt. I enjoyed his classes and learned much, but I also learned much from
him as a person of faith. When I think of faithful witness in ad-
versity, I think of Alan. He was a dear person.

I also enjoyed Dr. Andy Dearman. His basic Old Testament
course was fantastic; he made the old familiar stories new again,
and his insights about Scripture and the Hebrew people enriched
my life. He is a wonderful storyteller, a lively and entertaining
professor. I also took my basic Hebrew class from him; only
Andy could make Hebrew so interesting![13]

Farwell serves as associate pastor at Faith Presbyterian Church in
Sun City, Arizona, site of one Austin Seminary's extension programs.

A native of Fort Stockton, Texas, and a member of First Presbyterian Church in San Angelo, Fran Boggus had not planned to attend Austin Seminary. Having visited Union Theological Seminary–Presbyterian School of Christian Education (UTS-PSCE) in
Richmond, Virginia, her next visit was to be to Louisville Theological Seminary. However, at the urging of a co-leader at a church-
related retreat, Boggus visited the Austin Seminary campus. On the
basis of that visit, she decided to attend Austin.[14]

Of her work on campus she writes:

My campus job was in the business office. I enjoyed that job
tremendously because it put me in contact with people all over
the campus. My sole duty for three years consisted of running the
xerox machine; hence I was known as the Xerox Queen. It provided me with [the] wonderful opportunity to experiment with
Brother Lawrence's notion of practicing the presence of God in
the mundane as well as in major paper jams and deadlines!

Of her experience in taking Hebrew in the month of January, an intense experience not survived by every student, Boggus writes:

Hebrew was the turning point in my studies. For some reason
I had a strong desire to do well in this class. Therefore, when the

Rev. Jim Miles said that he held the secret to success in that class I listened closely—"a hard bench." I sat on that hard bench with great friends, Kathy Trevino, Kay Johnson and Alice Underwood, and we did well! After my final exam, I came home to two daughters hiding a bouquet of carnations (they had walked down to Eckerd's Drug) and a note written in Hebrew by their hands saying, "We love you!" Kids are grand! Instructor Donna Key provided me with a living image of God's grace and judgment. I was thrilled when she asked me to work as tutor. My children were equally happy because they saw other students going abroad in January and they did not want their mama to leave them.

Boggus recalls small acts of grace and generosity that might not have been noticed by everyone:

> Many may not have known that Herman Harren [vice president for business affairs] was Santa Claus in disguise. As a single parent on limited income, Christmas was a difficult time. With what would those stockings be filled? Herman gave me a Christmas advance each year in November that just coincidentally equalled my Hebrew tutor's pay. Easily enough, come February I would sign over my check to the business office. Looking back, I do not know of any other way I could have managed![15]

Boggus graduated in May 1993 and accepted a call to serve as associate pastor of First Presbyterian Church in Bryan, Texas. On November 26, 1994, she married Professor Bob Shelton, the academic dean of the seminary. On November 1, 1995, Fran Shelton became the associate pastor of the New Braunfels Presbyterian Church in New Braunfels, Texas.

Lemuel Garcia-Arroyo graduated from Austin Seminary in the Class of 1995. A native of the state of Veracruz, Mexico, Garcia graduated from the Presbyterian Pan American School in Kingsville, Texas, in 1986. He then matriculated at the National University of Mexico City, graduating in 1990. He entered Austin Seminary in the fall of 1992.

As a native of Mexico, Garcia writes of his experience at Austin Seminary among people much more familiar and comfortable with American culture:

I will be forever thankful to God and to Austin Presbyterian Theological Seminary for allowing me the invaluable opportunity of receiving the kind of theological training that has shaped my ministry as a servant of the Lord to God's people. Even when I considered myself an "outsider" coming from a different country and a different culture, I was never rejected or put down by anyone in the seminary community. On the contrary, ever since my wife, Egla, and I arrived on campus we felt welcome and accepted not only by faculty, staff and administrators but also by students themselves who went out of their way to make us feel at home and offer us their friendship and love.

Garcia found the faculty and staff particularly helpful:

All of our teachers were excellent but the ones I feel contributed the most to my pastoral formation were Andy Dearman, Stacy Johnson, and Terry Muck. From Andy I discovered a new level of appreciation for the Word of God. Every time we read a passage from the Hebrew Scriptures and were able to understand it as it was originally inspired became a sacred moment for me. Stacy challenged our faith and intellect as we struggled with theological issues and the way we could connect theory to praxis. From Terry's courses I was able to develop a new interest and sensitivity for other faiths, other cultures, and other peoples in their indefatigable search for the divine.

I had the blessing and privilege of counting on the support and wise counsel of people in the administration starting with the President Jack Stotts and the Dean Bob Shelton who were never inaccessible but found the time to talk to students and show genuine concern for us. John Evans, Dan Garza, and C. D. Weaver, also, were there for us ever since my wife and I arrived in Seminary and became very dear friends to our family. John referred us to the doctor who took care of Egla during her pregnancy and Dan and C. D. were the first ones to visit us at the hospital when our daughter was born.

Garcia concludes with thoughts on his experience of the seminary as a "family":

The seminary community became our family truly. Notwithstanding, I couldn't help wondering why there were but a few Hispanic students or students from Latin America who knew about or wanted to attend Austin Seminary. If only they knew that a Mexican student who thought he was an "outsider" spent the happiest and most rewarding three years in seminary with brothers and sisters in Christ. I believe that if they were told, they would consider Austin Seminary as the place where God might be calling them to study for the ministry.[16]

Upon graduating from Austin Seminary in 1995, Garcia returned to the Pan American School in Kingsville to serve as the chaplain. In June 1999 he accepted a call to serve the church in the Synod of the Sun as the associate for racial-ethnic ministries.

Dan Walker was raised "a Navy brat." Born in Kittery, Maine, Walker moved to Houston in 1974. Employed by a chemical company, he became active in the Sagemont Presbyterian Church. Responding to a sense of call to the parish ministry, Walker entered Austin Seminary in 1993. Among those faculty members who influenced Walker the most were those having to do worship and preaching. Citing Scott Black Johnston's "Introduction to Preaching" ("baby preaching") class, Walker recalls:

[O]ne of the first exercises he had us do was take a passage from scripture and re-tell it to the class in another method than just reading out of the Bible. My passage was the healing of the blind man of Bethsaida. I took the part of the blind man, acted as if I was blind and told the story from my point of view. This was very out of character for me, but very enjoyable and quite successful I might add. I have done similar first person narratives since and find them effective in the right situation.

Bob Shelton's senior preaching class had a significant impact on Walker:

The single most important item I learned from him, and it may be one of the most important lessons for my ministry, is that when we preach, it is not just us doing the preaching. Yes, we speak the words, but they are not just our words and there are meanings in our proclamation that we never realize but others do. My senior sermon in my opinion was a stinker. When I gave it before my class, I did not do a very good job and doubted that anyone would find anything of value in my "message." However, Bob and the class helped me to see that the Holy Spirit is at work if we let the Spirit work, and that in spite of ourselves the Spirit's work can be and is done.[17]

Upon graduation, Walker received and accepted a call to serve as pastor of St. Paul's Presbyterian Church in Needville, Texas.

Another student in the Class of 1996 was Martha Sadongei, a Native American. Although offered a full scholarship with all expenses paid by another seminary, she chose to attend Austin instead. She explains why:

But what attracted me to Austin were the titles of the course offerings. They were creative enough to get my attention and along with sound course descriptions spoke to me about the quality of the faculty. Not sure of what my ministry was about I also felt that in attending Austin, I would not be placed in a preconceived ministry. I did not want to be automatically placed in Native ministries just because I was a Native person. While at Austin, I was able to explore, question, struggle when my history as Presbyterian and love for the church clashed with my history as a Native person. Yet the understanding of ritual within the Native culture also led me to discover the rich liturgical history of the church, discovering some parallels between the gatherings. The explorations, the discoveries had their "a-ha" moments, some of which were joyful and at times left me in deep pain. But by journey's end, at least the seminary's journey, I knew that God had truly called this individual to a ministry, not limited to Native people but to the whole church.

Some of those persons particularly influential on Sadongei were Ellen Babinsky, Stan Hall, and John Alsup. But one person who proved especially helpful was Joe Haggard, computer systems manager for the seminary:

But when the academics were too much and I wanted to switch gears, as far as my thinking, I have to thank Joe Haggard for helping to make the switch. He, too, is a big fan of the NBA, especially of the Phoenix Suns! (My home team!) We kept up with scores, standings, trades in the off-season and looked forward [to] the start of the basketball season! On some days it was just a matter of giving each other the "thumbs up" sign across campus! But that was enough to calm the butterflies before a test, to lift my spirit when it was down, to remind me that there is a real world out there.[18]

Upon graduation, Martha accepted a call to serve the Indian Presbyterian Church in Livingston, Texas. In 1999 she returned to Arizona to take care of her ailing mother.

John Gallentine, a native of Broken Bow, Nebraska, received his M.Div. from Austin Seminary in May 1997 and accepted a call to serve the Peace Presbyterian Church in Yankton, South Dakota. Reflecting on the spirit of community that he found at Austin Seminary, Gallentine writes:

I remember the faith and the character of the people of Austin Seminary. I remember how President Stotts knew each student by name. President Stotts always had a warm smile, and most often a nurturing comment, for each student. Each faculty member was deeply involved in faith communities outside of his/her own academic responsibilities; their example motivated and nurtured my commitment to both study and embody the theological tenets of our Reformed heritage. ...

The *climate* of Austin Presbyterian Theological Seminary was mysterious—everyone seemed to feel valued and able to contribute according to gifts and talents given to him/her. Supporting staff consistently conveyed to me that each felt proud of what they were doing and expressed a positive attitude toward the broader seminary community. To what could this mysterious climate be attributed? I believe Dean Shelton revealed its cause very casually during the September (1994) new students orientation seminar.

Dean Shelton was explaining some of [the] tradition behind the seminary chapel and describing the meaning behind its many symbols. He pointed out that the chapel was at the center of the seminary campus and slightly elevated. The Dean made two comments about this: 1) the chapel's location was symbolic of the centrality of the Church to Austin Seminary, and 2) we should reflect that centrality by serving and worshipping in local congregations in conjunction with our study and work at the seminary. In my estimation, the commitment to Christ's Church which the Dean naturally displayed revealed an underlying dynamic that strongly contributed to the creation of the warm, caring, and at times challenging climate of Austin Presbyterian Theological Seminary—the seminary was under the fold of the church; and, in this climate, I was continually reminded that who I was and what I did was too.

It seems every seminary community offers classes, but the people who teach, administer, and serve create the memories that ministry is made of.[19]

The seminary began offering a master of theology degree (Th.M.) in 1945. In the 1978– 79 catalogue, one finds the following description of this degree program:

Intended for students who have completed a first theological degree, this program emphasizes a broad knowledge of all the theological disciplines—biblical, historical, theological, and church's ministry—and an increasing mastery of a particular discipline. Recently redefined, this program now requires residence during the nine-month period September through May.[20]

While anyone with an initial theological degree (B.D. or M.Div.) could apply, this program provided an excellent opportunity for international students to study in the United States and, in a relatively short period of time, earn a degree. Over the years, Austin Seminary has enjoyed the presence of many such students.

A native of Sri Lanka, Paul Benjamin studied at Austin Seminary from August 1975 through July 1997. After taking and passing several courses at the M.Div. level, Benjamin was accepted into the Th.M. program at the end of 1975. Of his experience at Austin Seminary, Benjamin writes:

I was impressed with the faculty. Since my major was Old Testament, I worked with Professors March and Williams. Dr.

Williams guided me in choosing the topic for the thesis. When he went away on sabbatical Dr. March became my thesis advisor. The experience of writing a thesis opened up for me many new areas to explore in the field of Old Testament.

The 75th Baccalaureate and Commencement Services in 1977 were unforgettable. The late Rev. Ross Dunn, who had played the role of a stand-up comedian in one of the year-end banquets, was the preacher at the Baccalaureate Service. The coming of the Honorable Leon Jaworski, after he had become well-known in the Watergate prosecution, to deliver the commencement address, was a cause of considerable excitement among the graduating classes of 1977.

Life at the informal level enhanced the quality of life at the seminary. When Thanksgiving came, there was the invitation from Ted Foote, Jr. When my family arrived at Dallas–Fort Worth airport, Jim Rigby and parents were there. When it was time to work out, there were several people to challenge at racquet ball and ping pong. My family and I were able to express our gratitude to the seminary community by hosting a "Sri Lanka Evening," serving ethnic food and showing a movie at the refectory in Feb. 1977.[21]

Benjamin went on to serve a United Methodist congregation in Burlington, Iowa.

Another international student was Intraporn Inchai, who came to Austin Seminary from Thailand. She received her master of arts degree in 1993. Of her experiences at Austin Seminary she writes:

It was a short time for me at APTS, but I learned a lot. I had a good time to be [t]here. I feel that I was welcomed into the family of Austin Seminary. During my time at APTS I was very impressed with the professors and students because they were so warm and friendly toward me. Everyone from the president (Jack Stotts) to the dean (Bob Shelton—I know that he is the president now), to the professors, to the dorm and the kitchen workers. Everyone was very help[ful] and kind. ...

My only frustration was the great difference in language. Translating Thai world view (Thai ideas—my ideas) into a language that does not include these ideas was very difficult.

I feel that I learned a lot by observing American culture and thinking about using those ideas in the Thai society and especially in the Thai church. In my current teaching and preaching I still use many of the methods that I learn[ed] in my seminary classes.[22]

Inchai now serves on the McGilvary Faculty of Theology at Payap University in Thailand.

The Master of Theology and the Master of Arts programs also enabled American pastors, in a variety of situations, to earn a second theological degree. One such person was Keith Hill, who received his master of theology in 1987. Having served as a pastor in Wichita Falls, Hill saw his experience in the Th.M. program at Austin as "an important waystation for me in the beginning years of my ministry. It was a year of both academic and existential searching for me as I determined whether I could carry out my ministry in the institutional church."

During that year, Hill recalls, two persons were of particular importance to him:

John Evans was admissions director at the time, and I remember his kindness and support as we went through the trying times of deciding whether to come and figuring out how to support a family. He connected me with the Brethren Church, for whom I was an interim pastor during that year, and by which I supported my family. The other person who was particularly helpful was Pete Hendrick. He was one of my two primary professors who supervised my thesis work, and was most helpful. He also offered encouragement and wise counsel as I sought a call.[23]

Hill went on to serve as co-pastor of the First Presbyterian Church in Douglasville, Georgia.

By 1996 the Master of Arts program had grown to the extent that ten persons were awarded that degree at the commencement exercises in May of that year. Five were Presbyterian, and five were non-Presbyterian.[24]

The international character of the student body has continued to develop over the years. In the fall of 1996, according to Acting President and Academic Dean Robert Shelton, persons in the entering class (for both the M.A. and the M.Div. programs as well as nondegree ecumenical students) included students from Germany, Hungary, Kenya, Korea, Malawi, Mexico, Nigeria, Peru, and Taiwan.[25]

The third degree program offered by the seminary is the Doctor of Ministry (D.Min.). This program is designed for those who have already earned an initial theological degree and are active in ministry. The D.Min. program was begun at Austin Seminary in 1974, four years after such a program had been started anywhere in this country.[26] Because of its quality, longevity, and growth, in the view of Tina Blair, director of the program, Austin Seminary's D.Min. program could be rated among the top four in the country.

This program draws persons in ministry from a broad spectrum of denominations and traditions, as well as from virtually every geographical region of the United States. It has also enjoyed a good reputation internationally, with persons from Canada and Cuba. Although it has evolved over its thirty-year life, the areas of concentration from which a candidate may choose are: Christian Nurture, Evangelism and Mission in a Multi-Cultural Context, and Proclamation and Worship. Within these areas, the seminary also offers special emphases in rural ministry and in spirituality.

Peter E. Roussakis of Alton, New Hampshire, received his D.Min. from Austin Seminary in 1986 and has written the following of that experience:

> I am very grateful for the opportunity to have studied at Austin Seminary. At the time they offered a track called "Particular Ministries," which afforded persons from varying backgrounds the opportunity to explore areas of ministry not specifically shaped as other tracks. In my case I was teaching church music at the time of my study as a professor at Southwestern University (Georgetown, TX)....
>
> I must say, in my opinion, the D.Min. program at APTS was rigorous; in comparison with models of D.Min. programs across the country, it may be excessively so. At any rate, the title is worth every word of praise, because of the integrity of the program. In my view, only Princeton's D.Min. program could compare with the quality and energy needed to complete Austin's degree.... Since earning the D.Min. I have earned an S.T.M. in Liturgical Studies and a Ph.D. in theological studies. Austin's D.Min. was highly regarded by the other institutions I've attended.[27]

H. R. (Lad) Anderson, Jr., a Presbyterian minister living in Bellingham, Washington, earned his D.Min. from Austin Seminary in 1990. He chose Austin Seminary because it was "the only Presbyterian seminary with an established curriculum and faculty in the area of worship." According to Anderson, Cynthia Campbell, Lewis Donelson, and Fred Holper were particularly important in his own theological growth and education.

The rich mixture of ecclesiastical traditions in the classroom became important to Anderson:

> The mix of students in the classroom experience was particularly beneficial to me. The range was from a very conservative Baptist to a modern-thinking Roman Catholic. There were Methodists, Lutherans, Church of God, and Episcopalians, in addition to a variety of Baptists, and, of course, Presbyterians. The challenge of discussions in this kind of mix was stimulating, enlightening, broadening.

The value of the education provided by the D.Min. program was twofold for Anderson:

> First it equipped me to function as a pastor-worship leader with a great deal more understanding of our heritage and history. Secondly, because of the projects that I completed in my church, it resulted in a congregation that had a growing understanding and appreciation of the place and power of worship in their life, and the life of the church.[28]

Don Joseph Sawyer, a Roman Catholic priest at Our Lady's Maronite Catholic Parish in Austin, received his D.Min. from Austin Seminary in 1991. Of his experience at Austin Seminary he writes:

> ... I am not only proud of the Doctorate that I received from Austin Seminary, but happy for the opportunity to take advantage of the experiences that Austin Seminary afforded me.
>
> I found the professors to be for the most part very open to me as a Catholic and respectful of my beliefs. They challenged me to analyze my ministry and to value myself and my expertise as a

pastor. The course load and expectations forced me to raise my goals and get back into the mode of thinking intellectually. The entire experience was very positive.

I will always be grateful to Austin Seminary and to the Presbyterian church for allowing me to go back to school and to obtain a doctorate. I look at those four years with warmth and appreciation.[29]

Although only a cursory sample, these views from Austin Seminary graduates reinforce the reality of community—both at the personal level and at the academic level—that has been a part of life at Austin Seminary in its first century of service.

CHAPTER NINE

Unsung Heroes

In the history of any institution, there are those whose service either remains in the background or perhaps goes unnoticed altogether, but whose commitment is no less fervent than that of those who are in positions of leadership. Some carry out their responsibilities with a winsome and humble spirit that reflects their preference for the shadows rather than the limelight.

In the 100 years of its life, Austin Seminary has been blessed with a host of servants who cared more for the witness of the gospel than for any attention that might devolve on them, who kept the purpose of the school to prepare men and women for the gospel ministry uppermost in their minds, who saw their own part in the life of the community as an expression of that same gospel, who were responsible for doing "the little things" that keep an institution operating well, and who often go unnoticed by others. While this spirit was also exhibited in the school's leaders, often too little notice is given to those who labored behind the scenes, as it were.

On March 31, 1994, Jack Hodges retired as superintendent of buildings and grounds of the seminary. Mr. Homer Bradish, a long-time employee in charge of maintenance, was named to succeed

Hodges. Having come to work in 1955, Hodges served Austin Seminary faithfully and saw students come and go for thirty-nine years.

In addition to overseeing the general maintenance and upkeep of the seminary facilities, he also oversaw some of the major building projects. For example, when the estimates from contractors for the renovation of Lubbock Hall were deemed prohibitive, Hodges offered to accept the job and the responsibility. Upon its successful completion in 1978, Hodges was presented with a resolution of appreciation from the Board of Trustees.

In 1991 the Lilly Foundation helped underwrite a "facilities evaluation" at Austin Seminary. With the $50,000 grant, the seminary engaged Mr. H. C. Lott, Jr., director of construction for the University of Texas, and his staff to do a facilities needs assessment. In his report to the Board of Trustees, Herman Harren refers to Lott's evaluation:

> In Mr. Lott's summary he says, "Austin Presbyterian Theological Seminary has done a commendable job through the years in maintaining its facilities. As a result, a major deferred maintenance problem does not exist; however, there are a number of minor repairs, as identified in this report, that need to be made to avoid major problems in the future."

At the end of his report Harren again cites Lott's report:

> "The physical plant staff at Austin Presbyterian Theological Seminary has done an excellent job in maintaining the various mechanical systems. Much of the equipment has outlived its expected service life due to the high degree of periodic maintenance." I share this quote to reiterate what I have mentioned in other reports to you, that the Seminary is most fortunate to have Jack Hodges as the Superintendent of Buildings and Grounds.[1]

But Hodges' impact went far beyond the diligence and efficiency with which he carried out his responsibilities. Shirley Howard, who herself worked for the seminary for twenty-two years, described Hodges as "a very special person," someone who "worked long hours, cared about the seminary, and knew everything about the buildings and equipment." She added that his thoughtfulness and caring attitude "added to the family atmosphere."[2]

In addition to Hodges, those who worked under his supervision should be included for their faithful service to the seminary and the spirit with which they carried out their duties: Willie Alexander, Elworth ("Pete") Wright, Ken Metcalfe, Vernon Batts, and Ulesly Conner, to name only a few. Homer Bradish continues the strong tradition of excellence as the manager of the physical plant. Working with him is Dennis Roetman, maintenance supervisor. With the expansion of the facilities, their responsibilities are daunting ones indeed.

Also on the list of "unsung heroes" over the past twenty-five years is the name of Ruth Metcalfe, director of food service for seventeen years (August 1, 1974, through June 30, 1991). She and her husband, Ken, contributed to the seminary community by their gracious spirit. Providing food for seminary students, faculty, and staff over the years in a kind and gentle way, Ruth and her staff endeared themselves to the seminary community. Among those who worked under Ruth's supervision were Ms. Bessie Maxwell and Ms. Willie Elizabeth Johnson. The latter died of cancer on April 25, 1993, having worked for Austin Seminary for almost nineteen years.

Jimmie Clark worked at Austin Seminary from 1958 to 1989. Having worked for the State of Texas, Clark moved to Dallas with her family. When her family returned to Austin, she applied for an opening at the Seminary and began work that would last thirty-one years. During her tenure she worked primarily in the Office of Supervised Practice of Ministry (formerly called "field education"). Her "bosses" included Henry Quinius (seventeen years), Bob Shelton, Carter King, and Pete Hendrick. When asked why she stayed so long, Clark replied, "Because I loved it. I loved every day I worked there. I loved those students as if they were my own." She added, "No one could have been happier in a job than I was."[3]

Shirley Howard shared Jimmie Clark's view of the seminary as "family." Employed by the seminary from June 1968 through May 1990, Howard worked first in the Office of the Director of Admissions (under Joe Donahue, Fred Morgan, and Ann Hoch) and later in the Development Office (for Joe Culver and Bill Hedrick). In addition to those for whom she worked directly, Howard has pleasant memories of both faculty and students: John Jansen ("dear, genuine; a good sense of humor"), Cathy Sautter ("Miss Seminary"), Stuart Currie ("brilliant, but down-to-earth"), Dick Junkin, Gene March, and Ross Dunn. Frank Ehman and Richard Culp both were student assistants in Howard's office and are fondly recalled by Howard. Upon graduation from Austin Seminary, Ehman accepted a call to be the associate pastor at Westminster Presbyterian Church in Austin, where Howard and her husband, Jack, were members.

Howard's love for Austin Seminary continues in her retirement, but she fears that with its growth, the sense of family and community will diminish. While she worked for Joe Culver in the Development Office, Howard participated in the arrival of the computer in the life of the seminary. Her fear is that the seminary will become more of a business and less of a family.

In May 1978 Fern Chester came to work at the seminary as the secretary to the academic dean, Dick Junkin. One of the dean's responsibilities was oversight of the Doctor of Ministry program. For the next twenty-one years, Chester became the chief contact person for anyone inquiring into the D.Min. program, guiding the students who went through the program and overseeing the program's growth and development.

Fern's husband, Ray, was in the seminary's first class of Doctor of Ministry students, which began in 1975. He received that degree in 1977.

The D.Min. program was directed first by Junkin and subsequently by Pete Hendrick, Cynthia Campbell, and Tina Blair. In addition to working with the D.Min. program, Chester assumed responsibility for assisting with the Continuing Education program, working first with Pete Hendrick and later with Blair and Dan Garza.[4]

According to a seminary publication, Fern Chester's "loyalty to the vocation of ministry and to Austin Seminary runs deep. She caught from Ray his enthusiasm for continuing education: 'I know I'm helping these students with something significant. Continuing their education does so much for pastors; it keeps them from burnout.'"[5]

Among the support staff who rendered faithful service but are no longer at the seminary, mention could also be made of Ida Forbes, Sharon Alexander, Evelyn Byrom, Dorothy Andrews, and Peggy Cockrum, among others. With new administrations, with growth, with the passage of time, a new generation of employees has the opportunity both to claim Austin Seminary as its own and to contribute to its life and sense of community.

At the meeting of the Board of Trustees in November 1997, President Shelton read a letter from Herman Harren indicating his intention to resign in order to retire, effective July 31, 1998. Harren, a native of La Feria, Texas, came to Austin Seminary in 1971 as the business manager. After ten years in that capacity, in 1981 the Board of Trustees elected him vice president for business affairs. He was in his twenty-seventh year of service to the seminary when, on April 12, 1998, he suffered a stroke.

Because of Harren's love for music and his several abilities in that field, the seminary purchased a six-foot-eight-inch Yamaha grand piano for the McCord Community Center in Harren's honor. It was dedicated at a program of recognition and dedication on October 23, 1998. On that occasion, President Shelton observed about Harren: "He is a friend I could trust and a colleague. His Christian witness has been inspiring." Continuing, Shelton said, "Herman never once thought of what he was doing as a job, but as a calling, his way of living out his own Christian faith. He was not only interested in what was going on in the business office. ... He never asked anyone to do anything he was not willing to do himself."[6]

After a music program including several hymns played by Kevin McClure, director of Chapel music, Academic Dean Andy Dearman offered a prayer of thanksgiving, expressing gratitude to God for "a faithful steward, cautious with the gifts of others and generous with his own."[7]

Genevieve (Gene) Luna came to work as a library secretary at Austin Seminary on February 1, 1968. After a year, she became the assistant librarian. After thirty-two years of service, Luna retired at the end of the 1999–2000 academic year. She saw the library grow from 50,000 volumes to 160,000 volumes. The collections were kept in card catalogs in 1968; by the time she retired, not only was everything automated, but the Stitt Library holdings could be accessed from one's home. In 1968 there were no copy machines; in 2000 several were available.[8]

In 1989 the Austin Seminary Association honored Luna for her service to the church through her work in the Stitt Library. Some of the words offered on that occasion were these:

"Mother confessor," friend, boss, "reference librarian," "circulation librarian," "book-find collector," library policy enforcer, hostess, messenger—Gene Luna, you have graced Austin Seminary (which you initially thought to be a monastery) for twenty-one years. You began your work as a secretary to the librarian, but from your first days demonstrated a keen interest in learning about the library and the Seminary.

And you were a fast learner. With no background in library work, you observed, asked questions, studied and read about the operation of the library. When the position of "circulation librarian" came open, you asked for the opportunity to take on that responsibility and fulfilled it so well that you were given the position of circulation clerk just over a year after your initial employment.

Your interest continued from that point on and your responsibilities grew with your interest. The more you learned, the more responsibility you asked for and were given, until now there are few, if any, aspects of the library's operations with which you are unfamiliar. Professors depend on you for their reserve books and to perform important bibliographic searches, students depend on you for locating books and periodicals, patrons outside the Seminary depend on you for information, research and assistance.[9]

Over her thirty-two years of service to the seminary, Luna served under three directors of the library. She noted that because it is a public place she had seen "lots of interesting and strange people go in and out." Among the many memories she has is that of locking Dr. Ernest Trice Thompson in the library. A visiting professor when Luna came to work in 1968, Dr. Thompson was hard of hearing and had closed the door to the room where he was working, and thus he was unable to hear any announcement that the library was being closed.[10]

Luna's quiet, patient, faithful service over more than three decades was a witness of its own to generations of students, pastors, faculty members, and persons having no connection to the seminary at all.

There is another group of persons who are vital to the seminary, but who, while perhaps achieving levels of distinction outside the life of the seminary, could go unnoticed—members of the Board of

Trustees. Included in the October 1996 minutes of the board are the following "qualifications for trustees" of Austin Seminary:

1) Demonstrated commitment to Jesus Christ and Christ's church;
2) Strong interest in Austin Presbyterian Theological Seminary and theological education;
3) Visionary attitude and skills;
4) Exhibited leadership ability;
5) Effective communication skills;
6) Knowledge about institutions;
7) Appreciation for and willingness to participate in fund raising;
8) Positive and hopeful about the future;
9) Willingness to serve;
10) Openness to the views of others.[11]

In the same set of minutes one also finds a list of the "responsibilities of trustees":

1) Attend faithfully and participate energetically in the meeting of the Board of Trustees;
2) Become and remain thoroughly informed about Austin Seminary;
3) Serve as a knowledgeable and enthusiastic ambassador for Austin Seminary;
4) Participate in institutional fund raising in accordance with your abilities and resources;
5) Develop an understanding and an increased knowledge about theological education;
6) Participate regularly in the evaluation of the seminary's president, and in the evaluation of other aspects of the seminary's personnel and programs when requested;
7) Become acquainted with the seminary's administrators, faculty and students;
8) Represent the seminary at events, conferences and programs; and serve as the seminary's presence on boards, agencies or committees when requested;
9) Be faithful in the further development of one's spiritual life;
10) Pray for the seminary and the seminary community regularly.[12]

Over the century of Austin Seminary's life, there have been many who have given of themselves freely and generously as board members. They come from a broad range of vocational backgrounds: clergy, business, education, law, medicine, politics, and homemaking, among others. Whether clergy or layperson, many have exhibited a winsome and sometimes courageous commitment to the gospel of Jesus Christ and the expression of that gospel in the mission of Austin Seminary.

The sense of devotion to the seminary and its mission is clearly evident in the remarks of some of those who have served on the Board of Trustees. For example, Weldon Smith served on the seminary's board for eighteen years (1970–79 and 1980–89), or as he says, "from Stitt to Stotts."[13] President of the Big "6" Drilling Company, Smith was a member of Second Presbyterian Church in Houston (which later became Grace Presbyterian Church) when he served on the board. In October 1998 Smith was honored as a "Distinguished Alumnus" of the University of Texas at Austin.

Smith believes that a good trustee recognizes that the appointment is an honor and that he or she should be grateful for that opportunity; needs to be a better Christian because of his or her role as a trustee; needs to believe that the associations will be pleasant and worthwhile; needs to be willing to give whatever time is required; needs to know when to decline a task or appointment; needs to continue to be active in one's church, representing the church on the board; and needs to love people.[14]

Clarence N. Frierson, an elder in First Presbyterian Church, Shreveport, Louisiana, served on the board for twenty-two years and was chairman of the board during much of Jack Maxwell's presidency, providing strong leadership at a very difficult time in the seminary's life. Of his experience he writes:

> In 1975 President Prescott Williams asked me to serve on the board of trustees at the seminary and I attended my first meeting that fall. At my first meeting I learned that Prescott was resigning and that a presidential search committee was already at work. Shortly thereafter a special meeting of the board was called to elect Tom Gillespie as president. Late on the night before the meeting Dr. Gillespie changed his mind and the search for a president had to be resumed. I am told that Dr. McCord [president of

Princeton Theological Seminary] had suggested two names to the search committee, Gillespie and Jack Maxwell. Not too long afterwards Jack Maxwell was elected president.

Frierson writes:

During some of the times when things were not going well, there were some "good and faithful servants" who stayed the course. They could have gone to greener pastures, such men as Herman Harren, Bob Shelton, Prescott Williams and others. Reflection on our history ought to acknowledge this kind of loyalty.

Frierson served as chairman of the Presidential Search Committee following Maxwell's resignation. Of this experience he avers:

We had in-depth interviews with five outstanding candidates, eventually and unanimously agreeing on Jack Stotts. This was the second major turning point in the life of the seminary, in my judgement [the first being the Jean Brown bequest]. People liked, trusted and respected the president of Austin Seminary! Jack possesses personal and political skills, integrity and has the respect of the entire church. His record as president speaks for itself.

And who could better succeed Jack Stotts than Bob Shelton? Well-liked by all, respected, knowledgeable, one who really loves Austin Seminary and wants the responsibility. Great choice![15]

Edward Vickery succeeded Frierson as chairman of the Board of Trustees in 1984. Recommended to the seminary administration by Weldon Smith, Vickery served on the board from 1977 to 1985 and 1987 to 1995. Vickery served as chairman from 1984 to 1985, and again from 1989 to 1995. A native of Forth Worth, Vickery graduated from the University of Texas law school with honors in 1948, moved to Houston, and joined First Presbyterian Church, where his membership has remained.

While many significant and positive changes in the life of Austin Seminary took place during his tenure on the board, including the call to Jack Stotts to serve as president, Vickery cites improvements in the physical plant as particularly important. Student houses that were old and worn out were torn down and new duplexes and apartments built; apartments for additional student housing was purchased; the dormitory was renovated; and, perhaps most significantly, the McCord Community Center was constructed.

Persons who played crucial roles in the life of Austin Seminary, in Vickery's view, include Herman Harren, "who basically supervised all the building projects"; Ellis Nelson, who "due to his reputation as an educator almost overnight restored credibility of the seminary as far as its Texas constituency was concerned"; Clarence Frierson "who was always a leader"; Weldon Smith, who provided wise counsel as chair of the seminary's Investment Committee; and, of course, Jack Stotts and Bob Shelton.

Reflecting on his service as a member of Austin Seminary's Board of Trustees, Vickery offers the following observation:

> Serving on the Austin Presbyterian Theological Seminary Board of Trustees was the most enjoyable and personally rewarding work I have ever done for the church, and it is the only church work that I regretted having to leave. What made it so was Ellis Nelson, Jack Stotts, Bob Shelton, Herman Harren, and the exceptional quality and dedication of the other trustees.[16]

Bruce Herlin, an elder in First Presbyterian Church in Palacios, Texas, was first elected to the board in 1981. He has served on the board for eighteen years (1981–90 and 1991–2000). Herlin's uncle, Robert B. Trull, moved to Palacios in 1927 and joined the Presbyterian church. The Trull Administration Building, built in 1962, is named after the Trull family. Herlin manages the family foundation in Palacios.

Dr. Ted Hartman, a member of the faculty of the Texas Tech University medical school, was a member of the Board of Trustees from 1989 to 1998. Although somewhat hesitant to accept the invitation to join the seminary board "because of the past turmoil at the Seminary and also because of my personal lack of knowledge as to 'what the Seminary was doing and where it was going,'" Hartman was influenced in his decision to join the board "through my close friend and former trustee, the late David Vigness."[17]

Hartman recalls his first board meeting:

The first time I attended a Board of Trustees meeting was in the fall of 1989. At that meeting, it became very clear to me that Jack Stotts was the embodiment of a strong Christian leader with a total dedication to education and to the future of the Church. In addition, Jack was a unique visionary. He saw what the Seminary could be for the future and communicated that very effectively!

Acknowledging the strength of the faculty of Austin Seminary and the attractive academic milieu in which the school finds itself, Hartman notes one element among faculty members that is conspicuous by its absence:

> Perhaps the one factor lacking when one recruits younger faculty is that so often they have not had significant experience as pastor of a congregation(s). That could be an issue that requires further study and consideration for the future inasmuch as these very faculty are expected to develop Seminary students into pastors for the congregations of the Church. And, as Bob Shelton stated in his presidential address, "Austin Presbyterian Theological Seminary is a school of the church."

Looking to the future, Hartman sees bright years ahead:

> In the description of the presidency that was developed by the presidential search committee, reference was made to a person who could move the Seminary to the "next level of excellence." Since being named president, Bob Shelton has shown a new vigor and vitality, vision, and leadership that is contagious. And I believe he will fulfill that statement from the presidential search. It is my personal belief that Austin Seminary will become the premier seminary among those Presbyterian seminaries not offering a terminal Doctor of Philosophy degree.[18]

Jo E. "Jed" Shaw succeeded Vickery as chairman of the board. A lifelong Presbyterian and a member of Memorial Drive Presbyterian Church in Houston, he first came onto the board in 1990. A native Houstonian and a real estate lawyer, Shaw had no ties to Austin Seminary prior to being asked by Jack Stotts to serve on the board. At the request of Ed Vickery, Shaw agreed to chair the capital campaign to build the McCord center. In addition to serving on the seminary board, Shaw served as chairman of the board of the Inner City Youth, Inc. of Houston, an experience that vies with his seminary experience in terms of personal satisfaction and fulfillment.[19]

Bessie Lou Doelling lives in Odessa, Texas, and was invited to join the Board of Trustees in 1990. Like Ed Vickery, Doelling writes that her experience on the board "has been the most educational, pleasurable and satisfying time of my life."[20]

Some of the seminary's best assets, according to Doelling, are the "real," "everyday" people who get things done, but rarely receive acknowledgment. Among those are Linda Cunningham, administrative assistant to the president, and Nancy Reese, secretary to the academic dean, both of whom will always "wear a halo," in Doelling's view. In addition, she writes,

> The receptionists, telephone answerers are always pleasant, helpful and accommodating. The faculty is the cream; each holds a special place in my heart and prayers. Of course, the students are very special. Without them a seminary would not be needed.

She concludes her thoughts:

> I believe that under the leadership of Bob Shelton, present staff, faculty and Board the Seminary will grow and grow and become even more important to God's work for all people, not just Presbyterians.[21]

Other board members who have given of their time, energy, and talents in a sacrificial way could be mentioned. Max R. Sherman, a former state senator, former president of West Texas State University, and retired dean of the Lyndon Baines Johnson School of Public Affairs, served on the seminary board from 1988 to 1997 and was reappointed in 1999. In 1999 Sherman, an elder at University Presbyterian Church, was named "Texan of the Year" by the Texas Legislative Conference. Rev. Joe B. Donaho, former director of admissions and pastor of Eastminster Presbyterian Church in Columbia, South Carolina, also served on the board from 1988 to 1997, and he was reappointed in 1999.

Stephen A. Matthews, an attorney from Pine Bluff, Arkansas,

and an elder at First Presbyterian Church there, served on the board for eighteen years and was named a trustee emeritus in 2001. The Rev. Dr. John M. McCoy, a 1963 graduate of Austin Seminary, was a board member from 1990 to 1999. With a Ph.D. from Princeton Theological Seminary, McCoy has served pastorates in Texas and North Carolina. After serving as pastor of NorthPark Presbyterian Church in Dallas, he served as interim pastor at Highland Park Presbyterian Church, also in Dallas. He served as co-moderator of the seminary's Centennial Committee.[22]

On November 13, 1999, President Shelton presented the Distinguished Service Award to William J. Murray, Jr., for having served on the Board of Trustees for twenty-seven years (1952–61, 1962–71, and 1972–81).[23] Such long and faithful service characterizes many, if not most, of those "unsung heroes" who love Austin Seminary and have been a part of its life for any period of time.

One "unsung hero" who played a particularly important role during and immediately following the Maxwell presidency was Allen Smith, pastor for many years of Second Presbyterian Church in Little Rock, Arkansas. He chaired the Synod Covenant Review team during the time leading to Maxwell's resignation. Smith, a graduate of Austin Seminary, not only led the Covenant Review team as a sounding board for those who expressed their concern for the seminary, but he also provided strong support for the listening meetings that went on throughout the synod following Maxwell's resignation. Bill Hedrick and members of the Covenant Review team traveled throughout the Synod of the Sun to make presentations and to listen to the church.[24]

Perhaps at least as much as these, "unsung heroes" should also include persons who, with their families, have responded to God's call to the ministry, have come here to prepare for that call, and have gone out to all parts of this country and throughout the world to live and proclaim the good news of the gospel. Often going to unglamourous places with little to offer other than an opportunity to preach, teach, and offer pastoral care as a representative of him who is the Good Shepherd, such persons also carry something of Austin Seminary with them.

Any effective and successful institution depends on those supporters who are willing to give of themselves in a sacrificial way, but who expect little or no recognition. Participation in a cause in which they believe and to which they are devoted brings its own satisfaction. Austin Seminary has certainly had, and continues to have, such persons as students, faculty, staff, administrators, board members, and constituents in the church. Such a spirit that combines humility with commitment to Jesus Christ surely will lead to one day hearing the words that all long to hear, "Well done, good and faithful servant; enter into the joy of your master."

CHAPTER TEN

Toward the Second Century

The first 100 years of Austin Presbyterian Theological Seminary's life have been rich and productive. In addition to equipping men and women for ministry in a variety of forms in the name of Jesus Christ, both in the Southwest and around the world, the seminary has seen its graduates assume positions of leadership in the church at the national level. Thomas White Currie (Class of 1911), the school's third president, was elected moderator of the General Assembly of the Presbyterian Church in the United States in 1930. James I. McCord (Class of 1942), having served as professor of systematic theology and academic dean at Austin Seminary, became president of Princeton Theological Seminary in 1959.

David L. Stitt (Class of 1936) became the fourth president of Austin Seminary in the summer of 1945 after serving as pastor of First Presbyterian Church in Haskell, Texas, and Westminster Presbyterian Church in St. Louis, Missouri. He served as president until 1971, when he accepted a call to be the associate pastor of First Presbyterian Church in Houston. He went on to serve as pastor of Bellaire Presbyterian Church in Houston. In 1980 Stitt was elected moderator of the General Assembly of the Presbyterian Church, U.S., at a meeting in Myrtle Beach, South Carolina.

Ellis Nelson (Class of 1940) taught at Austin Seminary and Union Seminary in New York. He also served as president of Louisville Theological Seminary from 1974 to 1981. His wisdom, experience, and availability made him an obvious and happy choice to serve as interim president of Austin Seminary following Jack Maxwell's resignation in November 1983. Recognized as one of the foremost authorities in the field of Christian Education, Nelson has lectured and published widely, and is the only person to have delivered the Jones Lectures on three different occasions at Austin Seminary's Mid-Winter Lectures.

Although not an Austin Seminary graduate, T. Watson Street taught church history and missions at Austin Seminary from 1949 to 1961. In 1961 he moved to Nashville, Tennessee, to become the executive secretary of the Board of World Missions of the Presbyterian Church, U.S.

In 1973 James E. Andrews (Class of 1956) succeeded James Millard as stated clerk of the Presbyterian Church, U.S., having served as assistant stated clerk for three years. When the two main branches of the Presbyterian Church reunited in 1983, Andrews was elected stated clerk of the General Assembly of the Presbyterian Church (U.S.A.) and remained in that position until his retirement in 1996.

Flynn Long (Class of 1952) served as assistant stated clerk of the General Assembly under Jim Andrews. Patricia McClurg (Class of 1967) was the first female Austin Seminary graduate to be ordained in the Presbyterian Church, U.S., went on to work in the Office of the General Assembly, and later served as executive of New Castle Presbytery, with offices in Wilmington, Delaware. The two most recent executives of the Synod of the Sun have been Austin Seminary graduates—William J. Fogleman (Class of 1953) and Judy Record Fletcher (1969).

Austin Seminary's leadership at the national level continued when Frank Diaz (Class of 1982) became interim executive director of the General Assembly Council in 1996. At the 1996 General Assembly meeting in Albuquerque, New Mexico, the executive director of the General Assembly Council, the Rev. James D. Brown, was to be confirmed for a second four-year term. In a stunning move, the assembly rejected the confirmation of Brown. Diaz, who had been serving as Brown's assistant, was elected by the General Assembly Council Executive Committee to serve as interim director.

It was Diaz's modest yet confident leadership, many believe, that contributed to a calm spirit as the search began for a new executive director. In an issue of the "Presbyterian Headline News," published by the Presbyterian News Service, Diaz is quoted as having said that he "felt that my first job was to hold the staff together in Louisville." The article continues:

> He began by instituting a daily prayer session at the Presbyterian Center (in addition to the daily chapel services that are held there) in which members of the national staff gathered and "prayed their way through the national staff—praying for individual staffers each day until we had prayed individually for every one of them."
>
> As word of the prayer "vigil" spread throughout the church, Diaz remembers, "The church began to see that we're emphasizing prayer and that Jesus Christ is at the center of what we do here ... and it was a breakthrough." Diaz says letters began pouring in from Presbyterians around the country—"They saw us as a praying people and they began lifting us up in their prayers and the tide turned."[1]

Diaz had come to Austin Seminary at the age of forty-six years after a successful career as an electronics engineer and owner and manager of a real estate firm. In addition, he served as chairman of the task force that desegregated the Dallas public schools. After graduation, Diaz served the Hispanic Presbyterian congregations in New Braunfels and San Marcos, Texas, in a yoked situation, from 1982 to 1987. In 1987 he went to El Buen Pastor in Austin, where, in addition to serving as pastor, he organized Manos de Cristo, a social service coalition of fifteen area churches. In 1989 Diaz was called to serve in the General Assembly offices in Louisville as associate director of policies and special projects. He remained in that position until 1994, when he agreed to serve as the associate executive director of the General Assembly Council. He was in that position when, in 1996, he became the interim executive director after James Brown's contract was not renewed. In 1999 Diaz was endorsed as a candidate for moderator of the Presbyterian Church (U.S.A.), but lost to Freda Gardner.[2]

As Austin Seminary begins its second century of service, it does so surrounded by this great cloud of witnesses, and many more who had an association with Austin Seminary and served Jesus Christ faithfully. But it does so also with considerable challenges before it. One which is facing the Christian enterprise in general is proclaiming the gospel in an increasingly dangerous world. Even though the last quarter-century saw the downfall of the Soviet Union and the threat that its form of communism represented, a new threat, in the form of religious fundamentalism, began to appear in various parts of the world.

Muslim fundamentalists, in particular, began open attacks on western institutions and countries in ways that killed indiscriminately. Such persons were connected with a bomb that sent a Pan American jet crashing to the earth over Lockerbie, Scotland, on December 21, 1988, killing all 259 persons on board the plane and 11 persons on the ground. On February 26, 1993, a car bomb was detonated in a parking garage beneath the World Trade Center in New York City. On September 11, 2001, four commercial jets were hijacked, presumably by Muslim fundamentalists, or representatives of them. Two crashed into the twin towers of the World Trade Center in New York City, causing them to collapse, killing thousands. A third took aim on the Pentagon in the nation's capital, killing not only all passengers on board the plane, but hundreds in the nation's defense center. A fourth jet went down in southwestern Pennsylvania, again killing all on board.

In addition, as the twenty-first century opened, the Presbyterian Church (U.S.A.) was challenged by a continued decline in its membership, a trend that had begun thirty years before.[3] The church saw itself torn apart by a debate over whether or not to ordain practicing homosexuals as church officers, a debate that had also persisted for twenty-five years.

A third challenge facing Austin Seminary as it began a second century of service was, paradoxically, its own success. The student body continued to grow. The faculty continued to grow. The administrative staff continued to grow. The seminary's investment portfolio continued to grow. The seminary enjoyed the goodwill not only of its Presbyterian constituency, but also of its ecumenical connections. After students who were members of the Presbyterian Church (USA), the United Methodist Church had the most students on campus. The office of vice president for student affairs, established by President Shelton in 2001, was filled by Dr. Ann Fields, a minister member of the United Methodist Church. Rev. Marvin C. Griffin, a Baptist pastor in Austin, was the first non-Presbyterian to serve on the seminary's Board of Trustees.

With all this goodwill and positive development, what room might there be for complaint? Perhaps none, except that of becoming too comfortable with the school's happy situation. If it is true that one creates not out of opulence, but out of the desert, then, it seems, one must be pushed and challenged, especially during prosperous times. While one would never wish to return to the days when the seminary's leaders struggled and had to wonder whether there would be a future for this school, at least those days were characterized by harnessing everyone's energy and focusing everyone's attention on making the vision of Austin Seminary a reality.

Instinct for survival can be a powerful force. Paradoxically, once an institution's survival seems to be assured, its life may be threatened by the comfort that accompanies the success. What will be the driving force behind Austin Seminary in the twenty-first century? Will it be a bigger investment portfolio? Will it be a bigger faculty and administrative staff? Will it be a desire to be bigger and better? Or, will it be a renewed sense of commitment to the gospel of Jesus Christ and the preparation of men and women for the gospel ministry? Will it be that same high calling that drove Sampson, Vinson, Currie, Stitt, and Williams, and the faculty and staff they led? Will it be the awareness that, while the seminary aims to produce the best scholarship possible, it is also, as President Shelton has said, a "school of the church"? Will it be a renewed commitment to the sense of community that has been such an important part of the seminary's life in its first 100 years, a community that had the Chapel and worship at its center?

Looking to the seminary's second century, another of its graduates who occupies a position of national prominence in the Presbyterian Church (U.S.A.) has reflected on Austin Seminary and its future. After serving several pastorates, Robert H. Bullock, Jr. (Class of 1971) became the editor of *The Presbyterian Outlook,* a national independent weekly publication, in August 1988. Uniquely positioned to look at theological education from a national perspective, as well as at Austin Seminary from a personal perspective, Bullock offered the following observations:

If the seminary is to build on the past and continue to offer major support to the Presbyterian Church (U.S.A.), it should be focusing in the following areas in the next 25 years:

1. Recruiting a strong president early in the new century with an authentic faith and the ability to articulate it clearly and winsomely, strong Presbyterian roots, theological depth with demonstrated knowledge of and commitment to the Reformed theological tradition, preferably with experience in the pastoral ministry, with an earned graduate degree (if possible), but most importantly one who sees the seminary as vitally related to the Presbyterian Church, and seeks in every way to nurture and expand relations with that constituency.

2. With the president, the seminary needs to have a board which shares that vision and those commitments, which together with the president, exercises effective control of the seminary in terms of its mission, identifies programs and curricula, [makes] faculty appointments and [encourages] student recruiting. Many Presbyterian seminaries are drifting toward detached divinity school status. This drift must be laid at the feet of presidents and boards. There is certainly a place for such schools of excellence that are non-aligned and function as an independent force in theological education, but this has never been the purpose of Austin Seminary, and should not become so either by design or by neglect.

3. The most important task of the president and the board, aside from setting the vision and mission of the seminary, is the recruitment of faculty. Most faculty members should have parish experience as well as the appropriate graduate degree. All faculty members should be persons of faith, who are able to articulate their faith, and among the Presbyterian faculty, who wholeheartedly support the confessional stance of the Presbyterian Church (U.S.A.) as contained in the *Book of Confessions.* In order, over time, to recruit and hold effective faculty, the seminary may need to challenge its ablest graduates to go on to graduate school, followed by significant parish experience, whereupon such persons would become faculty members at mid-life.... While there was a time when Austin Seminary needed to recruit more broadly geographically, if the seminary is to serve the Southwest, it would be helpful to recruit more faculty, over time, with ties to the Southwest.

4. The seminary must work much more closely with presby-

teries and churches in its region in challenging and recruiting the most competent candidates for ministry. This function has been sorely neglected for the past 30 or more years and the church is facing a major crisis within the next 10 to 15 years: a shortage of qualified, competent pastors for existing and new churches.

5. The seminary must continue to keep its financial house in order, expanding the endowment, containing costs, but not at the expense of adequately compensating the faculty and providing scholarships for the best students.

6. The seminary must keep abreast of changing trends in theological education, such as the growth of extension programs, but not so as to weaken its primary residential core program.

7. Insofar as resources permit, the seminary should provide opportunities for training the lay leadership of the church within its region. There are so many non-Presbyterians now serving as elders, that the need for training will overwhelm the individual pastor. Continuing education programs for laypeople with talent to become master teachers in the church should be made available.

8. The need for children and youth workers for our churches is critical. There still is an important need for professional church workers known as DCEs. Perhaps shorter training programs for 20-something young adults interested in spending a few years in such ministries could be instituted to replace training once provided by schools such as Presbyterian School for Christian Education.

9. The seminary should explore the possibilities for using new technology to make the best teaching available to churches and groups of churches.

Bullock concludes his thoughts and reflections on theological education, in general, and the future of Austin Seminary, in particular, with the following:

> Ultimately, the seminary is one of the chief guardians of the faith of the church. It is uniquely positioned to conserve the best of the tradition, to conduct ongoing discussions within the tradition on behalf of the church, and to equip the finest candidates for ministry in the Presbyterian Church in the coming century.
>
> The seminaries and the congregations are the two strongest in-

stitutions left in organized Presbyterianism. Their interests are closely related. Every effort to strengthen ties from both sides will be critically important to the seminaries, the churches and the Presbyterian Church (U.S.A.).[4]

In his report to the Board of Trustees in May 1998, John Evans, then vice president for development and church relations, quoted words from Barbara Wheeler, president of Auburn Theological Seminary in New York. Wheeler offered these words about Austin Seminary to the Board of Trustees, the faculty, and administration during a retreat in November 1995:

> ... you aren't the richest seminary; you don't harbor the most famous scholars; you're not the most aggressive in program or fund development. But your combination of advantages—adequate resources, enough students, a collegial faculty, programs of good quality—is unusual. Very few theological schools have so many positive factors in balance. The combination positions you, if you so choose, to become one of the institutional leaders in the next period.[5]

Austin Seminary enters its second century as a very healthy institution in virtually every respect. Many have labored and contributed generously and graciously to make it so. The opportunities before it are many. The challenges before it and the church are enormous.

The beginning of the twenty-first century has been filled with confusion and uncertainty. Terrorist attacks, the growth of Islam and other faiths, the decline of Protestantism, in general, and the Presbyterian church, in particular, and the rise of secularism all contribute to a daunting challenge that might discourage many. And yet, the cause of the gospel of Jesus Christ has rarely found comfortable surroundings. From his birth in Bethlehem to his death outside the walls of Jerusalem, Jesus encountered opposition and resistance to the good news he came to proclaim. Discipleship is always costly, but the prize is always more than worth the cost.

It is worth noting a letter that was written on March 30, 1906, from the Scotsman Marcus Dods to the Rev. Dr. W. Robertson Nicoll. Then in his later years, Dods reflected on the church and what lay ahead:

Our ecclesiastical affairs here are in a disgusting mess—no one is satisfied with anything. What is to come of it all I know not. Happily I enjoy my own work, and have good times with the students. I fear some of my moroseness and pessimism is due to age. I hope so, and that this generation is better and not worse than the last; but I do not envy those who have to fight the battle of Christianity in the twentieth century. Yes, perhaps I do, but it will be a stiff fight, and will require great concessions to be made.[6]

The view that "the battle of Christianity" would "be a stiff fight" in the twentieth century proved to be an accurate prediction. It appears to be just as true for the twenty-first century.

Mindful of its rich heritage and how far it has come in the past 100 years, this "school of the church" must look to the future trusting, as it has in the past, in him who is King of kings and Lord of lords, in him whose kingdom shall have no end, even Jesus Christ.

APPENDIX A

The Faculties

The Austin School of Theology, 1884–95

*Died while in office.

1884–95	R. K. Smoot, D.D.—Professor of Church History and Government
1884–95	R. L. Dabney, D.D., LL.D.—Professor of Theology
1884–85	George L. Bitzer, Licentiate—Teaching Fellow, Hebrew and Greek
1885–86	Archibald Alexander Little—Hebrew and Greek
1886–88	William Stuart Red—Hebrew and Greek
1888–90	Thomas Cary Johnson—Hebrew and Greek
1890–91	John McLeod Purcell—Sacred Rhetoric and Biblical History
1891–95	William Jared Tidball—Hebrew and Greek
1891–94	Jacob Amos Lefevre—Polemic and Didactic Theology and Exegesis

Austin Presbyterian Theological Seminary, 1902–2002

1902–15*	Thornton R. Sampson, D.D., LL.D—President (1900–1905) and Professor of Church History and Polity
1902–14	Samuel A. King, D.D.—Professor of Systematic Theology Professor Emeritus

1902–16   Robert E. Vinson, D.D., LL.D.—Professor of Old Testament
           Languages and Exegesis; Acting Professor of New Testament
           Language and Exegesis
           1906—Professor of English Bible and Practical Theology
           1906—President
1903–5*   Richmond K. Smoot, D.D., LL.D.—Professor of Church His-
           tory and Polity
1904–6   E. D. Brown, D.D. — Adjunct Professor of Hebrew and Greek
1904–5   E. D. Shurter—Adjunct Professor of Elocution
1906–14   Eugene C. Caldwell, D.D., LL.D.—Professor of Old Testa-
           ment Languages and Exegesis
1908–9   S. E. Chandler, D.D.—Professor of Greek
1910–13   James L. Bell, D.D.—Professor of New Testament Language
           and Exegesis
1911–43*   Thomas W. Currie, B.A., M.A., B.D., D.D., LL.D.—Associate
           Professor of English Bible
           1917–20—Chairman of the Faculty
           1921—President and Professor of Church History
1913–14   Samuel McPheeters Glasgow, D.D.—Instructor in Greek and
           Homiletics
1914–18   William Angus McLeod, D.D.—Professor of Systematic The-
           ology
1914–60   Robert F. Gribble, B.A., B.D., D.D.—Instructor in Hebrew
           and New Testament Greek
           1923—Professor of Old Testament Languages and Exegesis
           1923–1933—Director of the Spanish-Speaking Department
           1943–1945—Acting President Professor Emeritus
1915–18   Robert L. Jetton, D.D.—Professor of New Testament Lan-
           guage and Exegesis
1915–54*   Samuel L. Joekel, A.B., B.D., D.D.—Instructor in Church
           History
           1926—Professor of English Bible, Religious Education
1916–17   Neal L. Anderson, D.D.—Acting President
1921–27   Arthur Gray Jones, D.D., LL.D.—Professor of Systematic
           Theology; Professor Emeritus
1921–57   Daniel Allen Penick, Ph.D.—Instructor in New Testament
           Language and Exegesis
1921–23   Antonio Horatio Perpetuo, B.A., B.D., M.A.—Instructor of

Old Testament Language and Exegesis and Director of the Spanish-Speaking Department

1925–37 E. R. Sims, Ph.D.—Lecturer in the Spanish-Speaking Department

1925–27 Thomas Chalmers Vinson, D.D.—Instructor in Theology

1925–27 Lawrence Hay Wharton, D.D.—Instructor in Homiletics

1927–40 George Summey, A.B., B.D., D.D., LL.D.—Professor of Systematic Theology
Professor Emeritus

1928–33 Orin Conway Williamson, D.D.—Instructor in the Spanish-Speaking Department

1933–45 Robert Douglas Campbell, Instructor in the Spanish-Speaking Department

1936–37 Julian Sleeper, D.D.—Instructor in Homiletics

1937–40 Conway C. Wharton, D.D. —Instructor in Homiletics

1938–58 Eugene William McLaurin, B.A., M.A., D.D., Ph.D.—Professor of Systematic Theology and New Testament Language and Exegesis
Professor of Polity
Professor Emeritus

1940–44 C. Ellis Nelson, B.A., M.A., B.D., D.D., Ph.D.—Associate Professor of Christian Education
1948–1957—Professor of Christian Education
1984–1985—Acting President
1984—Visiting Professor of Christian Education
1987—Research Professor of Christian Education

1943–?? Glenn Maxwell, M.A., B.D.—Instructor in Theology

1944–59 James Iley McCord, M.A., B.D., D.D., LL.D.—Associate Professor of Systematic Theology and Dean
1946—Professor of Systematic Theology and Dean

1945–71 David L. Stitt, B.A., B.D., D.D., LL.D., D.Hum.—President and Professor of Church History, then of Practical Theology

1945–46 Gus J. Craven, B.A., B.D.—Director of Field Work and Instructor in Christian Education

1945–47 Ernest A. J. Seddon, Jr., B.A., B.D.—Instructor in the Spanish-Speaking Department

1946–47 W. Meade Brown, Jr., B.A., B.D.—Instructor in Church History and Missions

1946–47   G. Wendell Crofoot, B.A., B.D.—Instructor in the Spanish-Speaking Department

1946–48   Frederick Eby, Ph.D., LL.D.—Visiting Professor of Christian Education

1947–48   Thomas B. Gallaher, M.A., D.D.—Instructor in Christian Education

1947–61   T. Watson Street, S.T.M., Th.D., D.D.—Associate Professor of Church History and Missions
          1949—Professor of Church History and Missions

1950–56   Howard W. Townsend, B.S., M.A.,Ph.D.—Instructor in Speech

1952–59   James A. Millard, D.D., LL.D.—Professor of Homiletics

1952–53   Jack B. McMichael, B.D., Ed.D.—Visiting Instructor of Christian Education

1953–55   Bernard Citron, Ph.D.—Visiting Professor of Biblical Theology

1955–57   C. Ernest Best, Ph.D.—Visiting Professor of Biblical Theology

1955–56   William Ith Board, B.D.—Instructor in Bible

1955–65   Norman Dressel Dow, Th.M., M.A., M.L.S.—Assistant Professor of Bibliography and Librarian

1955–58   Carlyle Marney, Tb.D.—Guest Professor of Homiletics

1955–75   Henry Willard Quinius, Jr., B.B.A., Th.M., D.D.—Associate Professor of Church Administration and Director of Field Education
          1957—Professor of Church Administration and Director of Field Education

1956–95   John Robert Hendrick, B.A., B.D., Ph.D.—Instructor in Bible
          1981—Professor of Mission and Evangelism, Director of Professional Development
          1984—Director of Supervised Practice of Ministry and Continuing Education
          1993—John W. and Helen Lancaster Professor of Evangelism and Missions
          Professor Emeritus

1956–75   James Allen Wharton, B.A., B.D.,Th.D.—Assistant Professor of Bible
          1967—Professor of Old Testament

1957–58   Edward B. Paisley, D.D., Ph.D.—Visiting Professor of Christian Education

1957–62   John Rea Thomas, B.D., M.A.—Instructor in Pastoral Coun-
           seling
1957–58   Grover Cleveland Wilson, Jr., B.A., B.D.—Instructor in Bibli-
           cal Theology
1958–61   J. Donald Butler, Ph.D.—Professor of Christian Education
1958–83   John F. Jansen, B.A., B.D., Th.D—Professor of New Testa-
           ment Interpretation
           1959–1962—Acting Dean
           Professor Emeritus
1958–72   Dietrich Ritschl, Ph. D.—Visiting Professor of Biblical Theol-
           ogy
           1960–63 Associate Professor of History of Dogma
           1972—Visiting Lecturer in Theology
1958–59   Carl E. Schneider, Ph.D., I-L.D., Th.D.—Visiting Professor of
           Church History
1958–64   Earl Constantine Scott, B.S., B.D.—Assistant Professor of
           New Testament
1959–62   Lena Lea Clausell, B.A., M.R.E.—Visiting Lecturer in Christ-
           ian Education
1959–60   Paul Calvin Payne, Ph.D., D.D.—Visiting Professor of Christ-
           ian Education
1959–72   J. Rodman Williams, B.A., B.D., Ph.D.—Associate Professor
           of Theology and Philosophy of Religion
           1964—Professor of Theology and Philosophy of Religion
1959–60   Don Marvin Williams, B.A., B.D.—Teaching Fellow in
           Homiletics
           1970–71—Visiting Professor of Homiletics
1959–90   Prescott Harrison Williams, Jr., B.A., B.D., Ph.D—Assistant
           Professor of Old Testament Languages and Archaeology
           1961—Associate Professor of Old Testament Languages and
           Archaeology
           1964—Professor of Old Testament Languages and Archaeol-
           ogy
           1966–1976—Dean of Faculty
           1971–1972—Acting President
           1972–1976—President
           Professor Emeritus
1960–63   William J. Fogleman, B.A., B.D.—Assistant Professor of Prac-
           tical Theology and Director of Continuing Education

1961–62   Frank F. Baker, B.A., B.D.,Th.D., D.D.—Visiting Professor of Missions

1961–75*   Stuart Dickson Currie, B.A., B.D.,Ph.D.—Assistant Professor of Church History
1962—Associate Professor of Church History
1964—Professor of New Testament Language and Exegesis

1961–70*   W. Walter Johnson, B.A., B.D., Tb.M., Th.D.—Assistant Professor of Homiletics
1967—Associate Professor of Homiletics

1961–64   Charles Leonidas King, A.B., B.D., D.D. LL.D.—Visiting Professor of Homiletics

1962–63   Keith Renn Crim, B.A., B.D., Th.M., Th.D.—Visiting Professor of Missions

1962–68   John Brewer Spragens, B.A., B.D., D.D.—Assistant Professor of Christian Education and Dean of Students

1963–65   Grover Ellis Foley, B.Sc., S.T.B., Th.D.—Visiting Professor of Theology

1963–64   John Marshall Guthrie, B.A., B.D., Th.M.—Visiting Professor of Missions

1964–65   William Davidson Blanks, B.A., B.D., Th.M., Th.D.—Visiting Professor of Church History

1964–94   George Stuart Heyer, Jr., A.B., B.D., M.A., Ph.D.—Assistant Professor of the History of Doctrine and Director of Continuing Education
1966—Associate Professor of the History of Doctrine and Director of Continuing Education
1967—Associate Professor of the History of Doctrine
1988—Professor of the History of Doctrine
Professor Emeritus

1964–72   Jorge Lara-Braud, B.A., B.D.—Visiting Professor of Missions
1965—Assistant Professor of Missions
1966—Visiting Professor of Missions
1972—Visiting Professor of Theology

1964–82   Wallace Eugene March, B.A., B.D., Tb.D.—Instructor of Old Testament Languages
1966—Assistant Professor of Old Testament
1969—Associate Professor of Old Testament
1973—Professor of Old Testament

1965–72 Rachel Henderlite, B.A., Ph.D.—Professor of Christian Education
1971–72—Visiting Professor of Christian Education
Professor Emerita
1965–70 Ernest Trice Thompson, B.A., B.D., M.A., Th.M., D.D.—Visiting Professor of Church History
1966–89 Calvin C. Klemt, B.A., B.D., M.L.S.—Librarian
1977—Associate Professor of the Church's Ministry Associate Professor Emeritus
1967–84* Ross Denison Dunn, B.A., B.D.—Assistant Professor Christian Ethics and Director of Continuing Education
1976—Associate Professor of Christian Ethics
1967–68 Stanley F. Hogle, B.A., B.D., S.T.M.—Visiting Professor of Pastoral Care
1968–71 Ian F. McIntosh, M.A., B.D., Th.M., Th.D.—Assistant Professor of Pastoral Care
1969–71 Houston Hodges, B.A., B.D.—Visiting Professor in the Department of the Church's Ministry
1970–83 Edward Dixon Junkin, B.A., B.D., Th.D.—Assistant Professor of Church History
1973—Associate Professor of Church History
1974—Assistant to the Dean
1976—Academic Dean and Professor of Church History
1971 Alfred Frederick Swearingen, B.A., S.T.B.—Visiting Professor of Worship
1971 J. Randall Nichols, Th.D.—Visiting Professor of Homiletics
1971 Thomas F. Torrance, M.B.E., B.D., M. Theol.,Visiting Lecturer in Theology
1971– Robert M. Shelton, B.A., B.D.,Th.M., Ph.D.—Associate Professor of Homiletics
1975—Professor of Homiletics
1982—Jean Brown Professor of Homiletics and Liturgies
1982—Acting Dean
1983—Academic Dean
1996—Interim President
1997—President
1972–72 Thomas H. Cole—Visiting Professor of Pastoral Care
1972–75 David Jacques Ernsberger, B.A., B.D., S.T.M.—Visiting Professor of Christian Education

1973–2000 William Conwell Spong, B.A., M.Div., Th.M.—Adjunct Professor of Pastoral Care

1974–80 Merwyn S. Johnson, B.A., B.D., Ph.D.—Assistant Professor of Theology

1974–84 Carl Siegenthaler, B.A., M.Div., M.S.W.—Adjunct Professor of Community Ministry

1975–81 David Ng, B.A., M.Div., D.D.—Associate Professor of Church Program and Nurture

1975– John Edward Alsup, B.A., M.Div., Th.D.—Visiting Professor of New Testament
1976—Assistant Professor of New Testament
1977—Associate Professor of New Testament
1988—Professor of New Testament
1993—First Presbyterian Church Shreveport, D. Thomason Professor of New Testament Studies

1975–81 J. Carter King III, B.A., M.Div.—Visiting Professor of Ministry
1976—Assistant Professor of Ministry and Director of Supervised Practice of Ministry

1975–85 Hilmer Charles Krause, Jr., B.A., B.D., S.T.M.—Adjunct Professor of Hispanic Ministry

1975–92 Jack L. Whitehead, Ph.D.—Adjunct Professor of Speech Communication

1975–76 Rubén Pacillas Armendariz, B.A., M.Div.—Adjunct Professor of Hispanic Ministry

1976–83 Jack Martin Maxwell, B.A., M.Div., Ph.D.—President and Professor of Homiletics and Liturgics

1976–77 Ralph Erb Person, B.A., B.D. Th.D.—Visiting Professor of Church History

1977–87 Robert S. Paul, B.A., M.A., D.Phil.—Professor of Ecclesiastical History and Christian Thought
Professor Emeritus

1980–87 George W. Stroup, III, B.A., B.D.,S.T.M., M.A., Ph.D—Associate
Professor of Systematic Theology

1980–2001 Ralph L. Underwood, B.A., B.D., Th.M., M.A., Ph.D.—Associate Professor of Pastoral Care
1987—Profsssor of Pastoral Care
Professor Emeritus

1981–88 Cynthia McCall Campbell, B.A., M.Div., Ph.D.—Assistant Professor of Theology and Ministry
1984—Director of Doctor of Ministry Program
1987—Associate Professor of Theology and Ministry

1982– John Andrew Dearman, B.A., M.Div., Ph.D.—Assistant Professor of Old Testament
1985—Associate Professor of Old Testament
1994—Professor of Old Testament
1997—Acting Academic Dean
2000—Academic Dean

1982– Laura Jean Brooking Lewis, B.S., M.A., M.Div., Ph.D.—Assistant Professor of Christian Education
1991—Associate Professor of Christian Education
1999—Professor of Christian Education
2000—Acting Academic Dean

1983– Lewis R. Donelson, B.A., M.Div., Ph.D.—Assistant Professor of New Testament
1989—Associate Professor of New Testament
2000—Professor of New Testament

1985–96 Jack L. Stotts, B.A., B.D., M.A., Ph.D.—President and Professor of Christian Ethics
President Emeritus

1986–91 James Frederick Holper, B.A., M.Div., M.A., Ph.D.—Assistant Professor of Homiletics and Liturgies

1987– Ismael García, B.A., M. A., Ph.D.—Associate Professor of Christian Ethics
1997—Professor of Christian Ethics

1987–94* Alan Edmond Lewis, M.A., B.D., Ph.D.—Professor of Constructive and Modern Theology

1988–2002 Ellen Louise Babinsky, B.A., M. Div., M.11., Ph.D.—Assistant Professor of Church History
1994—Associate Professor of Church History
2002—Professor of Church History

1990– Christine Eaton Blair, B.A., M.A., M.R.E., M.Div., Ph.D.—Assistant Professor of Practical Theology and Director of the Doctor of Ministry and Continuing Education Programs
1998—Associate Professor of Practical Theology, Director of Doctor of Ministry Program

1990–94   Valerie R. Hotchkiss, B.A., M.L.S, M.A., M. Phil., Ph.D.—Director of David and Jane Stitt Library
1990–   Stephen Breck Reid, B.S., M.Div., Ph.D.—Associate Professor of Old Testament
             1999—Professor of Old Testament Studies
1990–2000 Terry C. Muck, B.A., M.Div., M.S., Ph. D.—Associate Professor of Comparative Religion
             1999—Professor of Religion and Director of Institutional Effectiveness
1992–   Stanley Robertson Hall, B.A., M.Div., M.A., Ph.D.—Assistant Professor of Liturgics
             2000—Associate Professor of Liturgics
1992–99   William Stacy Johnson, A.B., J.D., M.Div., Ph.D.—Assistant Professor of Systematic Theology
1993–2001 Michael Jinkins, B.A., M.Div., D.Min., Ph.D.—Assistant Professor of the Church's Ministry, Director of Supervised Practice of Ministry
             1999—Associate Professor of Pastoral Theology
             Director of Supervised Practice of Ministry
1993–   Scott Black Johnston, B.A., M.Div., Ph.D.—Instructor in Homiletics
             1994—Assistant Professor of Homiletics
             1998—Associate Professor of Homiletics
1993–96   Donna F. Wilson,, B.A., M. Div., Ph.D., Lecturer in Biblical Languages
1993–   Michael Nelson Miller, B.A., M.A., M.Div., Ph.D.—Lecturer in the Church and Higher Education
             1999—Research Professor of the Church and Higher Education
1994–   Timothy D. Lincoln, B.A., M.Div., M.S. (LIS)—Director, David and Jane Stitt Library
             2001—Director of Institutional Effectiveness
1994–   Cynthia L. Rigby, B.A., M. Div., Ph. D.—Instructor of Theology
             1998—Assistant Professsor of Theology
             2000—Associate Professor of Theology
1996–2001 Sherron Kay George, B.A., M.A., D.Min.—Assistant Professor of Evangelism and Missions
             2000—Associate Professor of Evangelism and Missions

1998–   William N.A. Greenway, B.A., M.Div., Ph.D—Visiting Professor of Christian Studies
          1999—Assistant Professor of Christian Studies
          2000—Assistant Professor of Philosophical Theology

1998–   Kathryn L. Roberts, B.A., M.Div., Ph.D.—Assistant Professor of Old Testament

1999–   Carol A. Miles, B.A., M.A., M.Div., Ph. D.—Instructor of Homiletics
          2000—Assistant Professor of Homiletics

2001–   David Hadley Jensen, B.A., M.A.R., Ph.D.—Assistant Professor of Reformed Theology

2001–   David W. Johnson, B.A., M.Div., Ph.D., Director of Supervised Practice of Ministry and Certificate in Spiritual Formation Programs

2002–   Arun W. Jones, B.A., M.Div., Ph.D.—Assistant Professor of Mission and Evangelism

2002–   Whitney Bodman, B.A., M.Div., M.A., Th.D.—Instructor of World Religion

Ever since Austin Seminary's Field Education program began, and especially after it was redesigned as Supervised Practice of Ministry in 1974, scores of pastors, chaplains, other ministers and professionals in related fields have augmented the seminary's educational enterprise by serving as "Non-Resident Faculty," "Lecturers," or members of supervisory councils. Their services have enriched and enhanced the theological education of its students, by the investment of their time, gifts, leadership, evaluations and energies in the preparation of leaders for the church.

These are all identified in the Seminary Catalogues in the sections "Non-Resident Faculty" and "Lecturers." We recognize their teaching and supervision as immense contributions to the fulfillment of Austin Seminary's function as "a school of the church."

May 2002, Prescott H. Williams, Jr.

Appendix B

Roster of Members of the Board of Trustees

1906–8   Mr. Henry Moore, Texarkana, Arkansas
1907–21   Rev. J. P. Robertson, Paris, Texas
1907–11   Rev. Thornton Whaling, Dallas, Texas
1908–10   Mr. C. A. Bridewell, Hope, Arkansas
1908–13   Mr. T. W. Gregory, Austin, Texas
1908–8   Rev. E. P. Kennedy, Monticello, Arkansas
1909–17   Rev. J. Leighton Read, Junction City, Arkansas
1910–31   Rev. Erskine Brantley, Antlers, Oklahoma
1910–16   Rev. T. S. Clyce, Sherman, Texas
1910–13   Rev. W. M. Lewis, Clifton, Texas
1910–13   Mr. E. R. Long, Batesville, Arkansas
1911–13   Mr. Rhodes S. Baker, Dallas, Texas
1911–13   Rev. A. H. P. McCurdy, Brownwood, Texas
1911–18   Mr. R. W. Porter, Little Rock, Arkansas
1912–16   Rev. J. M. Clark, Shawnee, Oklahoma
1913–37   Mr. A. N. McCallum, Austin, Texas
1913–19   Mr. Lauch McLaurin, Austin, Texas
1913–13   Rev. James I. Norris, Pine Bluff, Arkansas; 1920–1920
1914–16   Mr. R. F. Gribble, Waco, Texas
1914–16   Rev. W .S. Jacobs, Houston, Texas
1914–18   Dr. T .P. Junkin, Brownwood, Texas
1914–21   Mr. T. H. Williams, Austin, Texas
1916–16   Mr. G. E. McCelvey, Temple, Texas
1916–19   Rev. C. C. Weaver, Oklahoma City, Oklahoma
1917–44   Rev. E. T. Drake, Orange, Texas
1917–20   Mr. L. L. McInnis, Bryan, Texas
1917–27   Mr. J. A. Thompson, Taylor, Texas
1919–23   Rev. C. H. H. Branch (Chairman 1921–1922), Texarkana,
            Arkansas
1919–21   Mr. Ben Clayton, Houston, Texas
1919–21   Rev. John P. Kidd, North Little Rock, Arkansas
1919–20   Mr. B. C. Powell, Little Rock, Arkansas
1919–20   Mr. J. H. Rogers, Austin, Texas
1919–19   Rev. E. W. Williams, Bonham, Texas
1920–50   Rev. C. T. Caldwell (Chairman 1923–1945), Waco, Texas
1920–28   Rev. J. E. Latham, Oklahoma City, Oklahoma
1921–27   Rev. J. E. James, Gonzales, Texas
1921–40   Rev. W. R. Minter, Austin, Texas
1922–41   Mr. J. E. Jarratt, San Antonio, Texas

1922–25	Rev. Samuel L. Joekel, Waxahachie, Texas
1922–58	Mr. Robert Adger Law, Austin, Texas
1923–32	Mr. V. O. Alexander, Pine Bluff, Arkansas
1923–28	Rev. R. L. Jetton, Jonesboro, Arkansas
1923–32	Rev. John Van Lear, Little Rock, Arkansas
1925–25	Rev. James V. Johnson, Camden, Arkansas
1926–41	Rev. Julian S. Sleeper, Texarkana, Arkansas
1926–28	Mr. H. L. Ponder, Walnut Ridge, Arkansas
1927–36	Rev. T. M. Hunter, Beaumont, Texas
1928–44	Rev. R. L. Owen, Big Spring, Texas
1928–57	Rev. B. O. Wood (Chairman 1946–1950), San Angelo, Texas
1928–32	Rev. H. L. Paisley, Fayetteville, Arkansas
1929–41	Rev. W. McF. Alexander, New Orleans, Louisiana
1929–38	Rev. R. M. Firebaugh, Goodland, Oklahoma
1929–32	Rev. H. H. Thompson, Baton Rouge, Louisiana
1931–37	Rev. J. W. Moseley, Duncan, Oklahoma
1932–33	Rev. B. C. Bell, Shreveport, Louisiana
1932–45	Rev. J. H. Christian, Baton Rouge, Louisiana
1932–48	Mr. Mack H. Long, Little Rock, Arkansas
1933–33	Mr. D. L. McRae, Prescott, Arkansas
1933–47	Rev C. E. Newton, Pine Bluff, Arkansas
1934–70	Mr. W. C. Brown, Hot Springs, Arkansas
1935–35	Rev. S. D. Bartle, Fordyce, Arkansas
1935–37	Rev. S. E. McFadden, Ruston, Louisiana
1937–63	Rev. Charles L. King (Chairman 1951–1960), Houston, Texas
1938–43	Rev. Wade H. Boggs, Shreveport, Louisiana
1938–38	Rev. C. M. Campbell, Gonzales, Texas
1938–42	Rev. B. W. Downing, Wewoka, Oklahoma
1938–38	Mr. Joe E. Lawther, Dallas, Texas
1939–41	Rev. Fred I. Cairns, Conway, Arkansas
1939–43	Mr. M. B. Hughey, Charlotte, Texas
1940–44	Rev. John Knox Bowling, Duncan, Oklahoma
1942–44	Rev. R. Guy Davis, Wynne, Arkansas
1942–46	Mr. J. Adair Lyon, New Orleans, Louisiana
1942–45	Mr. J. S. Pulliam, Dallas, Texas
1943–46	Rev. M. E. Melvin, Oklahoma City, Oklahoma
1943–52	Mr. Arch S. Underwood, Lubbock, Texas
1944–45	Rev. Frank C. Brown, Dallas, Texas
1944–48	Rev. Hugh E. Bradshaw, Belcher, Louisiana

1945–62   Rev. Shirley C. Guthrie (Chairman 1961–1962), Kilgore, Texas
1945–45   Rev. L. Allen Holley, Wewoka, Oklahoma
1945–47   Rev. C. L. Power, Shreveport, Louisiana
1945–73   Mr. Glenn A. Railsback, Pine Bluff, Arkansas
1946–52   Rev. H. Grady James, Wewoka, Oklahoma
1946–48   Mr. D. D. McIver, Baton Rouge, Louisiana
1946–46   Rev. James E. Moore, Big Spring, Texas
1946–55   Mr. J. R. Scott, Jr., Falfurrias, Texas
1947–61   Mr. Roy L. Klein, Dallas, Texas
1948–51   Rev. W. L. McColgan, Pine Bluff, Arkansas
1948–48   Rev. Patrick D. Miller, San Antonio, Texas
1948–48   Mr. Marion R. Wellford, New Orleans, Louisiana
1949–74   Mr. Barton W. Freeland, Crowley, Louisiana
1949–67   Mr. Sam B. Hicks, Shreveport, Louisiana
1950–59   Mr. Tom A. Cutting, Fort Smith, Arkansas
1950–50   Mr. Earl Rawlins, Duncan, Oklahoma
1950–52   Mr. Tom Sealy, Midland, Texas
1950–51   Mr. W. J. Stebbins, Garyville, Louisiana
1951–58   Rev. H. A. Anderson, San Antonio, Texas; 1964–1964
1951–54   Rev. Walter A. Bennett, Oklahoma City, Oklahoma
1951–63   Rev. Marion A. Boggs, Little Rock, Arkansas
1951–63   Mr. Henry H. Bryant, San Antonio, Texas
1951–61   Mr. Franklin Flato, Corpus Christi, Texas; 1963–1973
1951–51   Rev. Ernest D. Holloway, Monroe, Louisiana
1951–57   Rev. W. L. McLeod, Lake Charles, Louisiana
1951–57   Mr. B. W. Trull, Palacios, Texas
1952–63   Mr. Tom G. Clark, Arkadelphia, Arkansas
1953–61   Mr. William J. Murray, Jr., Austin, Texas; 1963–1971; 1972–1981
1953–56   Mr. Myron Turfitt, New Orleans, Louisiana
1953–64   Rev. Claude D. Wardlaw, Lake Charles, Louisiana
1954–62   Mr. W. H. Gilmore, Midland, Texas
1954–56   Mr. J. W. Logan, Durant, Oklahoma
1955–64   Rev. J. Martin Singleton, Oklahoma City, Oklahoma; 1966–1971
1957–63   Mr. R. P. Gregory, Houston, Texas; 1966–1968
1957–65   Dr. O. L. Parsons, M.D., Lawton, Oklahoma
1957–57   Mr. Morgan L. Shaw, New Orleans, Louisiana
1958–59   Mr. David Crow, Shreveport, Louisiana; 1965–1967

1958–63　Rev. William M. Elliott, Jr., Dallas, Texas
1958–67　Rev. Albert B. Link, New Orleans, Louisiana
1958–65　Mr. Hamilton E. McRae, Jr., Midland, Texas
1959–61　Mr. Vannie E. Cook, McAllen, Texas
1959–65　Rev. John William Lancaster (Chairman 1962–1972), Austin, Texas; 1967–1973
1960–64　Rev. William A. Benfield, Shreveport, Louisiana
1960–62　Mr. Raymond Orr, Fort Smith, Arkansas
1962–67　Rev. Robert P. Douglass, Dallas, Texas
1962–69　Mr. James W. Hargrove, Houston, Texas
1962–67　Mr. Walter B. Howard, Texas City, Texas
1962–70　Mr. Robert B. Trull, Palacios, Texas; 1972–1980
1963–72　Mr. Allen H. Carruth, Houston, Texas
1963–72　Mr. Jack East, Jr., Little Rock, Arkansas
1963–71　Mr. Clarence L. Norsworthy, Jr., Dallas, Texas
1963–66　Rev. H. Edwin Pickard, Beaumont, Texas
1963–72　Mr. Leon Stone, Austin, Texas
1963–71　Mr. Gaston Williamson, Little Rock, Arkansas
1964–67　Rev. T. Chalmers Henderson, Arkadelphia, Arkansas
1964–65　Rev. James P. McCrary, Oklahoma City, Oklahoma
1965–73　Rev. Arch McD. Tolbert (Chairman 1976–1978), Baton Rouge, Louisiana; 1975–1983
1966–74　Rev. C. Ellis Nelson, New York, New York
1968–75　Rev. Joe M. Brown, Odessa, Texas
1968–79　Rev. William W. Hatcher, New Orleans, Louisiana; 1980–1988
1968–75　Mr. William G. Hazen, New Orleans, Louisiana
1968–70　Rev. Robert F. Jones, Fort Worth, Texas
1968–79　Rev. William S. McLean (Chairman 1974–1976), Little Rock, Arkansas
1968–73　Mr. Morrell F. Trimble, New Orleans, Louisiana
1969–77　Mr. Roy E. Glass, San Angelo, Texas
1969–73　Mr. L. Frank Moore (Chairman 1972–1973), Shreveport, Louisiana
1970–79　Mr. Weldon H. Smith, Houston, Texas; 1980–1989
1971–72　Mrs. Jack Boyd (Ruth), Sweetwater, Texas
1971–79　Rev. Patricia Ann McClurg, Pasadena, Texas
1972–73　Rev. Carlos S. Buck, Houston, Texas
1972–73　Rev. Walter M. Crofton, Jr., Fort Smith, Arkansas
1972–78　Mr. G. R. Hollingsworth, Dallas, Texas

1972–77   Mr. Robert S. Lindsey, Little Rock, Arkansas

1972–76   Mr. Collier Wenderoth, Jr., Fort Smith, Arkansas

1974–75   Mr. Emanuel M. Harrison, Baton Rouge, Louisiana

1974–76   Mr. Harold C. Harsh, New Orleans, Louisiana

1974–79   Ms. Patricia S. Huntress, Oklahoma City, Oklahoma

1974–81   Miss Cora V. Sylestine, Livingston, Texas

1974–81   Rev. William H. Tiemann, Dallas, Texas

1974–75   Rev. William Newton Todd, Hot Springs, Arkansas

1974–79   Mr. David M. Vigness, Lubbock, Texas

1975–77   Mr. Joseph H. Culver, Austin, Texas

1975–84   Mr. Clarence N. Frierson (Chairman 1978–1983), Shreveport, Louisiana; 1985 –1994; 1995–1997

1975–77   Rev. Ben Guiterrez, New York, New York

1975–81   Rev. David L. Jones, Shreveport, Louisiana

1975–83   Rev. Thomas H. Schmid, New Orleans, Louisiana; 1984–1993

1975–84   Rev. Don G. Shepherd, Amarillo, Texas

1975–84   Rev. Robert B. Smith, Midland, Texas

1976–85   Mrs. Mildred B. Dabe, New Orleans, Louisiana

1976–85   Mr. Edward D. Vickery (Chairman 1983–1985; 1989–1994), Houston, Texas; 1986–1995

1977–80   Mr. Robert F. Amundsen, Dallas, Texas

1977–86   Ms. Joyce Trapp LeMaistre, Houston, Texas

1977–86   Mr. Paul L. Offutt, Hot Springs, Arkansas

1977–80   Mr. Jack Q. Tidwell, Odessa, Texas

1978–87   Mr. Eleno Garza, Weslaco, Texas

1979–84   Ms. Virginia Joslin, Corpus Christi, Texas

1979–88   Mr. Stephen A. Matthews, Pine Bluff, Arkansas; 1992–2001

1979–88   Mr. Burnett B. Roberts, Levelland, Texas

1979–88   Dr. Kenneth W. Whittington, M.D., Oklahoma City, Oklahoma

1980–86   Ms. Jacque Goettsche, Houston, Texas

1980–89   Mr. John D. Miller, Dallas, Texas

1980–88   Mr. Louis Rochester, Odessa, Texas

1980–89   Rev. Jerold D. Shetler (Chairman 1985–1989), Dallas, Texas

1981–90   Rev. B. Clayton Bell, Dallas, Texas

1981–90   Mr. Ben T. Head, Austin, Texas

1981–90   Mr. Bruce G. Herlin, Palacios, Texas; 1991–2000; 2002–

1981–90   Rev. Edwin W. Stock, Jr., Wichita Falls, Texas

1983–91   Rev. James H. Monroe, Baton Rouge, Louisiana

1983–92   Rev. James W. Mosley, Hot Springs, Arkansas
1984–93   Mr. Roland Carpenter, Little Rock, Arkansas
1984–93   Rev. Charles Freeland III, Owasso, Oklahoma
1985–88   Ms. Nina W. Costley, Stillwater, Oklahoma
1985–94   Ms. Betty [Wilson] Jeffrey, New Orleans, Louisiana; 1995–
1986–95   Ms. Patricia H. Lee, Metairie, Louisiana
1986–93   Mr. Abraham Torres, Manchaca, Texas
1987–96   Rev. A. "Holly" Heuer, Ruston, Louisiana
1988–97   Dr. Donald R. Carter, M.D.,Oklahoma City, Oklahoma
1988–97   Mr. William Chapman, Madill, Oklahoma
1988–97   Rev. Joe. B. Donaho, Columbia, South Carolina; 1998–2001
1988–96   Rev. Wayne H. Sebesta, Fort Collins, Colorado
1988–97   Ms. Lidia Serrata-Ledesma, Victoria, Texas
1988–97   Mr. Max R. Sherman, Austin, Texas; 1998–
1988–95   Ms. Bobbie Young, El Paso, Texas
1989–95   Mr. Samuel K. Bradshaw, Houston, Texas
1989–98   Dr. J. Ted Hartman, M.D., Lubbock, Texas
1989–98   Rev. Cynthia Weeks Logan, Dallas, Texas
1990–99   Ms. Peggy L. Clark, Corpus Christi, Texas; 2000–
1990–99   Ms. Bessie Lou Doelling, , Odessa, Texas; 2000–2002
1990–99   Rev. John M. McCoy, Dallas, Texas; 2000–
1990–   Ms. Sydney F. Reding, Stillwater, Oklahoma
1990–99   Mr. Jo E. "Jed" Shaw, Jr. (Chairman 1994–1999), Houston, Texas; 2000–2002
1990–94   Rev. Thomas C. Truscott, Santa Fe, New Mexico
1990–99   Mr. Hugh H. Williamson, Greensboro, North Carolina; 2000–
1993–2001 Rev. Marvin C. Griffin, Austin, Texas
1993–2002 Rev. James D. Miller, Tulsa, Oklahoma
1993–2002 Mr. Carl V Williams, New Orleans, Louisiana
1993–2002 Rev. Louis H. Zbinden, Jr. (Chairman 1999–2002), San Antonio, Texas
1994–96   Mr. Finley Ewing, Dallas, Texas
1994–   Rev. Paul R. Debenport, Albuquerque, New Mexico
1994–   Rev. Lelia L. Power, Batesville, Arkansas
1994–99   Dr. Cervando Martinez, Jr., M.D., San Antonio, Texas
1994–97   Rev. John B. Rogers, Shreveport, Louisiana
1995–   Rev. David McKechnie, Houston, Texas
1996–   Ms. Jay Dea Brownfield, El Paso, Texas
1996–   Ms. Diane E. Buchanan, Denton, Texas

1997–	Ms. Carolyn W. Beaird, Shreveport, Louisiana
1997–	Mr. James W. Bruce, Oklahoma City, Oklahoma
1997–	Ms. Judye G. Hartman, Houston, Texas
1997–2000	Rev. George S. Heyer, Jr., Austin, Texas
1997–	Mr. James R. Hunt, Houston, Texas
1998–	Rev. William C. Poe, Little Rock, Arkansas
1998–	Ms. Elizabeth C. Williams (Chairman 2002–), Dallas, Texas
1999–	Mr. Giles C. McCrary, Post, Texas
1999–	Ms. Cheryl Covey Ramsey, Denver, Colorado
2000–	Ms. La Unah S. Cuffy, New Braunfels, Texas
2000–	Mr. Robert T. Herres, San Antonio, Texas
2000–	Rev. Jerry Jay Smith, San Antonio, Texas
2001–	Mr. Michael D. Allen, Tyler, Texas
2002–	Rev. Frank Diaz, Lewisville, Texas
2002–	Mr. J Carter King, Austin, Texas
2002–	Rev. Virginia L. Olszewski, West Chester, Pennsylvania
2002–	Mr. Rex C. Vermillion, Amarillo, Texas

The location of each member of the board is that from which he or she was first elected.

ENDNOTES

Preface

1. Craig Dykstra, *Growing in the Life of Faith: Education and Christian Practices,* p. 147, in the chapter entitled "Love's Knowledge and Theological Education."

2. Letter to JSC, dated November 18,1999, and in the hands of the latter.

3. Quoted in Currie, *Austin Presbyterian Theological Seminary: A Seventy-fifth Anniversary History,* p. 166.

4. Letter from Steve Plunkett to JSC, dated October 21,1998, and in the hands of the latter.

5. Letter from Jim Andrews to JSC, dated November 18, 1999, and in the hands of the latter.

6. Letter from Barbara M. Farwell to JSC, dated August 20, 1998, and in the hands of the latter.

Chapter One

1. Austin Seminary *Bulletin,* October, 1976, p. 6.

2. Ibid., p. 11.

3. Minutes of the Board of Trustees, October 7–8, 1976. The action of the board excised a sentence from Section VII.1 of the by-laws, which read: "No debts shall be incurred except for expansion of the Seminary's facilities whose income shall amortize the debt."

4. Figures are from data supplied by Timothy Lincoln and in possession of the writer.

5. Thomas White Currie, Jr., *Austin Presbyterian Theological Seminary: A Seventy-fifth Anniversary History,* p. 3.

6. Minutes of the Executive Committee of the Board of Trustees, April 7, 1978.

7. Minutes of the Board of Trustees, October 21–22, 1977.

8. Minutes of the Board of Trustees, May 20, 1983.

9. Notes from interview with Harren, September 14, 1998; notes are in hands of JSC.

10. This statement is based on conversations with several persons who served on the faculty at the time of Maxwell's arrival. Regrettably, Maxwell did not wish to be interviewed or submit his views and recollections in writing for this project.

11. Letter from Tom Schmid to JSC, dated December 12, 1999, and in the hands of the latter.

12. Biographical and publishing information is found on pp. 2–3 of the May 1978 issue of the Faculty Edition of the Austin Seminary *Bulletin*.

13. Letter from Tom Schmid to JSC, dated December 21, 1999, and in hands of the latter.

14. Letter from Hendrick to JSC, dated June 30, 2000, and in the hands of the latter.

15. Much of this information comes from a paper by Hendrick entitled "Toward the Third Millennium of Our Redemption: Evangelism at Austin Seminary: Recent Past and Near Future," pp.11ff. A copy of this paper is in the hands of this writer.

16. Schmid, op.cit.

17. Interview with Laura Lewis conducted by JSC in Lewis's office, January 21, 2000. Interview notes are in hands of JSC.

18. Letter of Tom Schmid to JSC, dated December 21, 1999, and in hands of the latter.

19. Austin Seminary *Bulletin*, June 1983, p. 4.

20. From notes of interview in Donelson's office on September 13, 1999. Notes are in hands of JSC.

21. Memorandum to JSC dated February 11, 1998, and in the hands of JSC.

22. Letter from Tom Schmid to JSC, dated December 21, 1999, and in hands of JSC. This position was funded by revenue from the Jean Brown bequest, the subject of chapter two.

23. From notes of interview with C. D. Weaver in his office on October 19, 1998. Notes are in the hands of JSC.

24. "Job Description for Vice-President," provided by Jerry Tompkins.

25. Interview with Joe Culver conducted January 11, 1999, on the campus of Austin Seminary. Notes from the interview are in the hands of JSC.

26. Faxed letter to JSC, dated December 21, 1999, and in the hands of JSC.

27. Letter from Frierson to JSC, dated January 20, 1998.

28. Vice President for Business Affairs Catherine Civiletto indicates that "investment portfolio" is a more accurate and preferable term to the more familiar term "endowment," because the figures include restricted

funds, unrestricted funds, and temporarily restricted funds, whereas "endowment" should refer only to restricted funds. Throughout this volume, therefore, "investment portfolio" will be used to refer to what used to be called the "endowment."

29. "The Maxwell Years: Random Reflections by Bill Hedrick, October 20, 1998," p. 1; sent to JSC and in the hands of the latter.

30. Ibid., p. 1.

31. Minutes of the Executive Committee of the Board of Trustees, November 20, 1980.

32. Minutes of the Executive Committee of the Board of Trustees, May 21, 1982.

33. Cf. Currie, *Austin Presbyterian Theological Seminary: A Seventy-fifth Anniversary History,* pp. 65, 94ff.

34. Letter to JSC, December 21, 1998, and in hands of JSC.

35. Notes from interview with Garza, February 1, 1999; notes are in hands of JSC.

36. Letter to JSC, received August 29, 1998, and in hands of JSC.

37. E-mail letter from Dick Junkin to JSC, dated August 12, 1998.

38. Written remarks from Ted V. Foote, Jr., to JSC, dated April 27, 2000.

39. Notes from interview with Shelton on January 11, 1999, on the seminary campus. Notes are in the hands of JSC.

40. Minutes of the Board of Trustees meeting, November 11, 1983.

41. E-mail letter from Dick Junkin to JSC, dated August 12, 1998, and in the hands of the latter.

42. Letter from Cynthia Weeks Logan to JSC, dated February 1, 2002, and in the hands of the latter.

43. E-mail from Dick Junkin, August 12, 1998.

44. Minutes of the Board of Trustees meeting, November 11, 1983.

Chapter Two

1. Currie, Thomas W., Jr., *Austin Presbyterian Theological Seminary: A Seventy-fifth Anniversary History,* pp. 16–17.

2. Ibid., p. 17.

3. For more information about Sarah Ball and Frank Lubbock and their contributions to Austin Seminary, cf. William K. Hedrick's paper "Presbyterians and Theological Education in the Southwest" in *Proceedings of the Xth Annual Meeting of the Presbyterian Historical Society of the Southwest, March 3–5, 1988,* pp. 95–109.

4. James W. Mosley, "A Legacy Greater Than Wealth: An Appreciative Appraisal of the W. C. Brown Family, Hot Springs, Arkansas" in *Proceedings of the Presbyterian Historical Society of the Southwest Xlth Annual Meeting, 10–11 March 1989,* p. 25. Most of the information regarding the Brown family will come from this paper.

5. Figures provided by Catherine Civiletto, vice president for business affairs, in March 2000.

6. Cf. Appendix II, pp. 260–61, in *Austin Presbyterian Theological Seminary: A Seventy-fifth Anniversary History.*

7. Mosley, "A Legacy Greater Than Wealth," p. 37.

8. Quoted in Mosley, p. 26.

9. Interview with Herman Harren, September 14, 1998.

10. Figures provided by Catherine Civiletto, vice president for business affairs, in March 2000.

11. The investment figures were: Princeton–$738.1 million, Union-Richmond–$101.7 million, Columbia–$155.7 million, Austin–$82.2 million, McCormick–$75.8 million, Louisville–$61.7 million, San Francisco–$47.0 million, and Johnson C. Smith–$8.6 million. The figures for Dubuque and Pittsburgh seminaries were not published in this report.

12. Minutes of the Board of Trustees, November 19, 1981.

13. Ibid.

14. Minutes of the Board of Trustees, May 22, 1982.

15. Memorandum from Ellis Nelson to JSC, dated February 11, 1998, p. 3.

16. Cf. "Austin Presbyterian Seminary Receives Pastoral Endowment," by Kim Sue Lia Perkes, in the *Austin American-Statesman*, March 8, 2001, p. B1.

17. Quoted in Spring 2001 issue of *Windows,* p. 12.

Chapter Three

1. Bruce Herlin in an interview in Palacios, Texas, June 1, 1999.

2. Letter from Frierson to JSC, dated January 20, 1998.

3. Letter from Hedrick to JSC, dated October 20, 1998.

4. Letter from Stroup to JSC, dated February 27, 1999.

5. This biographical information and that which follows about Nelson is taken from a presentation by former Austin Seminary president David L. Stitt to the Presbyterian Historical Society of the Southwest on February 29, 1992. It is printed on pp. 69–82 in the "Proceedings" of that date under the title "Carl Ellis Nelson: An Appreciation."

6. David Stitt's paper provides ample evidence of Nelson's success as president of Louisville. In addition to introducing computers and doubling the size of the library, increasing the budget by 60.7 percent, increasing the endowment by 116 percent, and securing grants to improve administration and educational programs, Nelson—with considerable assistance from his wife, Nancy—regained the support of Louisville's constituency. It should not go unnoted that during this period Nelson also published two books.

7. Memo from Nelson to JSC, dated February 11, 1998, p. 1.

8. Stitt, "Carl Ellis Nelson: An Appreciation," p. 72.

9. Nelson, memo to JSC, February 11, 1998, p. 3.

10. Ibid., p. 3.

11. Ibid., p. 4.

12. Ibid., p. 4.

13. In "The Plan Providing for the Reunion of the Presbyterian Church in the United States of America and the Presbyterian Church in the United States as The Presbyterian Church of the United States, May, 1943 (Issued for Study and Report Only)," the following statement is found on p. 2: "When the Plan of Reunion was formulated the late Reverend Thomas W. Currie, D.D., chairman, the late Reverend I. C. H. Champney, D.D., and the late Honorable Willis M. Everett were members of the Permanent Committee. Their successors on said committee are respectively the Reverend C. L. King, D.D., the Reverend G. W. Gideon, and Dr. J. R. McCain." Currie was the third president of Austin Seminary.

14. Minutes of the Board of Trustees, January 4, 1984.

15. Minutes of the Board of Trustees, March 1, 1984.

16. Ibid.

17. From notes of interview with Stotts on April 12, 1999, on the seminary campus.

18. E-mail from Jack Stotts to JSC, May 13, 1998.

19. "Report of the Interim President to the Board of Trustees," May 17–18, 1985, in minutes of the Board of Trustees, p. 1.

20. Ibid., p. 9–10.

Chapter Four

1. Austin Seminary *Bulletin,* Faculty Edition, April 1985, p. 10.

2. Ibid., p. 13.

3. Austin Seminary *Bulletin,* Faculty Edition, March 1986, p. 38.

4. Ibid., p. 7.

5. Ibid., pp. 7–8.

6. Ibid., p. 9.

7. "Annual Report to the Board of Trustees, May 24, 1986," in minutes of the Board of Trustees.

8. "Commentary on Enrollment" (including graphs), minutes of the Board of Trustees, May 21, 1983.

9. Ibid.

10. "Report of the Academic Dean to the Board of Trustees, May 24, 1986," minutes of the Board of Trustees.

11. "Annual Report—State of the Seminary," May 23, 1987, minutes of the Board of Trustees.

12. Jack L. Stotts and Jane Dempsey Douglass, editors, *To Confess the Faith Today,* p. 7.

13. Jack Rogers, *Presbyterian Creeds: A Guide to the Book of Confessions,* p. 233. This volume also gives an account of the process the com-

mittee followed in developing the Brief Statement. The collection of seven essays edited by Stotts and Jane Dempsey Douglass, *To Confess the Faith Today,* were written by members of the drafting committee, on the historical nature of confessions and on features of the Brief Statement.

14. Minutes of the Board of Trustees, May 24, 1986.

15. Interview with Garcia at APTS on October 26, 2000.

16. Information provided in the Seminary Catalogues of 1986–87 and 1987–88.

17. Minutes of the Board of Trustees, November 15, 1986.

18. Interview with Kay Lewis at Austin Seminary, November 2, 1998.

19. Austin Presbyterian Theological Seminary *Bulletin,* Faculty Edition, April 1988, pp. 31–45.

20. Interview, November 2, 1998

21. Kay Lewis, 'My Theology of Prayer,' in *Theology in Scotland* (Fall 1994), pp. 78–79.

22. "President's Report to the Board of Trustees," in minutes of the Board of Trustees, May 21, 1994.

23. Minutes of the Board of Trustees, May 21, 1994.

24. Lewis, *Between Cross and Resurrection: A Theology of Holy Saturday,* p. xi.

25. Ibid., p. 78.

26. Minutes of the Board of Trustees, May 23, 1987.

27. "Annual Report - State of the Seminary," in minutes of the Board of Trustees, May 23, 1987.

28. Undated text provided by Gene Luna, assistant librarian of the Stitt Library.

29. Letter from Prescott Williams to the Board of Trustees "through President Jack Stotts," dated December 28, 1988, and included in the minutes of the Board of Trustees, May 20, 1989.

30. Austin Seminary *Bulletin,* Faculty Edition: "God's Steadfast Love: A Festschrift in Honor of Prescott Harrison Williams, Jr.," Spring 1990.

31. 1989–1990 Catalogue, p. ii.

32. Campbell's resignation was accepted at the May 21, 1988, board meeting; Klemt's retirement was approved at the November 11–12, 1988, board meeting; Williams' letter, dated December 28, 1988, was announced at an executive board meeting on February 9, 1989; Sautter's resignation was received at an executive board meeting on May 19, 1989; Clark's retirement was announced at the November 11, 1989, meeting of the board.

33. Interview with Jimmie Clark, September 13, 1999.

34. Interview with Jacqueline Hefley, September 28, 2000.

35. Weaver received his new title in November 1987; the other actions were taken at the May 1988 meeting of the board.

36. Report of the Vice President for Business Affairs/Treasurer to the Board of Trustees, May 18, 1991, Appendix "J," p. 4.

37. "The Archives Project of the Stitt Library of the Austin Presbyterian Theological Seminary and the McCoy Historical Research Center: Declaration of Intent" in the minutes of the Board of Trustees, November 14, 1992, Appendix "B."

38. Information provided by Gene Luna, assistant librarian of the Stitt Library.

39. Interview with Blair at Austin Seminary, September 20, 1999.

40. Ibid.

41. Ibid.

42. Interview with Terry Muck, May 17, 1999.

43. Minutes of the Board of Trustees, May 23, 1992; interviews with Shelton on January 11, 1999; February 2, 1999; and August 20, 1999.

44. Minutes of the Board of Trustees, May 23, 1992.

45. Ibid.

46. Minutes of the Board of Trustees, May 22, 1993.

47. Ibid.

48. *Insights: A Journal of the Faculty of Austin Seminary,* Spring 1994: "A Festschrift in Honor of George Stuart Heyer, Jr."

49. This information is provided in Appendix III of Currie, *APTS: A Seventy-fifth Anniversary History,* pp. 264–66.

50. Minutes of the Board of Trustees, May 23–25, 1986.

51. Minutes of the Board of Trustees, May 23, 1987.

52. Interview with Jack Stotts on May 18, 1998.

53. Minutes of the Board of Trustees, May 23, 1992.

54. Minutes of the Executive Committee of the Board of Trustees, October 8, 1992.

55. Minutes of the Executive Committee of the Board of Trustees, November 12, 1993.

56. Minutes of the Executive Committee of the Board of Trustees, February 4, 1994.

57. Minutes of the Board of Trustees, November 11, 1995.

58. Interview with Jed Shaw, April 29, 1999.

59. President's Report to the Board of Trustees, November 12, 1993.

60. Minutes of the Board of Trustees, October 18, 1996.

61. Minutes of the Board of Trustees, May 20, 1995.

62. Minutes of the Board of Trustees, May 18, 1996.

63. Ibid.

64. Ibid.

65. President's Report to the Board of Trustees, May 18, 1996.

66. Interview with Linda Cunningham on November 16, 1998.

67. Interview with John Evans on October 5, 1998.

68. Letter from Clarence Frierson to JSC, dated January 20, 1998, and in the hands of the latter.

69. Minutes of the Board of Trustees, October 18, 1996.

Chapter Five
1. Minutes of the Board of Trustees, May 20, 1995.
2. Attachment to the minutes of the Board of Trustees meeting, November 11, 1995.
3. Minutes of the Board of Trustees, May 23, 1997.
4. Shelton's dissertation was titled "The Relationship Between Reason and Revelation in the Preaching of Harry Emerson Fosdick," 1965.
5. Interview with Robert M. Shelton, January 11, 1999.
6. An extended account of Shelton's acquaintance with Austin Seminary and his first contact with the school can be found in Thomas W. Currie, Jr.'s *APTS: A Seventy-fifth Anniversary History*, pp. 170–172.
7. Memo from Andy Dearman to Pete Hendrick, dated May 18, 2001, and made available to JSC.
8. Minutes of the Board of Trustees, May 24, 1997.
9. *Windows*, Summer 1997 (interview is on the inside cover).
10. For the complete address, cf. *Austin Presbyterian Theological Seminary: Speeches from the Presidential Inauguration, November 14, 1997*, pp. 2–14.
11. Ibid., p. 11.
12. Ibid., pp. 15–27.
13. Ibid., pp. 20–21.
14. Ibid., p. 22.
15. Ibid., p. 26.
16. Ibid., pp. 26–27.
17. Minutes of the Board of Trustees, October 18, 1996.
18. In the pamphlet "The Master Plan: Austin Presbyterian Theological Seminary."
19. Ibid.
20. Ibid.
21. Minutes of the Executive Committee of the Board of Trustees, March 3, 2000.
22. Report of the President to the Board of Trustees in the minutes of the Board of Trustees, November 10–11, 2000.
23. Minutes of the Board of Trustees, May 24, 1997.
24. "Civiletto Takes Charge as New Vice President" in *Windows*, Winter 1999, p. 17.
25. Interview with Catherine Civiletto, October 18, 1999.
26. Minutes of the Board of Trustees, May 23, 1998.
27. Information on Wilton taken from *Windows*, Winter 1998, p. 4.
28. Minutes of the Board of Trustees, May 23, 1998; additional information taken from "Roberts to Fill New Position in Old Testament" in *Windows*, Summer 1998, p. 11.
29. Minutes of the Board of Trustees, May 20, 2000.

30. Minutes of the Board of Trustees, May 23, 1998.
31. Minutes of the Board of Trustees, May 22, 1999.
32. *Windows*, Summer 2000, p. 18.
33. *Windows*, Winter 2001, pp. 10–11.
34. Report to the Board of Trustees, Vice President for Development and Church Relations, May 20, 2000.
35. Minutes of the Board of Trustees, May 20, 2000.
36. Minutes of the Executive Committee of the Board of Trustees, March 3, 2000
37. Interview with Garcia, October 26, 2000.
38. Ibid.
39. Letter from John R. "Pete" Hendrick to JSC, undated, and in the hands of the latter.
40. Letter from Bessie Lou Doelling to JSC, dated February 13, 2002, and in the hands of the latter.
41. Letter from Jed Shaw to JSC, dated March 5, 2002, and in the hands of the latter.
42. Letter from Jerry Tompkins to JSC, dated March 11, 2002, and in the hands of the latter.

Chapter Six
1. "Special Lectures Given at the Midwinter Convocations, 1945–" (pamphlet published by Austin Presbyterian Theological Seminary; undated, but the list of lectures goes through 1968).
2. E-mail from Stotts to JSC, dated February 21, 2001.
3. Robert M. Shelton, "Reflection on the Lecture Series at Austin Seminary," an informal paper provided to JSC.
4. E-mail from Stotts to JSC, dated February 21, 2001.
5. Shelton, op.cit.
6. E-mail from Thomas W. Currie, Jr., to JSC, dated August 18, 2001.
7. Currie, *Austin Presbyterian Theological Seminary: A Seventy-fifth Anniversary History*, p. 177.
8. Minutes of the Executive Committee of the Board of Trustees, Attachment D, May 19, 1995.
9. Thomas W. Currie, Jr., *Austin Presbyterian Theological Seminary: A Seventy-fifth Anniversary History*, p. 178.

Chapter Seven
1. Robert M. Shelton, "Possible Extension Program for Austin Seminary in Houston" (A Report from the Academic Dean), March 27, 1985; provided by Austin Seminary administration.
2. Undated Memo from Maxwell to himself ("JMM") regarding "Theological Education by Extension." Presumably, the reference to August 16

in the memo was in 1983, since Shelton refers to a trip he and Maxwell made to Houston in August 1983.

3. Shelton, op.cit. This document, attached to the former, is dated May 15, 1985.

4. Ibid.

5. "Proposal to Establish a Center for Ministry with Older Adults at Faith Presbyterian Church Sun City, Arizona," in minutes of the Executive Committee Meeting of the Board of Trustees, February 9, 1989 (Attachment B).

6. E-mail from Francis Park to JSC, dated April 9, 2001, and in the hands of the latter.

7. E-mail from Francis Park to JSC, dated April 17, 2001, and in the hands of the latter.

8. "Second Draft of Proposal," March 3, 1988, Midland, Texas, enclosed with a letter from Rev. Al Moreau to Dr. Robert Shelton; provided by Austin Seminary administration.

9. Others who taught in the West Texas Extension Program were: Rev. Ken Peters, Prof. Prescott Williams, Phillip Shuler, Prof. Ellis Nelson, Prof. Ismael Garcia, Prof. John R. "Pete" Hendrick, Prof. Robert Shelton, Steve Redi, Jerry Kelly, and Prof. Terry Muck.

10. Letter from Al Moreau to Dr. Robert Shelton, dated September 27, 1993.

11. Letter from Al Moreau to JSC, dated March 20, 2001.

12. Currie, *Austin Presbyterian Theological Seminary: A Seventy-fifth Anniversary History*, p. 558.

13. Background paper to the Board of Trustees, October 23, 1995.

14. This information is provided as an attachment to the November 11, 1995, minutes of the Board of Trustees. The information is printed as notes taken by Dan Garza.

15. Ibid., p. 5

16. Letter from Charlsie Ramsey to JSC, dated June 25, 1999, and in the hands of the latter.

17. Letter from Harry Slye to JSC, dated July 28, 1999, and in the latter's hands.

18. Letter from Shelley Craig to JSC, dated June 8, 1999, and in the hands of the latter.

19. Letter from Walt Faulkenberry to JSC, dated April 3, 2000, and in the hands of the latter.

20. Letter from Jim Gresham to JSC, dated April 9, 2000, and in the hands of the latter.

21. Letter from Marialice Billingsley to JSC, dated July 10, 1999, and in the hands of the latter.

22. Interview conducted May 17, 1999.

23. Interview conducted May 17, 1999.

24. Interview conducted September 13, 1999.

25. Interview conducted October 18, 1999.

26. Interview conducted January 21, 2000.

27. Interview conducted February 14, 2000.

28. Interview conducted October 26, 2000.

29. Currie's reflections on teaching in both the West Texas and the Houston extension programs are contained in a letter to JSC, dated March 28, 2001.

Chapter Eight

1. Letter from Ted Foote to JSC, dated April 27, 2000, and in the hands of the latter.

2. Letter from Jack Robinson to JSC, dated May 30, 2000, and in the hands of the latter.

3. Letter from Holly Heuer to JSC, dated December 4, 1998, and in the hands of the latter. Heuer has served as pastor of University Presbyterian Church in Ruston, Louisiana, and currently serves the Presbyterian Church in Nederland, Colorado.

4. Letter from Steve Plunkett to JSC, dated October 21, 1998, and in the hands of the latter.

5. Letter from Ken Peters to JSC, undated, and in the hands of the latter. Peters currently serves as pastor of the New Braunfels Presbyterian Church in New Braunfels, Texas.

6. Letter from Kenneth Jatko to JSC, dated June 19, 1998, and in the hands of the latter.

7. E-mail from Sally Sampsell Watson to JSC, dated February 19, 1999, and in the hands of the latter.

8. E-mail from Sallie Sampsell Watson to JSC, dated September 26, 1998.

9. Shelton himself maintains that a more accurate rendering of his words would be, "We rarely create out of the promised land. Creation comes more often out of the exodus."

10. E-mail from Sampsell Watson to JSC, dated September 26, 1986.

11. Letter from Clay Brown to JSC, dated February 29, 2000.

12. Letter from Kathy Neece to JSC, postmarked August 31, 1998, and in the hands of the latter.

13. Letter from Barbara Farwell to JSC, dated August 20, 1998, and in the hands of the latter.

14. E-mail from Fran Shelton to JSC, dated February 28, 2001, and in the hands of the latter.

15. Ibid.

16. Letter from Lemuel Garcia-Arroyo to JSC, undated, and in the hands of the latter.

17. Letter from Dan Walker to JSC, faxed August 31, 1998, and in the hands of the latter.

18. Letter from Martha Sadongei to JSC, dated January 18, 1999, and in the hands of the latter.

19. Letter from John Gallentine to JSC, dated January 5, 1999, and in the hands of the latter.

20. Austin Seminary *Bulletin, 1978–1979,* p. 50.

21. Letter from Paul Benjamin to JSC, received August 20, 1998, and in the hands of the latter.

22. Letter from Nitraporn Inchai to JSC, dated September 15, 1998, and in the hands of the latter.

23. Letter from Keith Hill to JSC, dated June 25, 1998, and in the hands of the latter.

24. Report to the Board of Trustees, October 18, 1996, by Eleanor Cherryholmes, Director of Vocations and Admissions. Cherryholmes resigned this position in February 1997.

25. Report of the Acting President and Academic Dean to the Board of Trustees, October 18, 1996.

26. According to Blair, the programs which received accreditation in 1970 were: San Francisco Theological Seminary, Claremont School of Theology, and the Chicago Divinity School (from interview conducted September 20, 1999, in Blair's office).

27. Letter from Peter Roussakis to JSC, dated November 7, 1998, and in the hands of the latter.

28. Letter from H. R. (Lad) Anderson, Jr., to JSC, dated June 16, 1998, and in the hands of the latter.

29. Letter from Don Joseph Sawyer to JSC, dated December 11, 1998, and in the hands of the latter.

Chapter Nine

1. Report of the Vice President for Business Affairs/Treasurer to the Board of Trustees, May 18, 1991, Appendix "J," pp. 1, 2.

2. Interview with Shirley Howard, September 13, 1999.

3. Interview with Jimmie Clark, September 13, 1999.

4. Interview with Fern Chester, October 19, 1998.

5. "Retirees Conclude Fifty-four Years of Service," in *Windows,* Summer 1999, p. 16.

6. "Herman Harren—a Friend of Austin Seminary," in *Windows,* Winter 1999, p. 15.

7. Ibid., p. 15.

8. "After Thirty-two Years, Respite for Librarian Overdue" in *Windows,* Winter 2001, p. 15.

9. From tribute to Genevieve R. Luna, made available to JSC by Gene Luna.

10. Interview with Gene Luna, January 21, 2000.
11. Minutes of the Board of Trustees, October 18, 1996.
12. Ibid.
13. Interview with Weldon Smith in Houston, August 26, 1999.
14. Ibid.
15. Letter from Clarence N. Frierson to JSC, dated January 20, 1998, and in the hands of the latter.
16. Interview conducted in Houston, November 6, 2001.
17. Letter from J. Ted Hartman to JSC, dated April 8, 1998, and in the hands of the latter.
18. Ibid.
19. Interview conducted in Houston on April 29, 1999. Shaw has since moved to Santa Fe, New Mexico.
20. Letter from Bessie Lou Doelling to JSC, postmarked November 30, 1998, and in the latter's hands.
21. Ibid.
22. E-mail memo to JSC, dated April 14, 2001.
23. *Windows*, Winter 2000, p. 19.
24. Letter from William K. Hedrick to JSC, dated February 5, 2002, and in the hands of the latter.

Chapter Ten
1. "Presbyterian Headline News" (Presbyterian News Service), 1998, No. 24.
2. Most of this information came from a telephone interview with Diaz on October 4, 2001.
3. For description and analysis of this decline, cf. Coalter, Mulder, and Weeks, editors, *The Mainstream Protestant "Decline": The Presbyterian Pattern* (Westminster: John Knox Press, 1990).
4. E-mail from Robert H. Bullock, Jr., to JSC, dated April 5, 1999, and in the hands of the latter.
5. "Report to the Board of Trustees" in minutes of the Board of Trustees, May 23, 1998
6. *Later Letters of Marcus Dods, D.D., 1895–1909* (London: Hodder and Stoughton, 1911), pp. 211–212.

INDEX

(Does not include faculty and board member appendices, pages 173-192)

Abrego, Angela, 113

Abzug, Robert H., 102

Aguirre, Thamar, 21

Ahlstrom, Sydney, 98

Alexander, Sharon, 153

Alexander, Willie, 152

Alston, Wallace, 99

Alsup, John E., 7, 49, 53, 54, 63, 142

Alumni Luncheon, 69, 87

Anderson, H. R. (Lad), Jr., 148

Andrew, Richard G., 29

Andrews, Dorothy, 153

Andrews, James E, xiv, xvi-xvii, 1, 3, 44, 47, 165

Anzaldua, Andy, 113

Apologeticall Narration: Editor of a Facsimile Edition of 1643, An (Robert S. Paul), 9

Arias, Mortimer, 102

Armendariz, Ruben P., 19

Asociacion para la Educacion Theologica Hispana (AETH), 89

Assembly of the Lord: Politics and Religion in the Westminster Assembly and the 'Grand Debate' (Robert S. Paul), 9

Association of Theological Schools (ATS), xiv

Atonement and the Sacraments, The (Robert S. Paul), 9

Augustine, Saint, 120

Austin Presbyterian Theological Seminary: alumni, 16, 68, 87; Board of Trustees. *See* Board of Trustees; capital campaigns, 68–69, 70, 81–82; Centennial, xi, 82, 94; and the church, xvii, 3, 11, 36, 37, 48, 78–80, 81, 95, 96, 103; as community, xiii–xviii, 141, 149, 152–53; Development Office, 15–19; Doctor of Ministry program, 11, 61-62, 147-149, 153; enrollment at, 46–47, 72, 87, 132 extension programs, 104–126; faculty and staff development at, 6–15, 49–66, 72, 82–89; financial contributions to, 25–30; Hispanic Ministry, 19–20, 89–90; image of, 72, 74, 80–81, 87, 91, 100, 159; international students at, 145, 146–147; investment portfolio (endowment) of, 18, 21, 27, 72; and Jean Brown bequest, 25–30; lectures, 95-103; Master of Arts program, 47, 146; Master of Divinity program, 46–47, 61, 72; Master of Theology program, 144; and Maxwell presidency, 1–24; and Nelson presi-

207

dency, 31–36; physical plant improvements at, 4–6, 17, 26, 35, 66–73, 77, 81–82, 151, 158; and Shelton presidency, 75–94; and Stotts presidency, 42–74; student perspectives on, 127–149; and technology, 17, 69–70, 82, 109, 121, 153, 154; vision statement of, 81–82; women at, 11–12, 65, 134

Austin Presbyterian Theological Seminary: A Seventy-fifth Anniversary History (Thomas W. Currie, Jr.), xi

Austin School of Theology, 4

Austin Seminary *Bulletin,* 8, 9, 10, 43, 48. *See also Insights*

Babinsky, Ellen, 54, 65, 115, 119, 137, 142

Baez-Camargo, Gonzalo, 96, 101

Baker, John, 108

Baldwin, R. Richard, 44

Ball, Sarah C., 25, 26

Barr, Browne, 99

Barr, James, 97

Barth, Karl, 120

Bass, Dorothy C., 98

Batts, Vernon, 152

Believing, Deciding, Acting (Jack Stotts), 39

Benjamin, Paul, 144-145

Berkhof, Hendrikus, 99

Billingsley, Marialice, 121-122

Blair, Christine (Tina), 61, 65, 88-89, 115, 147, 153

Board of Trustees: and budget, 27–29; Development Committee, 16; empowerment of, 91; Executive Committee, 5, 19, 36, 109; and faculty, 11, 12, 15; Institutional Development Committee, 68; Library Expansion Committee, 4; and master plan, 91; membership of, 155–162; and physical plant improve-

ments, 4–6, 17, 158; Presidential Search Committee, 36–38, 70, 76, 92, 158

Boggus, Fran, 138-139

Bohl, Robert, 70

Book of Confessions, The, 47-48

Book of Order, The, 48

Bradish, Homer, 150-151, 152

Brief Statement of Faith: The Presbyterian Church (U.S.A.), 47-48

Brock, Bill, 61, 87-88

Brown, Clay, 135-136

Brown, James D., 165-166

Brown, Jean, 26-30. *See also* Jean Brown bequest

Brown, Josephine, 27

Brown, Robert McAfee, 98

Brown, William Clark, 26-27

Brueggeman, Walter, 98

Buchanan, Diane E., 29-30

Bullock, Robert H., Jr., 168-171

Bush, Frank, 103

Buttrick, George Arthur, 101

Byrom, Evelyn, 153

Caldwell, Frank, 99

Calvin, John, 44, 120

Campbell, Cynthia, 11, 49, 57, 62, 65, 108, 115, 136, 148, 153

Campbell, R. D., 19, 113

Carter, Jimmy, 2

Chamberlain, Clark, 108

Charles I, 9

Chary, Ellen, 99

Chernenko, Konstantin, 42

Cherryholmes, Eleanor, 63

Chester, Fern, 62, 153

Chester, Ray, 61, 153

Church in Search of Its Self, The (Robert S. Paul) 9

Civil War, 3

Civiletto, Catherine (Cathy), 83

Clark, Jimmie, 59, 152

Clark, Peggy, 75

Cockrum, Peggy, 153

Come, Arnold, 32

communism, 167

Cone, James H., 102

Confession of 1967, 38

Conner, Ulesly, 152

Continuing Education office, 69

Continuing Education program, 17, 62

Costen, James H., 102

Council on Theological Education (C.O.T.E.), 83

Craddock, Fred, 99

Craig, Shelley, 116-118

Cromwell, Oliver, 9

Cross and Resurrection: A Theology of Holy Saturday (Alan Lewis), 53

Cross, Frank, 38

Culp, Richard, 153

Culver, Joe, 4, 16-18, 19, 22, 152, 153

Cumberland Presbyterians, 92-93, 136

Cunningham, Linda, 73, 161

Currie, David Mitchell, 67

Currie, Elizabeth Jeannette, 67

Currie Hall, 67, 69, 73. *See also* Single Students' Dormitory

Currie, James Stuart, xi, 109

Currie, Jeannette Roe, 67

Currie Lectures, 77, 97, 98-99

Currie, Stuart Dickson, xv, 7, 67, 77, 99, 153

Currie, Thomas W., 36, 67, 164

Currie, Thomas W., Jr., xi, 60, 67, 99, 100

Currie, Thomas W., III, 50, 112, 123-126

Danhof, John, 61

Davis, Donald, Jr., 60

Dearman, John Andrew (Andy), 12, 62, 75, 77, 83, 90, 108, 109, 115, 119, 136, 138, 140, 154

Development Office, 84

Diaz, Frank, 165-166

Dillard, Annie, 121

Dillenberger, John, 98

Doctor of Ministry office, 69

Doctor of Ministry program, 11, 61-62, 147-149, 153

Dods, Marus, 171

Doelling, Bessie Lou, 70, 91, 161

Donaho, Joe B., 161

Donahue, Joe, 152

Donelson, Lewis, 14, 59, 84, 107-108, 115, 119, 122, 136, 148

Douey, Ed, 38

Dunn, Ilene B., 44

Dunn, Ross, 7, 35, 49, 77, 129, 130, 145, 153

Dykstra, Craig, xiii-xiv, 97

E. C. Westervelt Lectures. *See* Westervelt Lectures

Easter, 52-54

Eckhart, Meister, 87

Edwards, Jonathan, 120

Ehman, Frank, 153

Elliott, William, Jr., 99

evangelism, 43-44

Evans, John, 36, 47, 63, 67, 70, 73, 86-87, 136, 140, 146, 171

F. W. Woolworth building, 6

Faith Presbyterian Church, Sun City, Arizona, 109-111

Farwell, Barbara M., xvii-xviii, 137-138

Faulkenberry, Walter, 118-120

Faulkner, Larry R., 103

Fernandez, Robert H., 105, 106

Ferraro, Geraldine, 42

Fields, Ann, 88, 168

First Presbyterian Church, Houston, 108

First Presbyterian Church, Odessa, 112

Flato, Edwin, 97

Flato, Mrs. Edwin, 97

Fletcher, Judy Record, 165

Fogleman, William J., 29-30, 44, 165

Foote, Ted, 22, 127-128, 145
Forbes, James, 99
Ford, Gerald, 2
Fosdick, Harry Emerson, 76, 93
Fowler, James W., 97
Fox, Quinn, 87, 88
Frierson, Clarence N., 18, 23, 31, 36, 44, 73-74, 157-158
Frobes, Ida, 153
Frye, Roland Mushat, 97, 100
fundamentalism, 167
Furnish, Dorothy Jean, 97

Gallentine, John, 143-144
Garcia, Ismael, 49-50, 59, 82, 89-90, 108, 119, 123, 134
Garcia-Arroyo, Lemuel, 139-141
Gardner, Freda, 166
Garza, Dan, 20, 49, 113, 140, 153
George S. Heyer, Jr., Distinguished Lectureship. *See* Heyer Lectures
George, Sherron Kay, 64, 65, 86
Gerrish, Brian, 99
Gillespie, Tom, 157
glasnost, 42
Gomes, Peter, 99
Gorbachev, Mikhail, 42
Grace Presbyterian Church, Houston, 108
Graham, Bobby, 77
Greenway, Bill, 89
Gresham, Jim, 120-121
Gribble, Robert F., 19, 32, 113
Griffin, Marvin C., 168
Growing in the Life of Faith: Education and Christian Practices (Craig Dykstra), xiii-xiv
Gustafson, Jim, 98
Guthrie, Shirley C., 99, 101
Gutierrez, Gustavo, 102

Haggard, Joe, 142-143
Hall, Stanley R., 63, 82, 88, 108, 119, 142
Hanson, Paul, 98

Hardie, James Finley, 101
Harned, David, 50
Harren, Herman, 4, 6, 24, 27, 35, 38, 40, 56, 60, 82-83, 139, 151, 154, 158, 159
Harren, Margaret, 83
Harris, Maria, 97
Hartman, Ted, 75, 159-160
Hedrick, William K., 18-19, 24, 31, 36, 40, 63, 86, 152, 162
Hefley, Jacqueline, 59
Henderlite, Rachel, 7, 11, 97-98
Hendrick, John R. "Pete," 10, 49, 59, 62, 63, 64, 91, 101, 116, 136, 146, 152, 153
Hendry, George, 98
Herlin, Bruce, 31, 159
Herron, Dawn, 134
Heuer, Holly, 129-131
Heyer, George S., 7, 37, 54, 64-65, 90, 102, 131, 132
Heyer Lectures, 102-103
Hill, Keith, 146
Hiltner, Seward, 62
Hoch, Ann, 152
Hodges, Jack, 5, 150-152
Holper, Fred, 54, 62, 63, 116, 136, 148
Holy Saturday, 52-54
Hotchkiss, Valerie, 60
Houston Baptist University, 108
Houston Extension Program, 105-109, 114-125, 126
Howard, Jack, 153
Howard, Shirley, 151-153
Hoxie Thompson Lectures. *See* Thompson Lectures
Hromadka, Josef, 96

Inchai, Intraporn, 145-146
Insights: A Journal of the Faculty of Austin Seminary, 48, 64, 66
Iranian Hostage Crisis, 3
Irving, John, 121

Jansen, John F., xiv-xv, 3, 7, 12-15,

54-56, 64, 107, 115, 129, 130, 152
Jansen, Mary, 55-56
Jatko, Kenneth, 133-134
Jaworski, Leon, 145
Jean Brown bequest, 25-30, 40, 74, 78, 158
Jean Brown Visiting Scholar Program, 28
Jefferys, William H., III, 103
Jensen, David H., 88
Jensen, Robert, 99
Jesus Christ for Today (George Stroup), 10
Jinkins, Michael, 64, 84, 88
Johnson, Daryl E., 44, 88
Johnson, David, 88
Johnson, Kay, 139
Johnson, Merwyn S., 7, 9
Johnson, Stacy, 88, 140
Johnson, Walter, 7, 77
Johnson, William Stacy, 63
Johnson, Willie Elizabeth, 152
Johnston, Scott Black, 30, 64, 84, 122, 141
Jones, Arthur, 61
Jones Lectures, xiii, 97-98, 165
Junkin, Dick, 7, 21-22, 23, 24, 62, 129, 130, 132, 153, 153

Key, Donna, 139
Khayyam, Omar, 55
King, Carter, 59, 152
Kingdom Come! (Robert S. Paul), 9
Kirk-Jones, Cheryl, 134
Klemt, Calvin (Cal), 4, 7, 57, 65
Kubatzky, Timothy A., 87

Lancaster, Helen, 10, 63
Lancaster, John William, 10-11, 63
Landrey, Jerald B., 111
Lara-Braud, Jorge, 19, 102, 113
Latourette, Kenneth Scott, 101
Law, Robert Adger, 26
Lawson, Jim, 38
Laycock, Douglas, 102

Lee, Sang Hyun, 102
Lehmann, Paul, 98
Leith, John, 99
LeMaistre, Joyce, 36
Let Us Worship God: An Interpretation for Families (John Jansen), 13
Lewis, Alan E., xvi, 50-54, 63, 64, 112, 137-138
Lewis, Kay, xvi, 50-53
Lewis, Laura Brookings, 11-12, 14, 59, 65, 84, 108, 115, 119, 122-123, 133
Lewis, Mark, 50, 52, 53
Lilly Endowment, 33, 36
Lilly Foundation, 151
Lincoln, Timothy, 60
Lindbeck, George, 99
Little, Sara, 97
Lockerbie, Scotland, 167
Logan, Cynthia Weeks, 23-24
Long, Thomas G., 101
Loomis, Charles, 56
Lord Protector: Religion and Politics in the Life of Oliver Cromwell, The (Robert S. Paul), 8
Lott, H. C., Jr., 151
Lubbock, Frank, R., 26
Lubbock Hall, 4-5, 17, 26, 66, 70, 77, 151
Luce Foundation, 70
Luna, Genevieve (Gene), 56, 154
Luther, Martin, 120
Lynn, Robert, 33
Lyon College, 26
Lyon, Taft, 37

Mabee Foundation, 40
Macbeth, 100-101
Mackay, John, 98
March, W. Eugene (Gene), 7, 12, 13, 21, 22, 129, 130, 144-145, 153
Marney, Carlyle, 77, 97
married student housing, 5, 66
Marsden, George, 98

Marty, Martin, 98
Master of Arts program, 47, 146
Master of Divinity program, 46-47, 61, 72
Master of Theology program, 144
Matthews, Stephen A., 37, 161
Maxwell, Bessie, 152
Maxwell, Jack Martin, 1-24, 33, 62, 66, 73, 105, 106, 128, 133, 157, 158, 165
Maxwell, Sandy, 21
McClure, Kevin, 154
McClurg, Patricia, 165
McCord Community Center, 69, 70, 73, 77, 80, 159
McCord, Hazel, 69
McCord, James I., 1, 3, 69, 77, 158-159, 164
McCoy Historical Research Center, 60-61
McCoy, John M., 162
McKechnie, David, 75
McMillan Foundation, 26
McMillan Memorial Classroom Building, 4, 17, 26, 66, 69, 82
Memorial Drive Presbyterian Church, Houston, 108
Metcalfe, Ken, 152
Metcalfe, Ruth, 152
Mid-Winter Lectures, xiii, 69, 87, 96-97, 100-101, 103, 165
Miles, Carol Antablin, 85, 86
Miles, David, 85-86
Miles, Jim, 139
Miles, Tom, 86
Millard, James, xiv, 165
Miller, Michael N., 63, 84
Miller, Patrick, 98
Ministry (Robert S. Paul), 9
Moffett, Samuel, 102
Mondale, Walter, 42
Montgomery, G. R. M. (Bob), Jr., 109
Moreau, Al, 111, 112
Morgan, Fred, 152
Mosley, James W., 27, 61

Mowrer, Orval, 97
Muck, Terry, 62, 86, 108, 115, 116, 122, 140
Muilenburg, James, 98
Murray, William J., Jr., 4, 162

Neece, Kathy, 136-137
Negron, Ebenezer, 89
Nelson, C. Ellis, 2, 14, 24, 28-29, 31, 40-41, 43, 49, 65, 72, 73, 98, 101, 159, 165
Nelson, Nancy Gribble, 14, 32
Nelson, Willie, 135
New Covenant Presbytery, 105, 106
Ng, David, 7, 12, 22, 98, 129
Nichols, James Hastings, 98
Nicoll, W. Robertson, 171
Niebuhr, H. Richard, 38, 96-97
Niebuhr, Hulda, 38
Nixon, Richard, 2

O'Connor, Flannery, 121
O'Connor, Sandra Day, 42
Office of Admissions and Financial Aid, 59
Office of Supervised Practice of Ministry, 88
Office of the Hispanic American Institute, 19
Oliver, Gary, 75
On the Growing Edge of the Church (T. Watson Street), 101
Opening the Door of Faith: The Why, When and Where of Evangelism (John R. "Pete" Hendrick), 10, 102
Osmer, Richard, 98
Owens, Pamela, 57-58

Pagels, Elaine, 98
Park, Francis, 110-111
Paterson, Katherine, 98
Paul, Robert S., 7-9, 49, 54, 134-135
Paul (the apostle), xvi, 86

Pense, Elizabeth, 75
Pentagon, 167
Percy, Walker, 121
Perpetuo, Antonio Horatio, 112-113
Peters, Ken, 132-133
Peterson, Eugene, 99
Plunkett, Steve, xv-xvi, 131-132
Poe, William C., 108, 109
Presbyterian church: denominations of, 3, 36; evangelism and, 43–44; membership in, 10; reunited, 3, 36; women in, 11, 12
Proctor, William, 109
Promise of Narrative Theology, The (George Stroup), 10

Quinius, Henry, 59, 152

Rainey, Homer Price, 96
Ramsey, Charlsie B., 114-115
Read, David H. C., 99
Reagan, Ronald, 3, 42
Reding, Sydney, 75
Reese, Nancy, 161
Reid, Stephen Breck, 62, 84, 122
Riccobene, Sam, 88
Rice University, 108
Richard of St. Victor, 137
Ride, Sally, 42
Rigby, Cynthia, 64, 65, 89, 123
Rigby, Jim, 145
Ritschl, Dietrich, 77, 98
Robbins, Fred S., 26
Robert F. Jones Lectures in Christian Education. *See* Jones Lectures
Roberts, J. J. M. "Jimmy," 84
Roberts, Kathryn L., 84
Robinson, Jack, 128-129
Roetman, Dennis, 152
Rogers, Jack, 48, 99
Roloff, Jurgen, 99
Rosewall, Ann, 134
Roussakis, Peter E., 147

Sadongei, Martha, 142-143

Salmon-Campbell, Joan, 47
Sampson Hall, 4-5, 66
Sampson, T. R., 16, 25, 39
San Antonio Extension Program, 112-114
Sarles, C. Harry, 44
Sauceda, Teresa, 134
Sautter, Catherine (Cathy), 27, 58-59, 62, 153
Sawyer, Don Joseph, 148-149
Scherer, Paul, 96
Schmid, Tom, 6, 9, 11, 12, 17, 20
Schweizer, Edward, 98
Seaman, Frank, 113
secularism, 171
Seminary Catalogue, 58-59
Seminary Chapel, 5, 6, 27, 66, 67, 82, 100, 168
Settles Lectures, 10, 101-102
Settles, Mrs. W. R., 101
Shakespeare, William, 56, 100
Shalom: The Search for a Peaceable City (Jack Stotts), 39
Shaw, Jed, 70, 71, 75, 91
Shaw, Jo E. "Jed," 69, 75, 160
Shelton, Barbara, 77
Shelton, Dean, 14
Shelton, Fran, 138, 139
Shelton, Robert M., 3, 7, 23, 28, 33, 35, 38, 44, 49, 59, 63, 64, 72, 75, 76-80, 82, 83, 87, 89, 90-94, 73, 98, 100, 105-106, 107, 110, 111, 113, 129, 130, 131, 135, 136, 139, 140, 141-142, 143-144, 145, 146, 152, 154, 158, 159, 160, 161
Sherman, Max R., 75, 161
Shetler, Jerold D. (Jerry), 37, 83-84, 87
Single Students' Dormitory, 26, 33, 35, 66, 67, 40. *See also* Currie Hall
Slye, Harry, 115-116
Smith, Allen, 37, 162
Smith, Janis, 38
Smith, Weldon, 157, 158, 159

Smoot Center for Continuing Education, 4, 17
Smoot, Richmond Kelley, 4
Soviet Union, 42, 167
St. Mary's School of Theology, 108
Stair, Lois, 1, 3
Stendahl, Krister, 97
Stitt, David L., 2, 3, 7, 16, 33, 36, 44, 93, 105, 129, 164
Stitt Library, 4, 17, 60, 61, 66-67, 77, 154
Stock, Edwin W., Jr., 36-37
Stotts, Jack Levin, 15, 38-39, 42-49, 51-52, 54-55, 58, 61, 64-65, 66, 67, 70-74, 81, 91, 97, 100, 109, 113, 115, 118, 136, 137, 140, 143, 145, 158, 159-160
Stotts, Virginia, 39, 42, 72, 137
Street, T. Watson, 101, 165
Stroup, George, 9-10, 31-32, 49, 78
Stuart Seminary, 25
Sun City (Arizona) Extension Program, 109-111
Supervised Practice of Ministry (SPM) program, 64
Synod Covenant Review Committee, 22
Synod of Mid-America, 73
Synod of Red River, 15, 20
Synod of Texas, 25
Synod of the Rocky Mountains, 73
Synod of the Southwest, 73
Synod of the Sun, 29, 37, 40, 41, 63, 73

Taylor, J. Randolph (Randy), 40, 47
Taylor, Marvin, 105, 106
terrorism, 82, 171
Tex-Mex Presbytery, 20
Thielicke, Helmut, 99, 101
Thomas White Currie Lectures. *See* Currie Lectures
Thompson, Ernest Trice, 96, 155
Thompson, Hoxie H., 103
Thompson Lectures, 103

Toma, Kris, 88
Tompkins, Jerry, 15-16, 17, 18, 22, 62, 92
Torrance, Thomas, 64
Trevino, Kathy, 139
Trinity Presbyterian Church, Midland, 112
Trinity University, 92
Trueblood, D. Elton, 96
Trull Foundation, 26
Trull Memorial Administration Building, 5, 6, 26, 66, 159
Trull, Robert B., 4, 159
Tshihamba, Mukome L., 102
Tyler, Anne, 121

Underwood, Alice, 139
Underwood, Ralph, 37, 49, 87, 108, 134
Union Seminary, New York, 2
Univeristy of Texas, 37
University Presbyterian Church, 100

Vaclavick, Larry, 69
Vickery, Edward D. (Ed), 36-37, 44, 70, 158-159
Vietnam War, 2, 32
Vigness, David, 159

Walker, Dan, 141-142
Watergate, 2
Watson, Sallie Sampsell, 134-135
Weaver, C. D., 15, 49, 59, 133, 140
Weaver, Rebecca, 64
Welborn, Elaine, 69
West, Ann Hoch, 35
West Lounge, 17
West Texas Extension Program, 111-112, 123-124, 126
Westerhoff, John, III, 97
Westerlage, Walker, 21
Westervelt Lectures, 97, 99-100
Wharton, James, 7, 100, 101
Wheeler, Barbara, 171
Whitman, Christine Todd, 85-86

Whittington, Kenneth W., 37
Whitworth, Andrea, 60
Williams, Jane, 57
Williams, Mary Ruth, xi
Williams, Prescott H., Jr., 1, 2, 7,
    15, 16, 44, 49, 57-58, 62, 64, 90,
    134, 135, 136, 144-145, 157, 158
Williams, Thomas, xi
Williamson, J. Gaston, 27
Williamson, O. C., 113
Willimon, William, 99
Wilmore, Gayraud S., 102

Wilton, John C., Jr., 84
Windows, xvi, 78, 85, 85-86
Wood, Ralph, 99
Word, the, xv-xviii, 94
World Trade Center, 167
Wright, Elworth ("Pete"), 152
Wright, George Ernest, 38
Wynne, Toddie Lee, 26

Young, Tim, 60

Zbinden, Louis, 70, 75, 92